Let's Go Outside

Monash University acknowledges the Boonwurrung, Bunurong and Wurundjeri peoples of the Kulin Nation as sovereign custodians of the lands on which we work, study and welcome visitors. We extend respect to ancestors and Elders, past, present and emerging, and to all First Nations people. We also acknowledge and celebrate connection to material and creative practice on these lands for more than sixty thousand years.

Let's Go Outside
Art in Public

A MUMA Reader

Monash University Museum of Art
Monash Art Projects
Monash University Publishing

Contents

8 Foreword
Charlotte Day and Callum Morton
12 Introduction
Amy Spiers
30 untitled (seven monuments)
Jonathan Jones
40 Making the Law of the Land Visible
Vicki Couzens interviewed by Amy Spiers
62 The Edge of Us: Regional Arts Development in the Settler Colony
Danny Butt
70 Interpreting Difficult Knowledge: What Difference Do Artists Make?
Alison Atkinson-Phillips
98 Monumental Lies, or Countering Cook
Daniel Browning
120 Responsibilities to Time
Callum McGrath
140 Art and the City
Mel Dodd
160 Women as Storytellers: Public Art in Sydney
Felicity Fenner
176 Becoming Molecular in Public
Emily Cormack
192 Public Art: A View from New York
Claire Bishop
204 Solidarity Grid
Blair French
214 The Art of Demonstration: A New Public Art in the City of Hong Kong
Michelle Antoinette interviews Oscar Ho and Clara Cheung

Contents

236 Living Lumbung: The Shared Spaces of Art and Life
A Conversation between Nikos Papastergiadis and ruangrupa
254 Deficit and Care
Zara Stanhope
264 Twich Women's Sewing Collective: Activism through Enterprise, Social Change through Culture
Grace McQuilten
280 Can You Be Your Whole Self Without Compromise?: Public Life, Public Accessibility, Public Art and Disability Justice
A Dialogue between Carmen Papalia and Sam Petersen
306 For a New Lexicon and Other Attitudes
Tania Bruguera
328 Our City in Summer
Mish Grigor
338 A Letter to Folkestone
Madeleine Collie
348 Making Publics
Sean Dockray
354 IT CONCLUDES WITH AN_EMAIL_AS_ART_QUEERING PUBLICS: A PERFORMANCE TEXT
Brian Fuata

Foreword

Charlotte Day* and Callum Morton**

The genesis of this reader was the symposium Let's Go Outside: Making Art Public, held on the Monash University Caulfield campus in Melbourne from 30 to 31 August 2019 and presented by Monash University Museum of Art (MUMA) and Monash Art Projects (MAP). Bringing together a broad cross-section of people interested in and involved in public art, this two-day event was born from the close affiliation that MUMA and MAP have with the topic as public art commissioners, producers, researchers and educators. It also arose from the longer commitment of Monash University—evident across more than sixty years—to art in the public realm. While the symposium afforded the opportunity to reflect on many projects associated with Monash and beyond, ranging from the significant to the speculative, and an occasion to review commissioning approaches and receptions to public art, we felt that the symposium only scratched the surface of a fast-growing and expanding field of practice in need of further critical discourse.

This reader is the result of further research and engagement across the field of public art practice undertaken since the event. It features transcripts from the original symposium, including artist Tania Bruguera's excellent keynote lecture in which she advocated for agitators, healers and allies, as well as underscored the difficulties involved in the implementation of projects. It also re-engages with a number of the original presenters, while also reaching out to a wider group of artists and thinkers—both within Australia and internationally—to delve into key issues that surfaced from the symposium. Most urgent among these is the importance of recognising First Nations knowledges, sovereignty and ways of being, as well as the role of public art in truth telling and as a counterweight to narratives of colonisation and oppression.

In the opening session of the 2019 symposium, Wardandi (Nyoongar) and Dadimaya (Yamatji) curator Clothilde Bullen reminded us that inside and outside are not only physical barriers. With inclusions and exclusions often systemically entrenched within institutions and across the public realm, addressing issues of equity and accessibility is an area for focus and concern that this reader attempts to negotiate. We have also explored the potential of public art projects to be a space (and a language) to be shared and in which to generate new forms of relationality and connectivity to place, resources and community, both temporal as well as permanent in nature. As we did for the symposium, we have privileged case studies and examples of processes that we hope can lead to better public art outcomes, in our joint commitment to emphasising the importance of practice-led research.

The ambition of this reader is that it opens up new critical possibilities across the entire field of public art practice, including the way is it conceived, who is included, how it is realised and how it is valued. We recognise that it is far from exhaustive and that there will always remain important things we didn't have the space to include here. Indeed, there were a number of case studies on our own wish list that are awaiting a further forum.

Publications such as this require a village to be realised: our thanks go to all the original presenters and attendees to the symposium Let's Go Outside: Making Art Public, which motivated the commiss-ioning of this publication, and especially to our co-editor, artist and academic Amy Spiers, who took on the task of crafting the content of this reader, and directly commissioned and liaised with the writers across a particularly difficult period, as she eloquently evokes in her introduction. Thank you also to MUMA's Curator Research Melissa Ratliff, who oversaw the final editing and production of this reader, working closely with our valued designers Stuart Geddes and Žiga Testen, copyeditor Evie Franzidis, and colleagues at Monash University Publishing. We would also like to recognise all the contributors to this reader and thank them for their generous and insightful reflections on projects they have been involved in, engaged with, and spent time thinking about.

Introduction

Amy Spiers*

Let's Go Outside: Making Art Public was a symposium on public art practices presented in Melbourne by Monash University Museum of Art (MUMA) and Monash Art Projects in August 2019. I was among the forty presenters and two hundred attendees who not only felt energised by the diverse topics and formal presentations featured in the symposium—including keynotes by Cuban artist Tania Bruguera and Public Art Fund Director and Chief Curator Nicholas Baume—but also the spirited corridor encounters and foyer discussions that took place between sessions with fellow public art peers from across Australia and beyond.

As a regular frequenter of public art conferences, I particularly enjoyed this symposium for the variety of practitioners from across the expanded field of public art who were represented in both the presentations and the audience. Over two days, directors of major art institutions and commissioning bodies, academics, commercial gallerists, public space consultants, local government and regional arts officers, independent curators, as well as both established and emerging public art practitioners of every ilk—from those who make large-scale permanent sculptural works to those whose works are more discreet, ephemeral, performative, discursive or community-engaged—all met, mingled and debated in proximity during the catered breaks.

Given the enjoyment I experienced in participating in the symposium, I was delighted to be invited to co-edit with Charlotte Day and Callum Morton this reader for MUMA. This project on public practices, however, was to be largely conceived, developed and realised while we were confined in our homes for long periods, unable to experience art or be outside in the same ways that we usually do.

Our first meeting in January 2020 was in person, held on a scorching day where the sky was filled apocalyptically with ash and smoke from the devastating Black Summer bushfires burning across Victoria. Given the air quality was so compromised that day, it seems retrospectively rather foolhardy to have embarked outside to travel across town without a mask. This was our last in-person editorial meeting for many months and just a small foreshadowing of the ensuing COVID-19 crisis to come.

As I write this introduction in October 2021, we are emerging from Melbourne's latest lockdown, which lasted seventy-seven days. Since the pandemic started, Melbournians have endured more than 250 days in lockdown—the longest period anywhere in the world.

Living through this much time governed by necessary but substantial public health restrictions—with access to the outdoors parcelled out into blocks of one to two hours; excursions confined to five, ten or fifteen kilometre radiuses, before curfew at 8pm or 9pm; and activities reduced to exercise or recreation with one other person, grocery shopping, or giving or receiving care—makes your nostalgia for times when going outside was less regulated and policed profoundly acute. With the benefit of hindsight, I think of the Let's Go Outside symposium as a momentous and auspicious gathering, given that the COVID-19 crisis would profoundly limit our capacity to travel and assemble in person a mere six months later.

Consequently, it has been our intention as editors from the outset to retain the spirit of the original symposium and to include a number of perspectives from across the diverse range of public art output in Australia and internationally. Taking up debates from Let's Go Outside, this edited reader reflects on the growing interest in making and presenting art outside of conventional gallery contexts and explores the opportunities and complexities of realising art in the public realm.

Our case studies expand on topics relevant to artists, designers, art consultants, policymakers, commissioners and curators working in this area, including indigenising the public realm; producing memorials to difficult pasts; placemaking and urban renewal; commissioning models; considerations of access, inclusion and diversity; and public art practices that are experimental, temporary and socially engaged. As well as case studies, the publication's twenty-one contributions include critical essays, artist pages, creative explorations, as well as interviews and features on key practitioners in the field. The book aims to situate and contrast Australia's unique approaches to public art by featuring essays on public art commissioning and practice internationally, including Hong Kong, Aotearoa (New Zealand), Indonesia, the US and the UK, and features the perspectives of twenty-five scholars, public artists and collectives.

Already a Place

We open the book with a thematic grouping of texts that centres on Indigenous sovereignty, connections to place, and ways of being and practicing, while exploring the fraught nature of situating art on stolen Aboriginal land. While commonplace discourses present public art as a positive force in 'placemaking', this reader is instead predicated on the understanding that in the settler colonial context of Australia, all 'places' always were, and continue to be, significant Country to First Peoples.

In 'untitled (seven monuments)', an edited transcript of the presentation given by Wiradjuri and Kamilaroi artist Jonathan Jones, a number of Wiradjuri principles are outlined that guide Jones's practice, including the notion of 'yindyamarra'—'to go slow'. Jones expands on the practice of yindyamarra through discussing the public art project untitled (seven monuments), 2019, a series of commemorative markers that skirt the perimeter of the important heritage site Coranderrk Aboriginal Reserve, which were created in collaboration with senior Wurundjeri Elder Aunty Joy Murphy Wandin AO and artist Tom Nicholson. Yindyamarra centres on a bearing of purposefulness, care and respect that can be at odds with the fast-paced requirements of the art world.

In the interview I held with Vicki Couzens, 'Making the Law of the Land Visible', Couzens thoughtfully extends on Jones's illuminating discussion about practicing respectful principles on others' Country. A Gunditjmara woman and master possum-skin cloak-maker, Couzens discusses what brought her to primarily make artworks for public spaces rather than galleries. She profoundly articulates that public art is foremost a mode of telling the 'Story of place' that centres First Peoples and makes sovereign unceded lands visible—a powerful conduit for summoning the Law of the Land. She expands the definitions of public artmaking and art itself through her preferred term, 'creative cultural expression', one she feels better encompasses her activities across sculpture and installation, multimedia production, language reclamation, possum-skin cloak-making, performance and community projects.

Scholar and artist Danny Butt closes this section with his contribution 'The Edge of Us: Regional Arts Development in the Settler Colony'. It details the regional township creative development project The Edge of Us, 2016–18, developed by Jessica Wilson with Jeannie Houghton and Mary Sullivan, and some of the issues that settlers face in situating art on sovereign, First Nations' lands. This project was aimed at creatively 'connecting', 'transforming', and generating a 'lasting legacy' among five economically disadvantaged towns skirting Western Port Bay on Boonwurrung Country. Butt, as a non-Indigenous settler and new resident of one such town (Grantville), raises questions in his text over who—on stolen Aboriginal land—has the mandate to commission and create such 'placemaking' developments of long-term legacy.

Truth-Telling and Commemoration

This next cluster of reflections considers how public artworks prompt public memory and bring visibility to difficult and disregarded histories and truths.

In the first text, 'Interpreting Difficult Knowledge: What Difference Do Artists Make?', cultural and social historian Alison Atkinson-Phillips analyses a range of contemporary Australian memorials that help the public consider the meaning of painful events such as the violence of war and forced migration, homophobia and sexual assault, devastating bushfires, as well as institutional failures to the Stolen Generations and Forgotten Australians. Most significantly, Atkinson-Phillips identifies that in such creative memory work, public artists, artsworkers and commissioners must carefully and respectfully interpret difficult knowledge, an effort that requires an expanded artistic skillset of listening, imagining and translating events to create engaging and affective spaces for public recognition and healing. Atkinson-Phillips presents this artist skillset—that carries the burden of memory—as an integral but under-acknowledged aspect of commemorative projects.

Bundjalung and Kullilli journalist, radio broadcaster, documentary maker, sound artist and writer Daniel Browning discusses the distorted public history that is upheld by colonial monuments and shapes the Australian national story and collective identity in his essay, 'Monumental Lies, or Countering Cook'. Reflecting on the 'alternative facts' that colonial monuments such as the statue of Lieutenant James Cook in Sydney's Hyde Park 'set in stone', Browning explores how First Nations artists Daniel Boyd, Reko Rennie, Yhonnie Scarce, Nicholas Galanin and Jacob Nash are challenging the falsehoods and effacements perpetuated by colonial statuary and icons and leading an empowered reclamation of public history.

These considered essays that reflect upon what is commemorated by and forgotten in public presentations of the past are followed by artist's pages by Melbourne-based Callum McGrath taken from his ongoing project Responsibilities to Time, 2019–. The series inserts snapshots of public memorials dedicated to the queer community's loves and losses into the pages of a domestic family photo album, as a way of questioning what is excluded by hetero-dominant modes of archiving and remembering.

In the City

Through three essays, this section considers the ways in which both temporary and permanent public art commissioning practices can shape, develop and activate the identity of city precincts and spaces.

In 'Art and the City', architect and academic Mel Dodd explores how urban regeneration and public art commissioning strategies have attempted to nurture culture and identity in new city precincts by examining two significant case studies in detail—the King's Cross regeneration in London and the still-in-development Melbourne Arts Precinct around Southbank. Dodd suggests that contemporary public art practice can be the critical 'software' that complements the 'hardware' of larger-scale infrastructural renewal, offering rich opportunities for fostering the messier, everyday practices that generate culture and enliven the city, especially in post-COVID-19 urban recovery.

Curator and scholar Felicity Fenner's essay 'Women as Storytellers: Public Art in Sydney' surveys public artworks made by women in Australia's largest city, outlining initiatives, figures, cultural events and partnerships that have defined public art commissions by women in Sydney since the 1990s. Fenner addresses the historical exclusion of female artists in Sydney's public spaces, arguing that women artists are particularly well placed to address the needs of city spaces by contributing inclusive visions, uncovering overlooked layers of history and generating compelling connections between people and places.

In 'Becoming Molecular in Public', curator Emily Cormack describes her unique approach to public art curation and commissioning. Drawing on the writings of Gilles Deleuze and his commentators, she describes how her aim is to produce an encounter with an artwork that invites the viewer to 'become molecular', working with architects and artists to capture the forces and energies within a site, and to transmit it as sensation to the viewer. Cormack's approach is elaborated through her descriptions of a series of recent artworks she commissioned by artists Isadora Vaughan, Jose Dávila and Céleste Bouriser-Mougenot.

Responses to Crises

The next section features three texts describing public art commissioning and creation in New York, Ōtautahi (Christchurch), and Hong Kong that have helped the public come to terms with political, natural and social crises, both in their aftermath or as a way to make sense of them during their unfolding.

In her essay 'Public Art: A View from New York', the New York–based British art historian and critic Claire Bishop reports on public art projects in New York and across the US produced during the turbulent year of 2020, which brought the COVID-19 pandemic and the election that toppled Trump. Bishop reviews projects by a range of New York's public art commissioning organisations, both established and lesser known, including Creative Time, Public Art Fund, Time Square Projects and the High Line. Bishop's snapshot, however, determines that the highlights were often self-initiated works produced on smaller budgets. She concludes that the defining public art of 2020 was the public visual culture of Black Lives Matter, including the repurposing of Confederate-era monuments such as the General Robert Lee memorial in Richmond, Virginia, that became powerful loci for activism, and for grieving and celebrating Black life.

In 'Solidarity Grid', curator and writer Blair French, who leads Sydney's multi-arts centre Carriageworks, discusses the site-specific and context-responsive Solidarity Grid, 2013–16, by Düsseldorf artist Mischa Kuball. The work comprises twenty-one streetlamps of differing designs and styles that were gifted by diverse municipalities from around the world and were permanently relocated to Ōtautahi (Christchurch) following the city's major 2011 earthquake in an act of rebuilding and solidarity. With insights as the project's curator, French describes how Solidarity Grid was driven by Kuball's desire to be an agent of international exchange and community building post-crisis, and developed with an openness in relation to the recovering city. The artist, for example, accommodated a change in the original proposed location following negotiations with the city, so the work could be situated where it would be of most use to the people of Ōtautahi.

'The Art of Demonstration: A New Public Art in the City of Hong Kong' is an interview held between academic Michelle Antoinette and Hong Kong artists, curators, and cultural workers Oscar Ho and Clara Cheung. Ho and Cheung discuss the shifting practices and changed significance of public art in Hong Kong following the period since the end of British sovereignty in 1997, the 2014 political street protests known as the Umbrella Movement, and the more recent 2019 Anti-Extradition Movement. The two describe a new form of public art that isn't necessarily artist-led but is forged out of civilian protest and necessity in response to shifting and charged political contexts.

Sharing Resources, Accessing Space

Through perspectives forged in Indonesia, Aotearoa (New Zealand), Canada and Australia, this section discusses a range of public art practices that encompass installation, performance, as well as socially and community engaged practices that sensitively consider questions about the capacity of public spaces to be inclusive, generate places of sharing, and address diverse collective needs.

'Living Lumbung: The Shared Spaces of Art and Life' is a transcript of an interview conducted by Melbourne-based cultural studies scholar and writer Nikos Papastergiadis with ruangrupa, an art collective (est. 2000) based in Jakarta that produces workshops, publications and multi-format events. The conversation centres around the concept of lumbung—a notion describing a collective distribution of surplus and resources derived from agrarian traditions in Indonesia, which, for ruangrupa, is a metaphor for sharing that guides their principles of collaboration and their curation of the upcoming documenta fifteen (2022).

In her essay, 'Deficit and Care', curator Zara Stanhope discusses the work of fellow Aotearoa-based artist collective Public Share and artist Shannon Novak, who engage with and contest conditions for workers and LGBTQI+ communities respectively through expanded public art practices. Stanhope discusses the gift relations and logics of care in operation in Public Share's site-specific ceramic-making and tea break events, which take place at a range of sites, including construction worksites and museums, and aim to claim a space for rest while reflecting on labour conditions. Stanhope also discusses Novak's work, including the ongoing, not-for-profit project the 'Safe Space Alliance', which encourages the caretakers of public venues to provide safe spaces to LGBTQI+ communities and to behave with responsibility and inclusiveness.

A case study about the Twich Women's Sewing Collective by scholar and curator Grace McQuilten discusses this Victorian-based social enterprise working with textile design and fashion that began in 2011 in direct response to the challenging settlement environment encountered by South Sudanese communities in Australia. Twich use art and fashion to engage with, challenge and transform mainstream representations of Sudanese Australian communities, existing on the margins of contemporary art practice and in spaces of the 'public' that range from the media sphere to trade, public events and community celebrations. McQuilten describes how Twich harnesses the symbolic power of public spaces for self-representation through their varied material and aesthetic practices.

In their candid dialogue drawing on lived experience, 'Can You Be Your Whole Self Without Compromise?', Vancouver artist Carmen Papalia and Melbourne artist Sam Petersen provide illuminating insights into the perils and opportunities of navigating public space and public life as artists living with disabilities. Papalia describes a variety of innovative creative practices that address the disabled community's access to public space, the art institution and visual culture, including his own collaborative performance and public intervention projects. Petersen describes limitations she has encountered in Melbourne arts spaces, and her inventive art practice which is focused on access—and the lack of it—to places, people's minds, and opportunities.

Art for the 'Not Yet'

This section takes its title from the words of Cuban artist Bruguera, describing art for the 'Not Yet' that is responsive to unfinished business, to politics and art-making conditions that are still taking shape. This collection of texts also reflects on public art that conceptualises alternatives, speculates possibilities, and produces visions of a future to come.

In an edited transcript of the keynote lecture that Bruguera delivered for the Let's Go Outside symposium, the artist speaks about the concepts and terms she has developed in order to define her unique approach to politically charged art practice, including Political-Timing Specific and Arte Útil (Useful Art). She also usefully describes how she alternates between 'positive energy' and 'negative energy' projects in the public sphere—from those that empower and fulfil needs within a community to those that position the artist as the promulgator of difficult truths. Bruguera elaborates her ideas through insightful descriptions of a range of her projects, from works that politically chafed and got her arrested in Cuba, such as Yo También Exijo, 2014, to ameliorative and community-engaged works, such as 10,148,451, 2019, at Tate Modern's Turbine Hall.

In 'Our City in Summer', established performance maker, writer and curator Mish Grigor looks back from her 'professionalised', mid-career position to reflect on the heady years between 2008 and 2012, when she was a young artist who worked with a 'motley crew' of art-making friends to initiate theatre shows, performances, visual art events and talks with a do-it-yourself ethic at semi-legal makeshift spaces across the inner-city suburbs of Sydney. Grigor describes pop-up works, performances and live events produced by The Imperial Panda Festival and Tiny Stadiums that were staged in carparks, empty shops and parks. For Grigor and friends, presenting works in public space provided possibilities outside of the conventional, established institutional gallery and theatre spaces that the group of emerging practitioners had not yet gained access to, and she wonders about what prospects emerging artists have now to work outside of institutional frames and seize such make-do public spaces for 'quick and dirty' artistic experimentation and development.

In 'A Letter to Folkestone' by former Folkestone resident and now Melbourne-based writer and curator Madeleine Collie, the author describes her encounters with temporary and permanent public artworks in the town that lays claim to being the UK's largest permanent collection of outdoor contemporary art. Collie's first-person account of art and place thoughtfully reflects on whether a place is special in spite of—or because of—its public art. She also provides incisive ruminations on the speculative nature of the town's artworks that produce competing outlooks for Folkestone: both imagining other poetic, community-activating and hopeful futures while also working to attract property speculators to a town experiencing decline and deprivation—developing prospects that exclude poorer residents from the town's changing fortunes.

Disrupting 'Public'

In this last thematic section, two writers who are also artists trouble easy notions of the 'public' of 'public art'. In 'Making Public', Sean Dockray considers the usefulness of the term 'public' in the context of the networked digital activity that proliferated after the widespread closure of physical gallery and museum spaces and shifts in programming during pandemic lockdowns. Dockray traces a longer history of artists working with media and communication platforms and makes the proposition that reaching and connecting audiences through digital means is now less important, or radical, than 'making publics'. Because digital networks entangle property and sharing, he suggests that to engage constructively online today means to create and renew communities, spaces, and protocols that collectively redistribute resources away from the control of institutions and corporate monopolies, and that engender publics through a 'generous and generative act of making and sharing spaces, tools and concepts'.

In IT CONCLUDES WITH AN_EMAIL_AS_ART_QUEERING PUBLICS: A PERFORMANCE TEXT, artist and improviser Brian Fuata contributes a performance text that says 'nothing and everything' about the idea of a 'Queer Public Art'. A sequence of episodic texts conjures scenes from the artist's beat cruising in sensorial, libidinal, public space, while questioning both the binary of inside-outside and the sanctioned objecthood of art. The text concludes, as its title forecasts, with an email performance that Fuata created in 2013 for all 'all the men in my address book', playing with identitarian categories and the theatrical fields of the public and private to, cc and bcc.

Ethnographer, filmmaker and author Phillip Vannini has recently observed that periods of COVID-19 quarantine and lockdown 'is a geography of what doesn't happen: of canceled events, of missed chances, of a shuttered consumer society, of shattered kinship'.[1] It is the missed chances and

1 Phillip Vannini, 'COVID-19 as

shattered kinship that our locked-down public art community has felt most keenly in the years since the Let's Go Outside symposium—all the things that sustained the field, the incidental encounters, chance introductions and mingling at openings and launches; the heated debates and exchanges between peers over refreshments after public art talks; the rehearsals, developments and co-creating corporeally in physical spaces together: seeing art in all its embodied, spatial and situated glory has for many months been severely curtailed.

I am not the first person to comment upon the irony of reflecting on the nature and significance of public art from lockdown. For instance, in the recent Artlink special issue In Public / Inside, editor Daniel Mudie Cunningham noted: 'Thinking through art's relationship to public life and civic space while inside, day after day, has never felt more urgent.'[2] As we emerge from our diminished situations, with promises from authorities that this is indeed the last lockdown and the end of cancelled life, our senses are heightened; public space, and our agency in it, feel somewhat strange and acute after many days spent inside. It is my hope this reader arrives at a timely moment, as we anticipate, renavigate and rethink what we want and need from public spaces, proximity with art and communality. As we rediscover our agency, begin to reassemble and speculate about what we want to create outside

Atmospheric Dis-ease: Attuning into Ordinary Effects of Collective Quarantine and Isolation', Space and Culture, vol. 23, no. 3, August 2020, p. 270.

2 Daniel Mudie Cunningham, 'Editorial', Artlink, vol. 41, no. 2, August 2021, p. 8.

post-crisis, the rich contributions contained here offer us much to think about how we might enable more just, engaging, radical and representative art for the public.

untitled (seven monuments)
Jonathan Jones*

* Jonathan Jones is an artist, curator and researcher. A member of the Wiradjuri and Kamilaroi nations of south-east Australia, he works across a range of mediums to create site-specific installations, interventions and public artworks that engage Aboriginal practices, relationships and knowledge. With the act of collaborating at the heart of Jones's practice, many projects have seen him work with other artists and communities, such as Dr Uncle Stan Grant Senior, Aunty Joy Murphy Wandin AO and Tom Nicholson. With the latter two, he produced the public art project (untitled) seven monuments, 2019, which traces the historical boundary of the Coranderrk Aboriginal Station in Healesville, Victoria.

Editors' note: This is an edited transcript of the presentation Jonathan Jones gave during the Decolonising the Public Realm panel session of the Let's Go Outside: Making Art Public symposium. The session explored how Aboriginal and Torres Strait Islander knowledge can inform discussions of national symbols and public strategies for contesting and reshaping cultural memory.

My name is Jonathan Jones. I am a Wiradjuri and Kamilaroi artist from New South Wales. Before I start, I'd like to acknowledge the Traditional Owners and thank Aunty Carolyn Briggs for her welcome. I'd also like to thank everyone involved in organising today's event and acknowledge the many extraordinary people presenting.

I will be talking about untitled (seven monuments), a public art project that was created over a number of years in collaboration with senior Wurundjeri Elder Aunty Joy Murphy Wandin AO and artist Tom Nicholson and which launched recently. I will talk about some of the ideas around that project from a Wiradjuri and Kamilaroi perspective. In particular, [I will talk about] the complications of being an artist while maintaining Aboriginal principles, including issues of dropping an artwork onto someone else's Country, and the cultural implications of that in terms of Aboriginal ways of being and doing—namely, respect.

How to act respectfully in a cultural sense while being an artist has troubled me for a long time. In fact, it has had a major impact on the way I can engage with exhibitions and projects both nationally and internationally, because before I start to work on a project, I need to ensure that there are legitimate cultural connections to the site; that there are meaningful relationships and approvals with the Traditional Owners, including a deep understanding of their histories and lived realities; and that my work contributes to these issues by empowering the local community. In today's fast-paced world, most projects don't enable you to establish or maintain these important relationships, but they are essential for my practice.

Because [a lot of] projects are not designed to encourage meaningful connections with the local community and environment, I'm often unable to work on many projects and respond to invitations with a no, which I rationalise by knowing that 'Wiradjuri' actually means 'no having', with wiray being 'no'. How we say no defines not only us but also many other nations along the Murray–Darling. In this way, 'no' is a good thing to say, but I still need to get better at saying it. Central to my understanding of cultural protocols has been [through working] with one of my senior Elders, Dr Uncle Stan Grant Snr AM, who is the language holder for our community. Over the years, Uncle Stan and I have not only collaborated on both art and on research projects but have also worked hard to create a Wiradjuri framework. From our process of working, we have produced a series of Wiradjuri principles, if you like—Wiradjuri gulbanha (philosophies), so Wiradjuri ways of thinking and knowing. They have been developed through practice, but also through teachings handed down through community. It's those principles that have really helped guide me as an artist.

For instance, marraga-la-dha means 'hold fast to community' or 'care for the community'. So this means everything we do needs to strengthen and bind community together. Nganga-dha nguram-bang

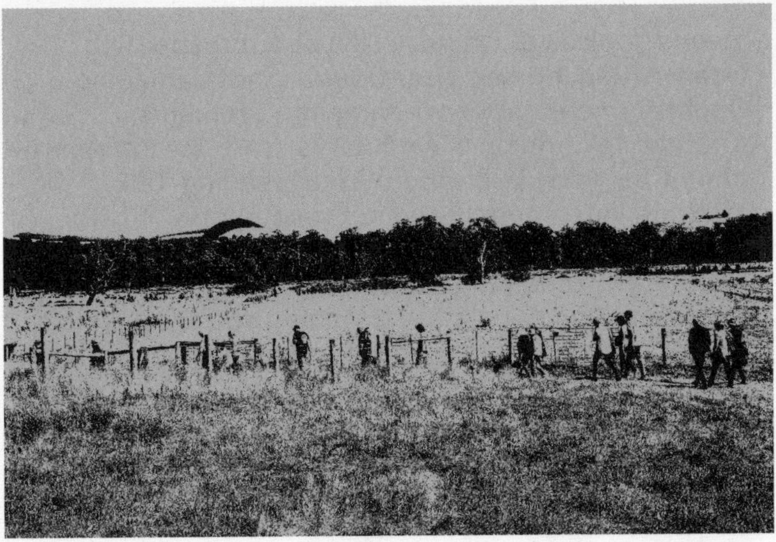

Attendees at the April 2019 launch of *untitled (seven monuments)*, a public art project by Aunty Joy Murphy Wandin AO, Jonathan Jones and Tom Nicholson that marks the historical boundary of Coranderrk Aboriginal Station. The project was commissioned by TarraWarra Museum of Art as part of the exhibition *Future Memorials* (2013–14), curated by Victoria Lynn, and was realised in 2019 with the support of Yarra Ranges Council, the artwork's custodian. Photo: Christian Capurro

means 'look after Country'; it's about respecting Country and looking after Country, not damaging Country or creating environmental problems. Another key principle is dhulu-ya-rra-bu wudha-gar-bin-ya-bu yindyamal-dhuray-bu, meaning 'talk straight, listen deeply and act respectably'. It's the idea that when you sit down and consult with people, you mean it; you are actually listening and you are telling people the truth and you are having a meaningful conversation. These are really important ideas, which I feel we need to properly engage with if we are to be serious about notions of decolonising.

But at the very heart of our Wiradjuri principles there is one word that we know by rote. You'll hear this word when spending time with old people; it's pretty much the first word you learn. The word is yindyamarra. When you're really young, you get told it means respect: 'Show some yindyamarra.' As you get older and learn our language, you start to realise that, in fact, yindyamarra literally means 'to go slow'; that is, to move with purpose, to think before you act, to think about everyone around you before you act. This idea of being purposeful is to be respectful to everyone and everything.

The idea of respect was demonstrated in Aunty Carolyn giving her welcome, and us acknowledging her. However, to have yindyamarra, to go slow in a world that seems to always be speeding up, is difficult. How we manage to hold on to our principles of going slow when working with deadlines, budgets and competing projects is a challenge, but it is absolutely essential to creating meaningful work that maintains our cultural principles.

I've been really lucky to work on untitled (seven monuments) with Aunty Joy and Tom. We've all collaborated in different ways, each bringing something unique to the table. We've worked with TarraWarra Museum, including its director Victoria Lynn and curator Anthony Fitzpatrick, and the success of this project has been yindyamarra, which I know was difficult for all of us to deal with at times, but respect has been an essential element of the project. It was a project that we had been developing over several years before we began working with TarraWarra; indeed, we had all collaborated with each other at different moments, but we came together for this project because of the enormous yindyamarra we have for the significant site of the Coranderrk Aboriginal Station and the marvellous Elders who made that place so special.

untitled (seven monuments) initially grew out of a number of visits that Tom and I, independently and together, made to Healesville to work with Aunty Joy. We knew that Coranderrk Aboriginal Station was part of that landscape, but while it is one of Australia's most important sites, it had been both physically and historically erased.

For those of you who don't know, the Coranderrk community was established in 1863 by displaced Wurundjeri people, who moved to the Yarra Valley with other displaced Kulin Nation people to establish a station. They were, in their own words, going to act like white men and take back some of their own Country. They cleared the land, farmed the land, and established what was one of the most prosperous communities of the time, attracting Aboriginal people from around that region with the support of the settler preacher John Green. It became a powerful base for Aboriginal self-organisation and political advocacy.

At its largest, Coranderrk was 4,850 acres, but then slowly, once the government realised how successful this project by Aboriginal people could be, it implemented policies aimed at reducing and undermining Coranderrk Station. This ultimately led to the dispersal and forced removal of the community to Lake Tyers in 1924, leaving only a handful of determined Elders. Government policies that continue to this day have been designed to slowly break up places like Coranderrk—chewing into it, biting into it—to the point where the only remaining section of Coranderrk that was left for Wurundjeri people was the cemetery. A small parcel of land was handed back to the Wurundjeri people in the 1990s. So, untitled (seven monuments) is really about engaging with that former larger site of Coranderrk and, as I said, [about] mapping out that entire footprint and connecting to important history and narratives drawn from it.

Tom and I had the identical experience of rolling up to the local information centre at Healesville and on asking 'Do you have any information on what is one of the most significant Aboriginal sites in Australia, this extraordinary station established in the Yarra Valley?', received blank stares from the information centre staff, who couldn't tell us where Coranderrk was or how to access it or any history about it. There were no books about Coranderrk in their shop. It was strange that this significant site and history is a mystery; like much of Australia's history, it has been unacknowledged.

That experience was the catalyst for the project. We sat down with Aunty Joy and started thinking about what it would mean to honour Coranderrk and what that might look like. After many trips, after much talking, researching and cups of tea, we eventually conceived of seven very small monuments that would mark the entire boundary of Coranderrk when it was at its largest.

The monuments themselves are little brick monuments or cairns—but, perhaps more importantly, we're asking people to have some faith in the fact that buried under each cairn is an upturned flagpole. To mark the site, we core-drilled into the ground and dropped in a flagpole to be buried in Country. The base of the upturned flagpole is encased within the brick cairn. Consequently, the only remaining memory of the flagpole is the small ring that you see on the top surface of the cairn. In this way, Country becomes the flag.

Around each small cairn are four bronze plaques. Importantly, one of those plaques describes one of the seven Wurundjeri seasons as written by Aunty Joy. In this way, untitled (seven monuments) was governed by the seven Wurundjeri seasons. Additionally, in proximity to each of the cairns are Coranderrk bushes, a flowering plant that the station was named after. The other plaques on each cairn include maps showing the different moments in Coranderrk's past, quotes and historical accounts of Coranderrk.

The bricks were part of a project that Tom had already been working on. One of the stories that really captured our attention was that when Coranderrk was officially closed, the township moved in and basically took everything, including the bricks, the corrugated iron, even the bell off the church. They literally consumed the station. Those materials were carried away and used to build the town of Healesville. Indeed, many of the old Healesville houses or buildings were constructed with Coranderrk bricks; that is, bricks made by Aboriginal people from local clay and fired on site.

Tom's project set up a dialogue in relation to that history, with a major call-out made to the local community to donate bricks. Strangely, a lot of bricks were donated—obviously not original Coranderrk bricks, but bricks from people living in and around Healesville who connected to the story. It was an extraordinary moment. I remember we spent a day sitting in the car park at TarraWarra while people showed up with car boots full of bricks, and stories connecting to the history of Coranderrk, and it felt as though people wanted to give something back to this story and help rebuild this story. It was a really important event. These bricks now make up the seven cairns: history making history.

Part of the untitled (seven monuments) project was also the creation of a website and a DL flyer (http://www.untitledsevenmonuments.com.au) that encourages people to go to each of the seven sites, to walk and spend time in that Country while considering this story. The flyer tells you how to get to each site and what to expect when you're there. You can find the flyer in the local information centre. I really encourage you to visit because it's some of the most beautiful Country and deeply significant in Australia's national story. While you're there, don't forget to nganga-dha nguram-bang (look after Country) by taking some water bottles and watering the plants and doing some weeding. If there's rubbish, pick it up, and in doing so, contribute in your own way to that site and that story.

The project started with acknowledging Country. It was designed to bring community together and to strengthen it, to provide a physical, tangible thing that people could connect to and talk about. But it was really about showing respect, yindyamarra. It was about showing respect to that Country, and showing respect to not just living people and not just ancestors but also future generations to come, so that they could actually start to learn about and think about Country in a different way.

Mandaang guwu. Thank you.

Making the Law of the Land Visible
Vicki Couzens* interviewed by Amy Spiers

* Yoolongteeyt Dr Vicki Couzens is a Gunditjmara woman from the Western District of Victoria, Australia, and acknowledges her Ancestors and Elders who guide her work. Her contributions to the reclamation, regeneration and revitalisation of cultural knowledge and practice extend across the arts and creative cultural expression, including language revitalisation, ceremony, community arts, public art, visual and performing arts, and writing. She is a Vice-Chancellor's Indigenous Research Fellow at RMIT University, Melbourne, developing her project 'watnanda koong meerreeng, tyama-ngan malayeetoo (together body and country, we know long time)', which investigates how revitalisation practices build resilience and capability towards sovereign nation-building aspirations, opportunities and realised living legacy. She is Senior Knowledge Custodian for the Possum Skin Cloak Story and language reclamation and revival in her Keerray Woorroong mother tongue.

Editors' note: This interview took place in April 2021.

Amy Spiers: Vicki, you are known for your powerful multidisciplinary artworks in public spaces, as well as for your work in possum skin cloak making revival and language reclamation. Can you start by telling me how you came to be making public artwork and about what kinds of benefits you have found in making work for public spaces rather than museums and galleries?

Vicki Couzens: I don't think of myself as making work for galleries, but I suppose I do sometimes—if invited, I might put an existing work in an exhibition. I'm not so often making work specifically for those spaces. I suppose the beginning of the story of my work in public spaces—the first public commission I undertook—was Birrarung Wilam (Common Ground), 2006, [with artists Lee Darroch and Treahna Hamm] down by the banks of the Birrarung, which ended up being a $1.1 million project.[1] From this huge commission, I learnt so

1 'Birrarung Wilam', meaning river camp, honours the traditions of tribes throughout Victoria. The artwork's components include a mound campsite, or puulwuurn, an eel pathway, two message sticks, five shields, a group of ancestor stones, interpretative panels, water vessels rendered in stone, wood, steel, bronze and nickel, as well as an audio installation. See https://citycollection.melbourne.vic.gov.au/birrarung-wilam-common-ground/.

much about public art and design and about space and place.

This opportunity came from a recommendation from the Reconciliation Report of 2000 about creating a public space recognising and celebrating Victorian Aboriginal culture.[2] The brief asked for stories of water, Aboriginal Victoria, reconciliation and place. To represent all of those things in a way that was meaningful, inclusive and respectful was a complex task. The site was designated in the area in front of and surrounding the ArtPlay building, which is on Wurundjeri and Boonwurrung lands.

Aboriginal Law and protocol mandates that you cannot bring your Story and put it somewhere else. This commission required us to engage and negotiate with the Traditional Custodians; we were developing a Story in their Country and we were wanting to ensure their Story of place was central to the conceptual thinking and design development of the artwork.

2 Editors' note: In December 2000, the Council for Aboriginal Reconciliation delivered its final report to the Australian Parliament, titled Reconciliation: Australia's Challenge. Among its recommendations was for symbols of reconciliation to be negotiated between governments, organisations and communities. See Appendix 1, National Reconciliation Documents, Reconciliation: Australia's Challenge, Council for Aboriginal Reconciliation, December 2000, http://www.austlii.edu.au/au/other/IndigLRes/car/2000/16/contents.htm. A number of Reconciliation Councils (Victoria in 2002) and public art strategies were established in response.

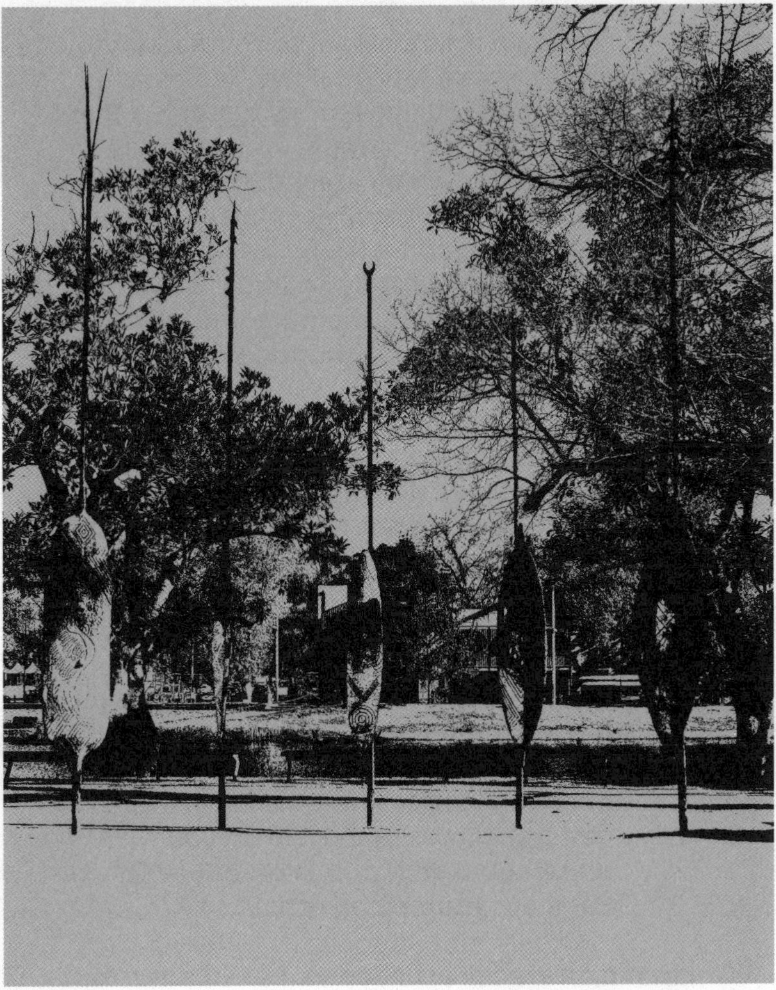

Vicki Couzens, Lee Darroch and Treahna Hamm, Birrarung Wilam (Common Ground) 2006, stone, wood, stainless steel, bronze, nickel and audio installation. A Commemorative Place Art Commission, jointly funded by the City of Melbourne and the Victorian government, 2006, City of Melbourne Art and Heritage Collection. Photo: Patrick Rodriguez

Because it was meant to represent the state, there was a lot of involvement with Traditional Custodians across Victoria. I think that's a bit different to most commissions that are offered, which are much more localised for a specific area or place. The Birrarung Wilam commission was where I first got to work with Jeph Neale and Hilary Jackman—two artists, mentors and friends whom I continue to collaborate with fifteen-odd years later.

Prior to this commission, the biggest three-dimensional sculpture I'd ever done was traditional basket weaving. I'm not a trained sculptor. In fact, I'm not trained in any specific artistic approach.

AS Right, that's interesting. It's evident that formal training in a specific artistic discipline has not held you back as you have developed a significant body of public artwork! I've also read that you describe yourself as working in 'creative cultural expression'. How do you understand your public practice? Do you consider yourself an artist?

VC To me, the label 'artist' is sort of limiting, as it doesn't adequately encapsulate the spectrum of the work I do nor does it indicate the intention of much of my work. I have no desire to be defined as that or in making work for the gallery and working in that 'fine arts' space in the arts and creative industries.

In my early years working in Aboriginal community affairs, I dabbled in creative work and artmaking as part of my role as project/program producer. I didn't consider myself an artist. It was when I was living on Gunaikurnai Country in the 1990s that I became involved in community arts activities in festivals such as the Mallacoota Festival and cultural reclamation practices like basket weaving. I made a few public artworks, performance pieces and murals and was also part of a group of founding members for the East Gippsland Aboriginal Arts Corporation, where I became interested in printmaking. While still in Gippsland, I became involved in the We Iri We Homeborn exhibition, a state-wide initiative led by Kimba Thompson and Maree Clarke. We Iri We Homeborn was my first exhibition and it was held at the Access Gallery at the National Gallery of Victoria. Kimba and Maree gathered works from artists from across the state; it was a turning point in Victorian Aboriginal arts. This occurred prior to moving home to Warrnambool in my Gunditjmara homelands. Still, I wasn't comfortably calling myself an artist. At some point, I thought 'Okay, alright, I'm an artist, I make artworks, yes.' But then it's come full circle and I now like to use the term 'creative cultural expression'; I can't remember where I heard it first, but I love it. For me, it embraces the breadth of the spectrum of my work across a whole lot of mediums in creating and producing public artworks and my own creative expression. I have been very fortunate and privileged to have had opportunities, especially in making public art, to explore different mediums that, unless you are a trained sculptor, you wouldn't get to work with.

Specifically, I've worked in digital media, projection, sound, stone, metals, timber—all with the help of others. I'm a 'Jill of all trades and master of none'. Oh no, I have to take that back—I am a Master Possum Skin Cloak maker and Knowledge Holder. I can say that emphatically. I've been fortunate and worked in slumped glass for a church window, as well as with cast iron and stainless steel. I am usually working in materials that come from the earth, even if they are in a different form—like glass is sand and cast iron is iron. More recently for my work at ACMI [Yanmeeyarr, 2020], we used a big acrylic carved and hand-polished lens. This has been our first move into a medium that is not 'natural'. Yanmeeyarr was an exercise in painting on the ceiling below which the lens was installed.[3] My family, my sister Lisa, her daughter Tarryn and my sister-in-law [Gina] all came to help—it was fun.

People often ask me why I do what I do, but I know what I do without having to actually articulate it. I'm also a very bad academic and don't write a lot of papers about what I do. Being busy, there's often not always time. It's good to sit down and yarn with someone like you to actually reflect on what I am doing and why.

3 'Yanmeeyarr' means 'flickering in the firelight' and the work reflects on the origins of the moving image. It depicts a painted scene of figures performing a ceremony. Viewers look at the scene through a large polished acrylic lens. See 'Yanmeeyarr', ACMI, accessed 28 October 2021, https://www.acmi.net.au/works/118030--yanmeeyarr.

My motivation to make public artwork is very much about place and the Story of place. It's about the opportunity to create presence and visibility of sovereign unceded lands and the Traditional Custodians and stewards of Country. We're not very visible in the cities or even in the rural landscapes. People are not generally thinking 'this is Aboriginal land', although that is beginning to change; there is momentum and greater awareness and consciousness with people, who, of their own volition, are finding out what Country they're on and acknowledging that in practice daily. But that change is still on the rise, it's not a given everywhere you go and for every person. My work in public spaces is aimed at raising awareness and visibility—creating a conduit if you like, or a point, where the Law of the Land and the continuous concurrency of creation can be discerned, hopefully experienced and people will be changed.

Through the artwork, that universal energy of creation and Aboriginal Law of the Land has a point to emerge and be embodied in and expressed. The Aboriginal Law of the Land and culture and people are ever-present, but it's not necessarily tangible—you have to encounter and engage with the public artwork and understand the Story.

As I mentioned earlier, I'm always negotiating with Traditional Custodians because you can't take your story and put it in someone else's Country. This is the long conversation we've had with colonial settlers: you can't bring your story and put it in someone else's place. This has been the modus operandi of colonisation—to impose a settler story and eradicate the rest. Sorry if that's offensive but it's the truth and something we must all address. The stakes are high. We know, for example, that Lidia Thorpe [a Gunnai Gunditjmara and Djab Wurrung woman who is the first Aboriginal Senator for the state of Victoria] is getting swastikas sent to her in parliament . . . so deep-seated racism is alive and well . . . But there are also good people with good hearts and good minds who are recognising and understanding First Nations position and privilege in first Belonging in these lands and who are becoming allies in support.

AS What you are saying about making sovereignty and the Law of the Land visible and tangible is deeply profound. Let's go back to what drives you to make public art. I was reading about <u>Wurrunggi Biik: Law of the Land</u>, 2019, the public artwork you made for the RMIT University Melbourne city campus—a 2.4 metre cast iron representation of a possum skin cloak. You describe that you wanted the work to effect conversations and facilitate education—which, as a lecturer at RMIT, I have certainly witnessed being activated among students. Can you talk about that more, and about how you see all of these activities that you're doing, and all the different mediums you're doing them in, as a way of generating a conversation?

VC Absolutely, it is about that encounter. A person has to, one would hope, think about it a little bit, or a lot, and they will then go home and literally have conversations: 'I've seen this thing, it's about this, did you know about that?' Also, obviously, that conversation is part of a larger social commentary and social conversations that are happening.

The RMIT work is certainly intended to assert the presence and the Story of place and the Traditional Custodians in place, to create presence, conversation and educate—all of those things—and/or annoy the hell out of the local rednecks, whatever. Whatever works, you know?

It is only recently that I have had the sense of 'freedom' to be able to speak in these terms and to articulate this through reflecting on my work. It's an assertion, a declaration of sovereignty never ceded, of Belonging and expression of, as I have said, our concurrent Creation, neverending and ever-present. It's a reclamation of public space, it's resistance and most importantly it's cultural expression for no other reason than the beauty of our cultures, our Stories and our Belonging to Country/ies.

Interestingly, hardly any of the works [I've been involved in making] have had any graffiti or vandalism—that I'm aware of. So that's good. I think—I hope—it shows respect for place and Story.

AS Public art such as yours often has this dual role of giving Indigenous people a sense of recognition—that they're being honoured—while at the same time they are meant to educate and confront the settler public. Do you always feel that you have to speak to two audiences at once? Or are you focused on Indigenous people foremost? How do you think of your publics?

VC That's a good question. I'm always doing the two because it's a public space, but the priority is, I think—well, for our Mobs—to strengthen and to give that presence. The education then is kind of a by-product, but with intent and purpose. We learn by osmosis, and that education will eventually sink in one way or another, and it will be normalised.

Imagine—that future is possible. For example, my grandkids don't know that I didn't grow up around possum skin cloaks; they just think they're ordinary, and possibly annoying sometimes when I'm making a mess with them at home.

With public art, you get to enjoy it and have fun because you're able to tell a story. Storytelling and people hearing other stories is really important, but there's a responsibility in a way, an obligation, to open those doors.

I've just been mentoring on a public art job, which was really good. I feel like the doors have been opened in numerous ways over the years through people's advocacy and work—obviously going back to Lin Onus, and his father Uncle Bill, and people like that—breaking down barriers into the arts and cultural world. My opportunities to do public art, the work that I do with Creative Victoria and people from the community, and the work that others have been doing, have helped push for change.

I have been fortunate to be sometimes on the front line with other people—opening those doors. You have a responsibility and obligation to keep the door open and to support the next generations and people emerging to be able to take up those opportunities. These days, there are so many opportunities! Someone emailed me another job the other day and I had to just send it out to people and encourage others to do it. There's a lot more support for that, even in policy. In the most practical terms, all government departments now have a minimum 1 or 2 per cent they must spend procuring Indigenous services—road management people, catering, and also public art!

AS That reminds me that I recently heard Badtjala artist Fiona Foley talking about her career in public art. Fiona explained that back in the 1980s and '90s, there weren't many people making work in public around Aboriginal perspectives and histories of colonial violence. She described that in order to realise the public work Witnessing to Silence, 2004, outside the Brisbane Magistrates Court, she had to keep secret from commissioning authorities for two years that the work was actually about ninety-four Aboriginal massacres that took place in Queensland.[4] I am wondering, because

4 See Amy Mitchell-Whittington, 'Brisbane Sculpture's Hidden Message about 94 Massacres', Brisbane Times, 24 April 2017, updated 25 April 2017, https://www.brisbanetimes.com.au/

you seem to be saying that things have gotten better, was there a time when you found it hard to make your public work? What sort of tensions and difficulties have you encountered in trying to realise works?

VC I haven't encountered that directly I suppose, but like you say back in the 1980s and '90s, Fiona was breaking new ground and her subject matter has always been very topical or very confronting, such as her words on the large stones piece [Lie of the Land, 1997, with Chris Knowles. The work comprises seven sandstone pillars etched with words describing the commodities John Batman traded with the Wurundjeri to secure land around Port Phillip Bay[5]].

My work is probably less confronting. It's centred on Indigenous culture and storytelling.

That being said, I would tell the commissioners the story that fitted the brief and fitted satisfactorily for myself and Traditional Custodians. But my underlying intent has always been to disrupt, to create that opportunity; it's not necessarily in your face, but my work's intention is to very subtly but [resolutely] be implacable, immovable . . . to influence, to bring about change and to

national/queensland/brisbane-sculptures-hidden-message-about-94-massacres-20170424-gvrb4n.html.

5 See 'Lie of the Land', City Collection, City of Melbourne, accessed 28 October 2021, http://citycollection.melbourne.vic.gov.au/lie-of-the-land/.

educate. [Most importantly, it is about] inserting a visible point of reference: we are still here!! I don't go smashing down things to make that statement but it's there and it's going to always be there.

I feel like that's always been my intent, but I've never actually discussed that much publicly; I have found better ways to articulate that. The increased use of terms such as 'indigenising' or 'decolonising' in the last few years has created that space, but it probably wouldn't have been as welcome previously, so I just didn't mention it.

Birrarung Wilam was meant to be a dedicated Indigenous space. There was no argument about that and so we weren't doing anything majorly radical in that sense. We've got spears and shields down there and they signal a lot of things—they're representative of the men and of defending Country—and nobody had a problem with that. Perhaps if we'd used different words at the time, it might have been harder for people to take.

AS Do you feel that you'd like to be able to talk more honestly to commissioners now about the radical, disruptive nature of the work?

VC Well, I can now, and I do, but ten to fifteen years ago, no, I didn't know how to articulate that in the same way that we do now. There's now room for settler uncomfortableness in the room. The discomfort was always there, but you can include it and reveal it now in a way. Not that you couldn't before; it's just whether you wanted to choose to be upfront radical or undercover radical. And at this time and at my age/stage of life, I don't care if I offend or create tension. I am comfortable in myself about that . . . it is the time of truth telling—so be it!

AS You already touched on it very briefly, but I wonder if you could talk about the kind of difficulties you encounter with working on other people's Country. How do you negotiate that? Do you find yourself having to turn down opportunities because there's not enough time to build relationships with the Traditional Owners?

VC Oh, there never is enough time, but commissioning organisations are getting a bit better at some of the processes. I recently did a gig where an outside public art curatorial company came in and facilitated the process, and I was the cultural advisor and helped with setting up the process. They were really good at sticking to the process and not trying to rush it. But often, the deadlines really constrain and try to box in the engagement and negotiation relationships with Traditional Custodians especially, and the time for respectful ways of working is compromised because of deadlines. We are always or almost always having to accommodate, be responsive, generous and agile . . . of course, now that there is greater awareness of cultural protocols and respectful ways of working, this has improved in many cases.

AS As a Gunditjmara Keerray Woorroong woman from the Western District of Victoria, do you have many opportunities to make public artworks on your own Country?

VC Not enough, I would love to do more down home. My first opportunity was in 2007, on Country out at the Budj Bim Cultural Landscape from the stone there. The sculpture [dry country/wet country] references the eel traps: it's a big spiral piece on a mound and a firepit out at the Kurtonitj property. It was a Regional Arts Victoria state-wide project titled Fresh and Salty, speaking to water and water use in your region/Country. It involved Indigenous and non-Indigenous artists. I worked with Carmel Wallace, an environmental artist from Portland on the south-west coast of Victoria. We also had four of our young people work on the project as a cultural mentoring, capability-building exercise. It was a really great experience and something that I had aspired to do was to learn the drystone walling technique, so we had drystone wall specialist Alistair Tune come and teach us. I really enjoyed learning about this and working with our young people.

Currently, I am working with Port Campbell on the town centre redesign—that's also on Country. It's easier in a way because you have the support of your community, Elders and also a level of authority as a senior person from that Country because you are on Country and it is your (collective we) Story to work with. I will be working with community and collaborating with and mentoring two younger Gunditjmara artists—one of my daughters and a cousin.[6]

AS As you've mentioned, you often collaborate, both with non-Indigenous artists (such as Jeph Neale and Hilary Jackman) and Indigenous artists (such as Maree Clarke and Treanha Hamm). Do you have particular ways of working with non-Indigenous people as opposed to Indigenous people?

VC It does depend on the project. Jeph and Hilary assist in the design development, in supporting my conceptual thinking as I move through the process of refining and translating an idea into a realised work and then we have technical discussions over the how and what of materials, production and fabrication. Our process has developed over time—I greatly value the knowledge base that they carry. I don't know anyone else like the pair of them. Jeph is a trained sculptor, he used to lecture in design, he's done engineering, he's got the whole bit. Hilary's the director of our colour department because she's the painter and the drawer. So if we need any sketches in situ or whatever, she can do it, because I can't draw (life drawing, that is).

6 See 'Former South-West Resident Vicki Couzens's Artwork Will Be Part of the Port Campbell Town Centre Project', The Standard, 11 July 2020, https://www.standard.net.au/story/6828919/coastal-town-project-is-close-artists-heart/.

They're very respectful and while they acknowledge they are learning about Aboriginal culture, they provide creative insights and expertise that has been accumulated over five or six decades of lived experience. They truly are amazing and wonderful human beings, and I am indebted to them for their friendship and generosity. They have been working with quite a few other Aboriginal artists, such as Mandy Nicholson and Maree Clarke and Sally Gabori and family, to name a few.

Working with Maree, Treanha and others is a negotiated space. We all bring our different views, perspectives, knowledges and skills. At the same time, there is a baseline from which you are working . . . you're kind of on the same page fundamentally because you're Indigenous, so there's a lot of collectively known protocols, conventions and the like that you don't have to explain. This collaborative space is a space of freedom when compared to mainstream working environments where we are in a constant position of justification and compromise and often on the end of unconscious bias, institutional racism or direct personal racism. In mainstream settings and working with non-Indigenous people, we have to contend with the structures, processes and protocols of a system that is generally the antithesis to how we work in our creative collaborations and within our communities.

These days I don't collaborate as much as I used to with Maree and the others, but I'm looking to younger people—my nieces, my daughters, my cousins. We're doing a work for Port Campbell involving sound and song. Brett

Clarke is a singer songwriter, and my daughter Yaraan Bundle and I both do traditional songs and dance, so we're going to write something for a sound piece, a whale song. I'm looking forward to that.

AS You sing and dance as well—it's striking how your creative expression moves so comfortably across a variety of forms and mediums. This connects to another question I had. I was reading about your work in the reclamation of possum skin cloak making and how you were the Artistic Director of the 2006 Commonwealth Games Possum Cloak Project, which brought together communities from across Victoria to wear the cloaks at the opening ceremony. Would you consider this as an extension of your public art practice?

VC Yes, performance and community arts are 'public' and so are an extension.

I've done performance work in both theatre and music over the years here and there. I co-wrote a theatre piece with a group of friends/colleagues that we performed at the Mallacoota Festival in the late 1990s; I also performed with a group called Earth Tribe and Yakkan Wimmun around East Gippsland in the '90s as well. When I moved home to Warrnambool in 1999, I established our Gunditjmara Women and Girls Cultural Dance group and choreographed dance and wrote songs in language for this as well as 'performed' at community events and ceremonies. More recently, my daughter Yaraan Bundle, my sister-in-law Gina Bundle and I collaborated with women from the Indian diaspora, Dr Priya Srinivasan and her colleagues Nithya and Uthra Vijay. We co-wrote, choreographed and performed a hybrid work which comprised elements of Aboriginal and Indian song, dance, movement and story/spoken word. These were woven together in an intertwining two-way narrative as an Earth Honouring, performed at the opening of the Jaipur Literary Festival as part of the Melbourne Writers Festival. It was then developed further to engage with shared/similar creation stories overlapping and intertwining, addressing issues of identity, racism and colonisation. This work, Serpent Women Dreaming, was performed as part of Multicultural Arts 'Mapping Melbourne' 2017.

I really enjoyed this collaboration and wish that I had been able to travel to India with Gina, where our group toured this work, which was again further developed and included two Aboriginal women from NT. Priya and I spoke about the importance of sharing in our respective cultural contexts. Through this, we were able to 'meet' and to create a space for reciprocal learning. It's like the sacred geometry of the circle: a shape that holds, embraces, enfolds and nurtures. We respect those things that we have in common and honour our differences.[7]

7 See Vicki Couzens and Priya Srinivasan, 'On Being, Knowing and Doing', Contemporary Theatre Review, 13 June 2021, https://staging.contemporarytheatrereview.org/2021/on-being-knowing-and-doing/.

Possum skin cloaks are very much part of my 'public' work especially when we are doing ceremony in community or in public events. The 2006 Commonwealth Games in Melbourne was certainly the largest and most public community arts and cultural development project I have been involved in.

AS Finally, is there a particular public artwork that you have in mind that you'd like to make that might be too difficult or ambitious to do at the moment?

VC Oh yeah, I'd love to do a language festival. What that would look like would be all of the things we've talked about: music, sculptural installation, performance, writing, everything. It's not impossible: it's the global decade of Indigenous languages starting next year [2022], so I'm working towards that. What I am thinking and talking about with the Victorian Aboriginal Corporation for Languages—the peak body for Aboriginal languages in Victoria, on which I am a Board member—is developing a concept of a public artwork that honours our Australian/Victorian Aboriginal languages. This idea is inspired by and reproduced from the Wyndham Council Mother Tongue Public Art project that is currently under commission . . . They are honouring Mother Tongue for and on behalf of the Bangladeshi people and other diverse cultures that make up the communities around Tarneit and Wyndham shire. I was inspired by this and thought that as Aboriginal people we should do this for our languages as an Aboriginal-led project.

The other really important public project I still want to do is to have a memorial honouring our Old People who fought and died defending our Country during the homeland wars and massacres during the first contact period of invasion. My father Ivan Couzens, an esteemed Elder of the Keerray Woorroong, expressed to me his vision to see memorials to our Peoples across the Country, especially in our homelands of Gunditjmara Country. This wasn't achieved in Dad's lifetime and so it is one that I will keep working towards in honouring his memory and of course those who have gone before us.

The Edge of Us: Regional Arts Development in the Settler Colony

Danny Butt*

* Dr Danny Butt is Associate Director (Research) at Victorian College of the Arts, University of Melbourne, where he also convenes graduate research in design and social practice. His book _Artistic Research in the Future Academy_ was published by Intellect/University of Chicago Press in 2017. He is the editor (with Jon Bywater and Nova Paul) of _PLACE: Local Knowledge and New Media Practice_ (Cambridge Scholars Press, 2008) and _Internet Governance: Asia Pacific Perspectives_ (Elsevier, 2006). He works with the Auckland-based art collective Local Time, whose work engages the dynamics of visitor and host in the context of mana whenua and discourses of self-determination.

In The Lure of the Local, critic Lucy Lippard contrasts 'hopeful integration' and 'hopeless fragmentation' in diagnosing her own nomadic, 'serially monogamous passion for place'.[1] Throughout her text, art holds a potential key to reconciliation between the communities that Lippard has come from or moved into. But Lippard's integration is via an aspirational figure of art, rather than the political economy of how art is made: funding for art is rarely mentioned in the book. In real life, art sometimes only makes social fragmentation more palpable.

Governmental art funding works in two broad directions. Firstly, it subsidises venues and professional artistic works that service the nation through the cultural uplift of representation. Secondly, it allows people and communities to gain skills and engage civic life through the therapeutic benefits of participatory artistic creation. In the settler colony, the first mode of art is associated with urban centres that hold a critical mass of taste publics that are 'cultural', while regions typically become sites for therapeutic participation. They inherit artistic genres rather than shape them, and transformations in the aesthetic perception of the community are pictured rather than staged.

Regional Arts Victoria, like many organisations emerging from the neo-liberalisation of government arts development from the 1980s, has forged a larger and more diverse range of activities and income streams across the public and private sector to deliver on its mandate of a measurable impact on

1 Lucy R. Lippard, The Lure of the Local: Senses of Place in a Multicentered Society, New Press, New York and London, 1997, p. 6.

place. Small Town Transformations is a Regional Arts Victoria program whose second iteration funded six groups to produce a 'significant artistic project with lasting legacy'.[2] Five small townships in Boonwurrung Country—from Pioneer Bay to Coronet Bay on the shores of Western Port—applied as a group for their project The Edge of Us, 2016–18, under the guidance of artist and Bass Coast Mayor Jordan Crugnale. The project, connecting the towns on the 'edge' of the bay, was led by Melbourne-based artist Jessica Wilson and assisted by resident artist Jeannie Houghton and regional artist Mary Sullivan.

I had moved to one of these towns, Grantville, in 2013, but my engagement with the immediate community was limited, for, like a number of residents, I worked one hundred kilometres away in Melbourne. As with many small, largely white towns in Australia, the community infrastructure in Grantville mostly involved maintaining legacy forms: keeping the barely used town hall viable and retaining membership of the residents and ratepayers association. At meetings held to discuss these issues, I was by far the youngest person in attendance. In accordance with the transition from state- to market-led infrastructure, the residents association has now merged with the business association. Grantville has a reputation as being more working class in origin than some of the other towns, and methamphetamine remains a strong sector of the economy. There is no artistic infrastructure in the immediate area, and I didn't

2 'Small Town Transformations', Regional Arts Victoria, accessed 20 December 2020, http://www.rav.net.au/statewide-projects/small-town-transformations.

hear about The Edge of Us until the community consultations in the region were well underway.

Attending the community steering committee meetings for The Edge of Us curiously felt less like participating in an art project and more like sitting in on the aforementioned resident committees. Senior male voices dominated, and questions directed to the women on the artistic team mostly took the form of 'How are you going to spend the money?' and 'When will you have a proper plan?' With little community experience of, or interest in, artistic autonomy, the grant was imagined as a large pile of cash being siphoned from roading, rubbish or other local government services even though it came from the Victorian state government. Despite the grant being designed specifically to provide artists jobs in the community, paying artists was seen as unnecessary or even undesirable.

Eventually, the artists persevered to deliver the first phase, Luminous Streets, in 2017, using school and community workshops to develop temporary illuminated public sculptures made out of plastic materials and LED lights. The opening nights in the five towns provided rare night-time family-friendly activities. While this event was perceived as a success, there was concern in the community committee that the artistic team's proposed second phase of performances would fail to deliver a 'lasting legacy'. Community aspirations for the second phase moved toward sculptural formations that would demonstrate visible and lasting return on investment in physical structures. A compromise was found in the construction of ground-embedded uplights in each town, conceived as Luminous Galleries that could be activated by the local community for light installations and events.

However, a continuing presence for The Edge of Us on the land raised questions of the status of the sites as Aboriginal land, issues the community constituted around the project had little experience in navigating.[3] Boonwurrung artist Steve Ulula Parker was engaged for the Welcome to Country and launch of the 2017 event in conjunction with Boon Wurrung Foundation Founder and Elder N'arweet Dr Carolyn Briggs AM. Parker was then engaged to develop the concept for the composition of gallery lights, which were installed in the form of constellations, reflecting customary techniques of celestial navigation used by First Peoples in the region. However, in 2017 the Victorian government appointed the Bunurong Land Council Aboriginal Corporation to be the Registered Aboriginal Party for the area, bringing to a close a period of competitive applications between them and the Boon Wurrung Foundation to be the settler government-approved organisation with authority on Aboriginal issues in this area. Those involved in The Edge of Us found that their auspicing group, non-Aboriginal environmental organisation Bass Coast Landcare, was keen to ensure that work with the settler government-approved Aboriginal representatives took priority in the project, even though this compromised the ongoing engagement

3 For a nuanced account of the problematics of Aboriginal engagement by non-Aboriginal practitioners in regional south-east Australia, see Amy Spiers, 'Miranda Must Go: Rethinking the Generative Capacities of Critique, Discomfort and Dissensus in Socially Engaged and Site Responsive Art', PhD diss., University of Melbourne, 2018, https://minerva-access.unimelb.edu.au/handle/11343/216507.

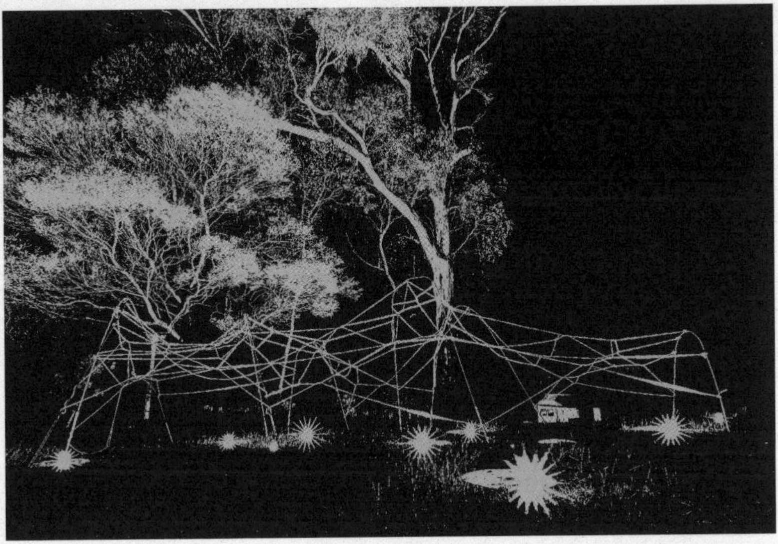

An illuminated public sculpture produced for the event Luminous Streets, April 2017—one of the outcomes of the project The Edge of Us 2016–18, a joint initiative of five townships (Pioneer Bay, Grantville, Tenby Point, Corinella and Coronet Bay) located on Boonwurrung Country around Western Port Bay, south-east of Melbourne. Supported by the Victorian Government's Small Town Transformations program, the project was led by artist Jessica Wilson and assisted by artists Jeannie Houghton and Mary Sullivan. Photo: Anna Carson

with an Aboriginal artist from the area, with the plans to involve Parker in programming falling aside. The tension highlighted again how the efforts of The Edge of Us to localise the process of community engagement fell afoul of larger-scale problems—in this case, the government's colonial anxiety to promote 'stability' in recognition of Aboriginal authority by endorsing competitive Aboriginal governance structures according to non-Aboriginal criteria.

The Edge of Us may have had largely positive effects for non-Aboriginal residents, but this benefit was perhaps incremental rather than 'transformative'. The project fostered a platform and intermittent opportunities for creative artists to connect in some of the towns. But there are larger problematics of who small waterline towns are for today, and what mandate they have to create a legacy. The towns' establishment as Victoria's first settlements in the nineteenth century was part of the genocidal dispossession of local Aboriginal peoples. Aboriginal 'placemaking' is what settler colonial culture set out to destroy, and this mindset is sedimented intergenerationally into local governance in ways that art is not well suited to address or repair, despite settler hunger for narratives of reconciliation.[4] As cities become increasingly hostile to artists through gentrification and the COVID-19 pandemic, settler-colonial artistic

4 The way colonial inclusionary cultures and settler hunger for Indigenous content ultimately suppress Indigenous self-determination is articulated in Dylan Robinson, Hungry Listening: Resonant Theory for Indigenous Sound Studies, University of Minnesota Press, Minneapolis, 2020.

attention is turning to Indigenous culture outside the city for aesthetic experiences grounded in place and in distinction from default settler colonial norms. Projects such as The Edge of Us have a lot to teach us about the problems of figuring 'community' in artistic work in this domain.[5]

5 For Marina Vishmidt, 'the constitutive indeterminacy of the aesthetic driving the speculative mode of production can become an active negativity, essential both for a rupture with that mode of production and for instituting the speculative as social change'. See Vishmidt, Speculation as a Mode of Production: Forms of Value Subjectivity in Art and Capital, Historical Materialism series, vol. 176, Brill, Leiden, Netherlands, 2018, p. 13. This figuration of art's speculative potential is the opposite of the managerial/ameliorative mode.

Interpreting Difficult Knowledge: What Difference Do Artists Make?

Alison Atkinson-Phillips*

* Dr Alison Atkinson-Phillips is a public historian based at Newcastle University, UK, where she serves as the University's first lecturer in public history. Her practice uses oral history along with visual and other sources to explore such areas as mutual aid responses to COVID-19, food poverty, deindustrialisation and the history of public commemorative practices. Her doctoral research was published as Survivor Memorials: Remembering Trauma and Loss in Contemporary Australia (UWA Publishing, 2019), and she has had a long involvement in social justice advocacy at a community level, including campaigns on prison justice and responses to asylum seekers in Australia.

Introduction

Memorials provide a public space for private grief. But as public artworks, they do more than simply offer a physical space; they also provide an emotional and conceptual one by interpreting the meaning of a painful event. The best public memorials do this in a way that is open enough to allow both survivors (those directly impacted) and the wider public to engage with a difficult history. A growing number of memorials in Australia and elsewhere move beyond the commemoration of death, and remember painful experiences people have lived through. The creators of these memorials are tasked with interpreting topics that were previously considered private or taboo in the public realm—histories of colonisation, genocide, child institutionalisation and sexual abuse, as well as civic and natural disasters and violent conflict. The work of acknowledging these events and experiences in public spaces, respectfully and carefully, is both important and difficult. However, the impact on those who take on the burden of this memory work is rarely discussed. In this essay, I explore the role of public artists and commissioners in respectfully and powerfully bringing traumatic histories into the public realm. Drawing on interviews with artists and arts workers who have been responsible for some of these challenging memorial projects, I consider what it means to interpret the past in this way. Memorial artists bring creativity to the project, but alongside their artistic skills they must be willing to listen to the pain of others and to interpret it in a public space, in a way that honours the experiences of survivors.

Historicising This Discussion

Recent debate about commemorative public art has tended to focus on figurative statues of colonial figures, mostly installed during the 'monument mania' of the late nineteenth century. The #Rhodesmustfall campaign that began in Cape Town, South Africa, during March 2015 has been followed by multiple waves of discussion and protest in cities around the world, including in Australia. During the British summer of 2020, this debate was re-ignited when Black Lives Matter protesters in Bristol pulled down the statue of former slave-owner Edward Colston and dumped it in the local harbour. Public debate about the kinds of histories we should be celebrating in our public spaces is vital, but the discussion of whether or not to keep or remove old statues ignores a fundamental shift that has taken place over the last thirty years in the kinds of histories being commemorated in public spaces. As Malcolm Miles wrote, memorials and public art 'both define and make visible the values of the public realm, and do so in a way which is far from neutral, never simply decorative'.[1] Many of the newer memorials demonstrate a democratising of the public realm. These memorials recognise the pain suffered by people who have been pushed to the margins, and whose experiences would not previously have been acknowledged publicly in this form, or perhaps at all. In Australia, this includes families and communities harmed by government policies of assimilation and social engineering (Aboriginal Stolen Generations, Commonwealth child migrants and those impacted by forced

1 Malcolm Miles, Art, Space and the City: Public Art and Urban Futures, Routledge, London, 1997, p. 61.

adoptions until the 1970s) and the thousands of children impacted in various ways by the child institutionalisation of the twentieth century, particularly those who were sexually assaulted while under the 'care' of these institutions. Twenty-first-century memorials also acknowledge the harm suffered by people living through bushfires and floods.

Such a shift did not happen overnight, but is rather the result of decades of memory activism as well as the creative work of artists who were willing to re-imagine the possibilities of the public memorial. Among these artists is Maya Lin, whose ground-breaking (literally) Vietnam Veterans Memorial (VVM) in Washington DC, dedicated in 1982, is commonly cited as marking a postwar shift in the memorial form. The VVM does not celebrate war, but is designed to be 'read' as a book of names, with all those killed listed in the chronological order of their death, regardless of their role in the war. Because the names begin in the centre of the 'book', memorial participants must walk a long way to physically read each one; the highly polished surface of the memorial means they see themselves literally reflected as they reflect on the meaning of war. Memorials since the VVM are usually designed to be democratic and experiential.[2]

James E. Young has suggested that the VVM served as a catalyst for the German artists of the 1980s and 1990s, 'for the expression of their own national shame, for their revulsion against

2 For more about the experiential nature of contemporary memorials, see Quentin Stevens and Karen A. Franck, <u>Memorials as Spaces of Engagement: Design, Use and Meaning</u>, Routledge, London, 2015.

traditionally authoritarian, complacent, and self-certain national shrines'.[3] In Australia, the 1980s and 1990s saw a similar re-imagining of the memorial form and the emergence of what SueAnne Ware termed the anti-memorial.[4] Having rejected the monumentality of earlier commemorative public art, many such projects were ephemeral in nature, but nonetheless made an impact on other artists and the public. We can see this by tracing one particular project that has survived—the Noble Park Peace Park Mosaic, created in 1994 through a community arts project involving first- and second-generation migrants and refugees from Melbourne's south-eastern suburbs.

This project came about because the local branch of the Returned Services League (RSL) was seeking funding to revitalise the green space near their building, where the local war memorial is located. The council supported this idea, but wanted to develop 'a more inclusive commemorative space, given the cultural make-up of the area, with a large number of refugees in recent years and many migrants in earlier waves of settlement'.[5] Melbourne's south-east had attracted many new migrants in the postwar era, drawn to jobs in the manufacturing industry. In the neighbouring suburb

3 James E. Young, The Stages of Memory: Reflections on Memorial Art, Loss, and the Spaces Between, University of Massachusetts Press, Amherst, 2016, p. 4.

4 SueAnne Ware, 'Anti-Memorials and the Art of Forgetting: Critical Reflections on a Memorial Design Practice', Public History Review, vol. 15, August 2008.

5 Kitty Owens, email to the author, 12 February 2016.

of Springvale, the Enterprise Migrant Hostel ran as an arrival point from 1969 to 1992, first for assisted migrants and later for refugees. Engaging with migrant history through a community oral history project meant that a more inclusive commemoration was created, with the lived experiences of local residents inspiring a mosaic depicting civilian experiences of war. Originally a single wall-length mural on the side of the RSL hall, it was restored a decade later and re-positioned as a series of discrete panels. A plaque written in the voice of the migrants reads as follows: 'This mural is dedicated to the friends and relatives of this area who died in war and to those people we have been separated from in the process of migration. It is also a celebration of peace.'[6]

While not exactly ephemeral, the original project had the primary aim of building an inclusive community, rather than creating a permanent memorial. Such an approach was not unique at the time (the mid-1990s), although it is unusual that the artwork was maintained and even restored—a testament to its local significance. My point here is that contemporary memorials do not always look as we expect them to look or exist where we might traditionally expect them to be located. In the development of many contemporary memorials, there are unacknowledged participants, council workers or memory activists who play a significant role in bringing the project to fruition.

6 Kitty Owens, Libby McKinnon, Christine Mae Chua, et al., Peace Park Mosaic, ceramic mosaic, Noble Park, City of Greater Darebin, Victoria, 1994, restored by Libby McKinnon in 2003.

What Does It Mean to Make Difficult Knowledge Public?

In the twenty-first century, the changes in commemorative forms started in the 1980s and 1990s have become established. As I have outlined elsewhere, the end of the last century saw the emergence of some significant grassroots memory work in Australia, which has solidified over the last two decades into established bureaucratic processes through which memorials can be developed.[7] Some older traditions continue, such as the use of materials associated with mourning—rock (particularly, granite), water and certain plants—the engraving of names and the creation of pathways. However, the commission briefs and calls for expressions of interest that artists respond to are increasingly steering them away from traditional forms—especially figurative statuary—and asking for creative interpretation.

These days, by the time an artist is commissioned to create a memorial, the event or experience is almost always already publicly known. In particular, I am referring to memorials created in response to government inquiries and most recently the Australian Royal Commission into Institutional Responses to Child Sexual Abuse. And yet, we could equally argue that the experiences and issues discussed in these public inquiries were already public. The history of the child migrants in the 2001 Lost Innocents report[8] had already been told in

7 Alison Atkinson-Phillips, Survivor Memorials: Remembering Trauma and Loss in Contemporary Australia, University of Western Australia Publishing, Perth, 2019.

8 Commonwealth of Australia, Lost Innocents: Righting the Record—Report

numerous ways, including through the 1992 miniseries The Leaving of Liverpool[9] and Margaret Humphreys's 1994 book Empty Cradles (later interpreted on film as Oranges and Sunshine).[10] Similarly, Anna Haebich makes a compelling argument that 'evidence of Aboriginal child removal has been circulating in the public arena from early colonial times to the present'.[11] The work we ask memorial artists to do is not the work of the investigative reporter or the public inquiry. What then is it?

Writing about Peru's civil conflict in which the government, army and police were implicated, Cynthia Milton notes the 'double scandal' articulated by truth commission president Salomón Lerner: first the human rights abuses; and second the indifference of those who could have stopped them. Milton writes, 'The latter scandal endures in public forums: indifference to past violence continues in the form of quasi-denial mixed with a rewriting of

on Child Migration, 30 August 2001, https://www.aph.gov.au/Parliamentary_Business/Committees/Senate/Community_Affairs/completed_inquiries/1999-02/child_migrat/report/index.htm.

9 The Leaving of Liverpool, two-part television miniseries, directed by Michael Jenkins, written by John Alsop and Sue Smith, first aired 8 and 9 July 1992 in Australia on ABC TV.

10 Margaret Humphreys, Empty Cradles, Doubleday, London, 1994; Oranges and Sunshine, directed by Jim Loach, written by Rona Munro, Icon Film Distribution, Bristol, 2011.

11 Anna Haebich, '"Between Knowing and Not Knowing": Public Knowledge of the Stolen Generations', Aboriginal History, vol. 25, 2001, p. 71.

the past.'[12] This sentence could equally have been written about the experiences of human rights abuse suffered by those whose experiences have been the subject of Australia's various public inquiries and Royal Commissions. In response to that double scandal, Milton claims that artist Lika Mutal's El Ojo que llora (The Eye that Cries), 2005, 'acts as a countervailing force' against those who would rather ignore or deny the past by inscribing it in the landscape.[13] Similarly, this is the work that artists who take on Australia's public memory work are being asked to do.

The Artist's Role as Historical Interpreter

Government-funded memorials at the state or national level are usually commissioned in response to specific recommendations of public inquiries, and only after those findings have gained widespread public acceptance. Memorials instigated at a more local level, either by local government or individual institutions, are more likely to be driven by an individual 'memory activist' who is skilled at building consensus. In either of these situations, public art processes usually involve experienced public art administrators or consultants, whose role is to shape ideas about what the memorial is about into a design brief that an artist can respond to. These professionals also play an important role as a point of contact between the community of memory and the artist, as well as sometimes taking on more practical project management roles. Projects often develop through a call for artists to submit an

12 Cynthia E. Milton, 'Defacing Memory: (Un)Tying Peru's Memory Knots', Memory Studies, vol. 4, no. 2, 2011, p. 193.

13 Ibid.

expression of interest. Sometimes, this involves the submission of a draft design, but more often shortlisting takes place based on evidence of their past work. Public art workers, whether employed by local government or working as consultants, understand that artists need a range of skills beyond their creative practice to respond to these briefs. Increasingly, this is taken into account at the project initiation stage.

I have written elsewhere that memorials are a form of testimony.[14] However, in contrast to traditional forms of testimony, which try to directly represent the voice of the oppressed, memorials are created by artists who are only rarely the direct survivors of the experiences they give voice to. Instead, their work is an act of interpreting the testimony of those survivors, whether directly or mediated through previous memory work.

Another way of thinking about this is to consider the role of the artist as an 'outsider-witness', whose role is to listen to the testimony of survivors of trauma and reflect back to them in a way that assists them to recognise their own agency. This idea comes from Rosanne Kennedy and Tikka Jan Wilson's article, 'Constructing Shared Histories', in which they draw on the model of narrative therapy developed by psychologist Michael White for addressing trauma.[15] In contrast to

14 Alison Atkinson-Phillips, 'Material Testimony: Memorials Bearing Witness to Experiences of Loss and Trauma', in Cristina Santos, Adriana Spahr and Tracy Crowe Morey (eds), Testimony and Trauma: Engaging Common Ground, Brill, Leiden, 2019, pp. 13–35.

15 Rosanne Kennedy and Tikka Wilson, 'Constructing Shared Histories: Stolen

the psychoanalytic model (in which the traumatised person tells their story to a therapist), in narrative therapy the survivor tells their story to a third party (the outsider-witness). Kennedy and Wilson make the crucial point that testimony is 'an inherently social process, requiring a community that shares and participates in the discourse—both retrospectively and prospectively'.[16] I think of the memorial creator as an active listener whose role is to hear the story of the survivors and to re-tell that story back to them—their pain but also their strength and resistance—in a way that assists them to move forward into the future. At the same time, the process and finished project needs to acknowledge that the past continues to have an impact in the present. The depth and complexity of this role, and its impact on the artist, are hugely underestimated and should not be undertaken lightly.

Memorial artists often talk of the need to create 'space' for meaning in their work. This reflects a shift away from the didactic, educative role of earlier times. Contemporary memorial artists draw on an expanded repertoire of elements, including space and time, to open up meaning—or at least, to avoid the closing down of meaning. This means avoiding a sentimental over-identification with the pain of others. In Lauren Berlant's terms, sentimentality involves 'the presumption of emotional clarity and affective recognition in the

Generations Testimony, Narrative Therapy and Address', in Jill Bennett and Rosanne Kennedy (eds), World Memory: Personal Trajectories in Global Time, Palgrave Macmillan, London, 2003, pp. 119–39.

16 Ibid., p. 132.

scene of the mediated encounter'.[17] Rather, memorial artists need to find a way to acknowledge the gap between past and present, and to acknowledge the uniqueness of each survivor's experience, while also finding a way to build a sense of shared community and connectedness.

The Process of 'Listening'

The way artists listen varies from project to project. In some situations, listening is literal, direct and immediate; in others, it is mediated.[18] When memorials are created in response to various kinds of public inquiries, a listening process has already been undertaken, as survivors have given their testimony in written submissions and in person. Beyond this, there is often an intermediate process of listening that takes place with a selected group of survivors and a trusted government worker who may or may not have an arts background. In the example of the Western Australian state memorial to the Forgotten Australians, this person was Marie Waldeck from the Department for Child Protection,

17 Lauren Berlant, The Female Complaint: The Unfinished Business of Sentimentality in American Culture, Duke University Press, Durham, 2008, p. 271.

18 Even when listening is a direct embodied experience between the artist and survivor(s), it is always mediated by social and cultural factors in ways that I am still working towards understanding. See, for example, Dylan Robinson, Hungry Listening: Resonant Theory for Indigenous Sound Studies, University of Minnesota Press, Minneapolis, 2020. See also Leah Bassel, The Politics of Listening, Palgrave Pivot, London, 2017.

who played a liaison role between the Forgotten Australians Committee and the other participants in the memorial process. In particular, she acted as a conduit between their ideas and desires for the memorial and Andra Kins, who was appointed as a public art consultant to frame the call for expressions of interest.

Judith Forrest and Terri-ann White, respectively the creator and writer responsible for the resulting memorial artwork, Unfolding Lives, 2010, both conducted detailed research by reading the existing published accounts, including personal and collective memoirs, and the Forgotten Australians and Lost Innocents reports.[19] Later in the process, they were also able to hear directly from care leavers. White met the care leavers committee once in an 'informal setting' and again with Forrest for two more formal workshops, where they presented the ideas for the memorial and received feedback (both facilitated by Waldeck).[20] For both Forrest and White, that research was a painstaking process. Rather than a collaboration from the beginning,

19 Commonwealth of Australia, Forgotten Australians: A Report on Australians Who Experienced Institutional or Out-of-Home Care as Children, 30 August 2004, https://www.aph.gov.au/parliamentary_business/committees/senate/community_affairs/completed_inquiries/2004-07/inst_care/report/index; Commonwealth of Australia, Lost Innocents: Righting the Record—Report on Child Migration, 30 August 2001, https://www.aph.gov.au/parliamentary_business/committees/senate/community_affairs/completed_inquiries/1999-02/child_migrat/report/index.

20 Terri-ann White, oral history interview with the author, 6 May 2014.

Forrest produced a design into which White's text would be incorporated. The workshops with the care leavers happened after Forrest's design—a large-scale model of a 'chatterbox' toy—had already been approved by a committee of high-level government stakeholders. Reflecting on the process, and despite having only limited direct engagement with the care leavers themselves, Forrest said she had needed to draw on a range of life skills and wondered if artists with less experience would have managed. She didn't know if that wider experience was part of the criteria on which she was selected for the commission, 'but it should have been'.[21]

Artist Mikala Dwyer detailed a similar process when working with the City of Sydney on A Lamp for Mary, 2010, a rape memorial in Surry Hills. Early research involved looking at images of the original laneway murals, created in the immediate aftermath of the hate crime, a homophobic rape attack on Mary as she was leaving a lesbian nightclub. Replacing the murals that had 'carpeted' the laneway where the rape took place, Dwyer's memorial is a giant, hot pink lamp through which light reflects in disco rainbows. Her aim was to bring the comfort of an internal space, represented by the lamp, out to the potentially threatening street. Both Forrest and Dwyer spoke in almost mystical terms of a moment when they knew that their design offered 'what was needed'. For Dwyer, it was a 'lightning fast' moment of intuition, whereas for Forrest, the process involved weeks of experimentations and some false starts. For both, however, the initial concept was then honed by

21 Judith Forrest, oral history interview with the author, 7 April 2014.

interactions with a wider community of memory—in Dwyer's case, not only Mary herself but also the LGBTQI+ community of Sydney.

Another common element of these projects is the incorporation of text that fundamentally shapes the public's encounter with the memorial itself. In the case of Unfolding Lives, the text is integrated into the artwork, appearing as handwriting directly onto the chatterbox form. Memorial participants are invited into the intimate space of the memorial, having to move closer to read the words on the inside folds of the chatterbox, or inscribed on the ground within three diagrams. Never attempting to tell a full, closed narrative of 'what happened', the text reflects the fragmentary and sometimes contradictory experiences of life in institutional 'care'. In contrast, the text that is part of the Lamp for Mary is bright, immediately visible, and offers no protection to the reader when it narrates what happened in that space. In her research for the artwork, Dwyer watched Melissa Lee's Mary's Place video documentary, which features interviews with Mary herself and outlines the wider context of the attack.[22] Dwyer became convinced that text was needed to counter the sense of safety the artwork attempted to create, and so invited writer Michael Taussig to contribute. His text, influenced by Mary's words, narrates the brutality of the attack, and had to be carefully negotiated with the City of Sydney and local residents and businesses. While it does not shy away from naming the attack as rape, it offers, in Dwyer's words, 'space' for interpretation.

22 Mary's Place, documentary directed by Melissa Lee, Queer Screen, Sydney, VHS tape, 50 minutes, 1998.

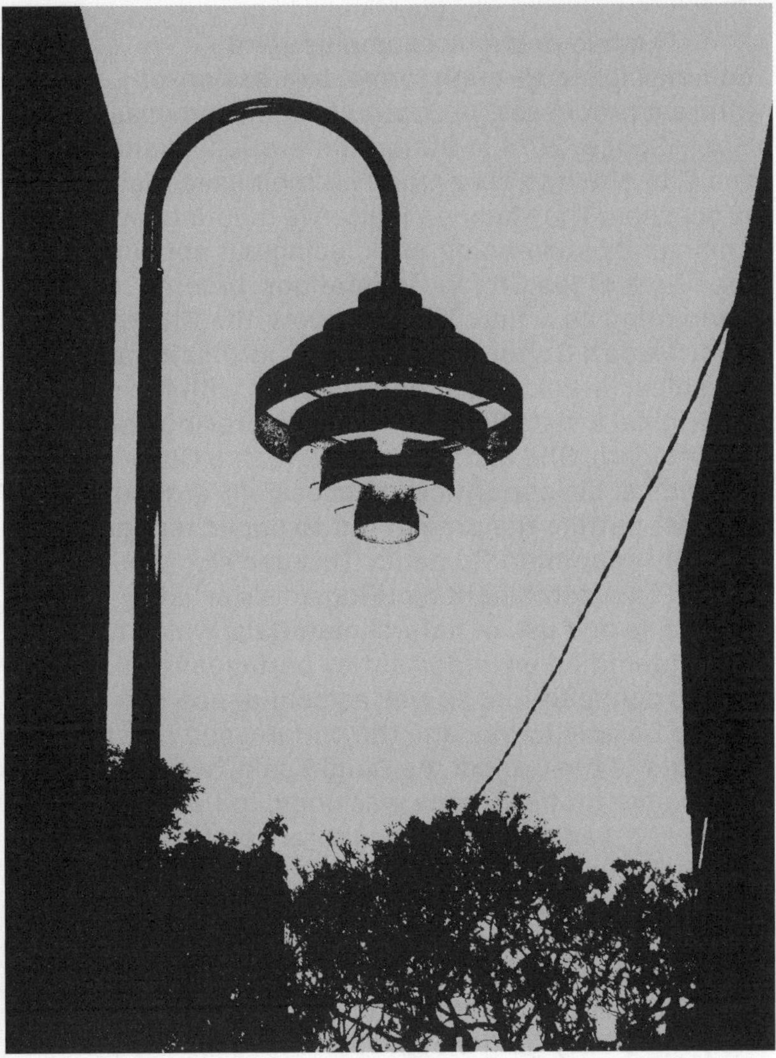

Mikala Dwyer, A Lamp for Mary 2010. City of Sydney commission, installed 2011 in Mary Place in the Sydney suburb of Surry Hills. A text contributed by writer Michael Taussig accompanies the lamp on an adjacent brick wall in pink laser-cut lettering. Image courtesy of the artist

The two previous examples were commissioned through formal expression-of-interest processes. In contrast, when commissioning Sorry Space, 2014, a Stolen Generations memorial, the City of Whittlesea modified their usual public art processes. They held consultative meetings with community stakeholders, including but not limited to members of the Stolen Generations, before appointing an artist. Sandy Caldow, the City of Whittlesea's Cultural Collection Coordinator and herself an artist, had already worked with the Aboriginal artist Glenn Romanis on previous public art projects. She and Donna Wright, the City's Aboriginal Liaison Officer, successfully argued against putting the project out to public tender and directly appointed Romanis. This decision was based on a combination of Romanis's artistic expertise and use of natural materials, which had been identified as important by participants in a public consultation, as well as confidence that he would be able to manage the cultural and emotional aspects of the project. As Wright said, 'we needed to make sure that everyone was going to be okay, and everyone was safe, from a cultural point of view and emotionally as well'.[23]

Romanis, who has been creating public art for over twenty years, uses an established process that involves working with the story of the physical site as well as the story of the community itself.[24] He also has a very gentle approach that seeks to draw people into the story of a space, rather than making bold statements that may confront or alienate them.

23 Donna Wright, oral history interview with the author, 24 November 2014.

24 Glenn Romanis, oral history interview with the author, 20 November 2020.

In the case of Sorry Space, the process involved meeting with the Wurundjeri Traditional Owners and Elders to make sure what was created was appropriate on their Country, as well as to Stolen Generations survivors and their families. Wright facilitated many of these meetings, and emphasised that Romanis's background as an Aboriginal artist was important in terms of people being able to trust him with their stories. The location outside of the City of Whittlesea offices also complicated the brief, because Sorry Space needed to be a place of contemplation but also fit in with the wider civic complex.

Romanis explained the challenges of this work, saying, 'When you're interpreting someone else's story, they're not your thoughts . . . and you're trying to do the best you can with making sure it's right. It can be challenging when you're dealing with a really full-on story.'[25] Rather than attempting to directly tell the 'layered hurt and history' he was hearing, Romanis used wood and stone to map the landscape to show the meeting of two rivers (the River Plenty and Darebin Creek) as a representation of the Wurundjeri people and those who have come from other places. In the finished memorial, two wooden benches in the shape of gum leaves edge a tear-shaped stone mosaic in a meeting place designed for both private contemplation and public ritual. According to Wright, the tear represents 'Tears of joy when the families were reunited and tears for families that were never reunited.'[26] On National Sorry Day, a custom wooden bowl is brought out expressly to be used for smoking

25 Ibid.
26 Wright, oral history, 2014.

ceremonies. Again, the success of the work is in the space it leaves for memorial participants to encounter the layers of meaning.

Whereas Romanis sought to tell the Stolen Generations story through a mapping of land and Country, one of the lead artists whose work forms the Colebrook Reconciliation Park, Silvio Apponyi, opted for figurative statuary. With its first plaque dedicated in 1997, Colebrook is Australia's first memorial to acknowledge the pain and loss of the Stolen Generations. At the time, there was no established process for this kind of commemoration of lived experience. An extensive time of listening preceded the formal memorial creation. This happened in a very grassroots way over a few years, through a relationship between ex-residents of the Colebrook Home for Aboriginal Children (the Tji Tji Tjuta[27]) and the Blackwood Reconciliation Group (BRG). Apponyi, an established sculptor, happened to live locally and regularly walked through the site, which was at that stage vacant land. He was approached by the BRG to work with them. The commemorative sculptures on the site, the Fountain of Tears, 1998, and the Grieving Mother, 1999, were created by Apponyi working with Kaurna artist Sherine Rankin and with two Tji Tji Tjuta members, Yankunytjatjara artists Kunyi McInerney and Jane Pole, in an advisory role. McInerney also painted the Reconciliation Mural, 2005, a later addition to the site.

The idea for the Fountain of Tears emerged out of an organic process of meetings and conversations. In an effort to save on costs, Apponyi carved the four faces of the Fountain of Tears directly into the

27 This name, meaning 'all the children', refers to the formalised ex-residents' group.

stone as the models sat and shared their stories. This created a more immediate and intense process of listening than any of the projects described so far, since three of the four faces are ex-residents of Colebrook. When Apponyi spoke about the impact the four different models had on him, he had especially fond memories of carving Yankunytjatjara Elder Mona Olsson, one of the oldest survivors from the Home, who has consistently emphasised the need for forgiveness and reconciliation. Carving Ngarrindjeri woman Doris Kartinyeri, on the other hand, was a much more confronting experience. Kartinyeri told Apponyi she didn't want to be sad, she wanted to be angry,[28] and while there were moments of lightness during the sittings, the emotional impact of attempting to honestly translate her pain and anger into sculptural form weighed heavily on him.[29] Apponyi was again the lead artist for the Grieving Mother in 1999, and by the end of the two-year process, his physical and emotional health was seriously impacted—he contracted pneumonia about the time of the dedication of Grieving Mother, and said he felt that it was as a direct result of the demanding work of listening and trying to carefully represent the Colebrook survivors' experience through his artwork.

Artists in the Immediate Aftermath

Very occasionally, artists themselves are the ones to instigate a memorial project. The idea for AFTER

28 Doris Kartinyeri, oral history interview with the author, 23 April 2015.

29 Silvio Apponyi, oral history interview with the author, 23 April 2015.

(Art From the Extended Region), 2010, which commemorates the Black Saturday bushfires in the Victorian country town of Kyneton, came from Kathryn Portelli, a local artist whose husband was one of the volunteer firefighters involved in putting out the blaze. Having spent the day in a state of alertness, worried for her partner and ready to leave their home if necessary, Portelli attended an artists' gathering in Melbourne on the Sunday. Those present came together in a minute's silence for the people affected by the fires. Portelli described being moved by the empathy and solidarity expressed by artists from other places who had not directly been impacted by the fires. One of the older women in the group asked, 'what can we do?', which started Portelli thinking about her role as an artist. She described how the memorial idea came to her as she slept that night:

> I have the drawing actually, the very first sketching drawing . . . And it never really changed from this because now it was going to be art-directed rather than artist-directed. You know? It was going to change dependent on contributors, so I didn't make my drawing any more sophisticated, but this is the image I saw overnight after the fires and then this conversation, this group, the silence and the impact that had on me.
>
> And in my mind I saw, I walked along that wall, so I saw the square windows above, I saw the bricks, I saw the shape, I saw my design suited that wall. I saw the fire scene, I saw dark, I saw transitioning to light. I saw a jagged beginning and end and I saw this black and white row through the middle. And I walked it in my mind that Sunday night after the Black

> Saturday. So from then on I'm a worker. Because it's already invented, it's already designed for me, so I don't have to plan a different shape or anything.[30]

While Portelli's account emphasises the serendipitous way the design came together (indeed, later in the interview, she said she felt she 'received' the design), her ability to carry out the project was built on many years of experience as an artist. The local shire workers to whom she went with the design had confidence in her ability to carry out the project, because of her existing track record as a public artist, including knowing how materials respond to the weather conditions of the Victorian hills. The gumleaf motif fits the idea of the memorial well, and was already ready to use, thanks to an earlier project that Portelli was working on for a local business.

Perhaps equally important, Portelli knew her limits. She understood that her enthusiasm for the project and her 'art language' was sometimes difficult for those who were grieving:

> You get all those sort of emotional rollercoaster conversations that without any skill—no psych skill, no art therapy skill, no anything skill—you're in the deep end all the time. And sometimes I've had the right response, and other times I'd think, 'Whoa, I hope I was okay with that.' I sounded so artist and not counsellor . . . so I was in the deep end. Not drowning but floundering many times.[31]

30 Kathryn Portelli, oral history interview with the author, 27 November 2014.

31 Ibid.

The Macedon Ranges Shire Council devised a system that enabled people to participate without always approaching Portelli directly, and empowered intermediaries such as counsellors to raise the question of memorial involvement when the time was right. Rather than listening directly to people's stories, Portelli and her team of volunteer mosaic artists received small fragments of the material of their lives and carefully, painstakingly created beauty out of the destruction of the fires. For each commemorative tile on the public memorial, a duplicate was made for the fire-affected person as a private keepsake.

Spaces for Sharing Stories

As seen in Sorry Space, memorials increasingly incorporate opportunities for participants to rest a while, to talk and to listen to each other's stories. Sometimes, that opportunity comes in the making of the memorial itself. For example, the Stolen Generations Memorial and Healing Garden, 2014, at Andrews Farm in South Australia is a native garden with a path of coloured rock. Mosaic leaves punctuate the path at certain points, and in the central area is a circular mosaic. These are made of many individual circular rocks painted by members of the Stolen Generations and their families in community workshops. The workshops offered an opportunity for intergenerational sharing. Participants are drawn to the space to find their tile, and bringing together the many individual expressions creates a sense of their shared experience being valued.

Another example of a memorial project involving community art is the Kambah Firestorm Storytree Memorial, 2005, created by artist Bryan

Carrick working with the community of the Mount Taylor Estate in the aftermath of a severe bushfire that burned through 70 per cent of the Australian Capital Territory in January 2003. The memorial is the trunk of a tree that was killed by the fire, carved and painted with imagery that imagines what it might have seen in its two hundred years of life. The base of the trunk and nearby seating is covered in mosaic tiles created by residents. The <u>Firestorm Storytree</u> carving shows the skill of the artist, both in the technical aspects of the carving and the composition of the design. However, part of the artist's skill was also his ability to understand the nature of the loss suffered by the community, and to the find an appropriate way to engage with it. As is the case for the painted rocks of the Andrews Farm memorial, the quality of the individual elements might not necessarily be high, but a skilled artist can bring these together to create something that is meaningful for the community of memory.

Public Art Practicalities

Managing the cost of any public art project is a careful balancing act, but particularly so when commemorating a trauma with ongoing impacts. Survivors may appreciate their experiences being acknowledged through public art, but they don't want to see money wasted that could be spent on reparations or other more practical healing work. Many of the artists I spoke with acknowledged the challenges of fulfilling the brief within a very limited budget. The need to ensure the work is weather-proof and vandal-proof often absorbs much of what might originally seem like a generous budget, particularly when working with subcontractors. Partly because of the seriousness with which they take on the responsibility, memorial artists often work well beyond what they are paid for. They also take on an unpaid responsibility (with others) to maintain the memorial. Both Dwyer and Forrest mentioned writing to the council to inform them of maintenance issues, and when I interviewed Portelli in Kyneton, she had with her a feather duster for cleaning AFTER on her way past.

Conclusion

Artists play an integral and under-researched role in the creation of meaningful memorial spaces. As Hilde Hein points out:

> Artists do not have privileged vision, but they do have a practiced eye and the ability to speak in a rich variety of languages—verbal, visual, conceptual, sensual, serious, humorous, figurative, and rational. Sometimes and somehow they break through ordinary expectation and cause people to venture upon new perspectives.[32]

The more practised and skilled they are at their craft, including the parts of their craft that involve listening to people and context, the more an artist is able to create work that 'breaks through' in some way. Nonetheless, this work does not come without personal cost.

In preparing this essay, I returned to interviews I had conducted with artists and arts administrators five years ago, for a project that was eventually published as Survivor Memorials.[33] At that time, I

32 Hilde Hein, 'What Is Public Art?: Time, Place, and Meaning', The Journal of Aesthetics and Art Criticism, vol. 54, no. 1, 1996, p. 5.

33 Atkinson-Phillips, Survivor Memorials.

had interviewed the two council workers (Donna Wright and Sandy Caldow) involved in commissioning Sorry Space, which had only recently been dedicated. Both women were more than happy to participate in an interview and to speak to me about the development of the project, but were reluctant to put me in touch with the artist. Indeed, they emphasised that the project had taken 'a lot out of him emotionally', a statement which chimed with what I had heard from other artists and so I did not attempt to take things further.

Five years later, I thought enough time had passed, and hoped to hear more about the project from the artist's perspective. As is clear from the earlier discussion, while somewhat uncomfortable talking about himself, Glenn Romanis was eloquent in discussing the way he sees his role as an 'interpreter' rather than an artist. We spoke about the challenge of balancing competing demands of story, site, technical and emotional requirements, and the burden that such interpretive work places on the artist. However, when I asked how the project was different from other commissions, the conversation came to a stop. Romanis eventually replied simply, 'It's really, really hard.'

Not all artists do what Romanis did, and engage directly with survivors to listen to their stories in person. But all artists who work on commemorative artworks, whether self-instigated or commissioned, are taking on the burden of memory. They use their skills of listening, imagining and interpreting to create spaces where difficult knowledge is brought into the public sphere. Such spaces not only need to be meaningful for the community of memory, including direct survivors and others impacted by painful experience, but also need to allow a wider public to engage with this history. Such work is—as Romanis reflects—really, really hard. It has a physical and emotional impact on artists that is rarely acknowledged, and almost never fully remunerated.

Monumental Lies, or Countering Cook

Daniel Browning*

* Daniel Browning is a Bundjalung and Kullilli journalist, radio broadcaster, sound artist and writer. Host of The Art Show on ABC Radio National, he has worked with ABC since 1994, where he leads the Indigenous Radio Unit and previously presented Radio National's Indigenous art and culture program, *Awaye!*. Browning is a former guest editor of *Artlink Indigenous*, an occasional series of the quarterly Australian contemporary arts journal, and a widely published freelance writer on arts and culture. He is the inaugural curator of Blak Box, an award-winning, architect-designed sound pavilion commissioned by Urban Theatre Projects (UTP), Sydney.

In June 2020, as outrage grew over the destruction by mining giant Rio Tinto of the Juukan Gorge rock shelters in the Pilbara region of Western Australia, and as Black Lives Matter demonstrators gathered in Sydney, a squadron of riot and mounted police drew a protective circle around the statue of Lieutenant James Cook in nearby Hyde Park. The colonial monument, with its rather blunt inscription—'discovered this territory'—has been at the epicentre of a debate about the shortcomings, the blindspots and ellipses in Australian public history. Public history, as opposed to academic history, is that version of events fortified by monuments and statues—a history that is hegemonic and largely established according to an agreed set of facts, consolidated in a coherent national story.[1] This national story, an apparently pragmatic but wilfully amnesiac metanarrative, was articulated most clearly over a decade prior by the former Prime Minister John Howard, who drew the ideological battle lines in the so-called 'history

1 Editors' note: Although it has become an academic discipline in itself, public history is described as existing outside of universities and in the broader community. It is how the past is made knowable in the public sphere and becomes national memory—whether through films, historical fiction and podcasts or heritage organisations and public memorials. Although it is the domain of 'multiple pasts jostling for recognition' (as Jenny Gregory describes in her article 'Dark Pasts in the Landscape: Statue Wars in Western Australia', Public History Review, vol. 28, 2021, p. 4, quoting Jane Jacobs), dominant narratives can become mainstream and entrenched.

wars'. Howard argued that 'blemishes' in Australian history—presumably, the invasion and theft of the continent, the brutal and protracted frontier wars and the trauma of the Stolen Generations—should not alter the metanarrative, which he defined in heroic terms as the 'overall story of great Australian achievement'.[2] As if history were an algorithm or a ledger of moral transactions, Howard declared that:

> The 'black armband' view of our history reflects a belief that most Australian history since 1788 has been little more than a disgraceful story of imperialism, exploitation, racism, sexism and other forms of discrimination . . . I believe that the balance sheet of our history is one of heroic achievement and that we have achieved much more as a nation of which we can be proud than of which we should be ashamed.[3]

Despite the national reckoning and truth-telling implicit in the findings of the National Enquiry into the Separation of Aboriginal and Torres Strait Islander Children from their Families and the shaming of the Cronulla riots in the intervening years, Howard was entirely unreconstructed ten years later when he addressed the National Press

2 See Australian Government Department of the Prime Minister and Cabinet, 'Transcript of the Prime Minister the Hon John Howard MP: Opening Address to the Australian Reconciliation Convention Melbourne', PM Transcripts, 26 May 1997, https://pmtranscripts.pmc.gov.au/release/transcript-10361.

3 John Howard, 1996 Sir Robert Menzies Lecture, 'The Liberal Tradition: The Beliefs and Values Which Guide the Federal Government', PM Transcripts, 18 November 1996, https://pmtranscripts.pmc.gov.au/release/transcript-10171.

Club on Australia Day in 2006. Here, Howard again invoked a sense of national 'balance' in almost fiscal terms. Citing an attitudinal report which found that fewer Australians were 'ashamed' of our collective past than in the previous decade, Howard trumpeted: 'I welcome this corrective in our national sense of self. It restores a better balance between pride in our past and recognition of past wrongs'.[4]

Almost singlehandedly, Howard declared and inflamed the history wars. He politicised history teaching by taking the matter into his own hands and drafting a national history curriculum—an overtly political intervention in what is essentially the business of the states and territories. In 1999 he constituted a national inquiry into school history, led by Associate Professor Tony Taylor, a history educationalist then based at Monash University. Then in the 2006 National Press Club address, Howard announced a 'root and branch renewal' of the way Australian history was being taught in schools. He convened a national history summit in Canberra, and appointed a committee including—among others—the conservative historian Geoffrey Blainey, who invented the term 'black armband view of history' so skilfully propagated and weaponised by Howard.[5] Before being unseated in the 2007

4 John Howard, A Sense of Balance: The Australian Achievement in 2006, Australia Day address to the National Press Club, 25 January 2006, https://parlinfo.aph.gov.au/parlInfo/search/display/display.w3p;query=Id:%22media/pressrel/AZVI6%22.

5 Among the few non-historians invited to attend the National History Summit held in Canberra on 17 August 2006 were the conservative social commentator Gerard Henderson; the

election, Howard prescribed a compulsory national history curriculum and, in a bid to force compliance, made it a condition of the Commonwealth schools' funding agreement. He dismissed criticism from Professor Taylor, who suggested that the scheme was 'overly prescriptive'.[6] Owing to his electoral defeat, Howard's scheme was never implemented, but even in retirement the former Prime Minister maintained his rage. In his 2010 autobiography, he declared that the teaching of Australian history needed 'a major repair job'. His lobbying continues to this day: Howard is chairman of the Ramsay Centre, endowed to 'advance education by promoting studies and discussion associated with the establishment and development of western civilisation'.[7] A member of the board is Howard's ideological successor, former Prime Minister Tony Abbott. In 2020, with funding from the Ramsay Centre, the University of Wollongong offered a full bachelor's degree in 'Western Civilisation'—as if we weren't steeped in it already. And make no mistake: in terms of public history—the history that is enacted in traditions such as Anzac Day and

editor-at-large at The Australian, Paul Kelly; former New South Wales Premier Bob Carr; and curator Margo Neale.

6 As conveyed by a reporter in John Howard's 'Doorstop Announcement' at Moorebank High School, Sydney, 11 October 2007, Australian Government Department of the Prime Minister and Cabinet, PM Transcripts, https://pmtranscripts.pmc.gov.au/release/transcript-15609.

7 'About Us', The Ramsay Centre for Western Civilisation, accessed 29 July 2021, https://www.ramsaycentre.org/about-us/about-the-ramsay-centre/.

monumentalised in official precincts and public spaces such as Sydney's Hyde Park and Melbourne's Fitzroy Gardens—we are deeply enmeshed in 'Western civilisation', a singularly Eurocentric imagining of the national story.

We are entitled to ask: what claim do colonial monuments and statues make to historical truth? Are they objective history—or an unreconstructed, one-sided version of it? Such monuments tell a story that is literally set in stone. In 2017, a new battle line was drawn in the history wars when ABC journalist and television broadcaster Stan Grant, a Wiradjuri and Kamilaroi man, suggested that the inscription on the statue of Lieutenant James Cook in Hyde Park was 'a damaging lie'. In an opinion piece for ABC News,[8] Grant argued for simple historical accuracy over the myth that Cook 'discovered' the continent in 1770—proposing that a counter-inscription might go some of the way in fixing the error. The gold inscription on the base of the Cook statue reads 'discovered this territory, 1770'—but perhaps the postscript should be 'at least 60,000 years after the fact'. How can you discover a populated continent, inhabited for millennia, unless you don't count the indigenes of that continent as people?

This spot fire in the history wars was initiated by Grant in the interests of healthy public debate and in light of a movement to dismantle Confederate statues in the United States, that would be inflamed

8 Stan Grant, 'America Tears Down Its Racist History, We Ignore Ours', ABC News, 18 August 2017, https://www.abc.net.au/news/2017-08-18/america-tears-down-its-racist-history-we-ignore-ours-stan-grant/8821662.

by strident editorialising in the conservative flank of the Australian media. Grant wrote that while 'Americans are tearing down the monuments to hate . . . we remain oblivious to ours'.[9] The then Prime Minister Malcolm Turnbull and his political nemesis Abbott both weighed into the fervid moral panic, sounding the alarm over the 'rewriting of history', Stalinism and what Abbott would decry as 'political correctness on steroids'. The comedian and radio host Michael Hing brought some levity to the overheated dialogue. In a satirical video for SBS Viceland, set in the fictive Department of Un-Australian Activities, Hing declared that 'there is nothing more Australian than statues of British people'.[10] As the conservative media fulminated, the politics editor at The Monthly, Sean Kelly, wrote a lucid defence of Grant's article.[11] Speaking on ABC Radio National's Awaye!, Kelly explained that:

> It is impossible to both believe—or understand as we do now—that Indigenous people have been on this land for tens of thousands of years, and to believe that a white man discovered the land. Those two facts don't sit side by side.[12]

9 Ibid.

10 'Department of Un-Australian Activities', The Feed SBS, YouTube video, 29 August 2017, https://www.youtube.com/watch?v=sHYNBW-rn4Q.

11 Sean Kelly, 'A Dishonest Debate about Dishonest History', The Monthly, 25 August 2017, https://www.themonthly.com.au/today/sean-kelly/2017/25/2017/1503644404/dishonest-debate-about-dishonest-history.

12 Sean Kelly with Daniel Browning, Awaye!, ABC Radio National, broadcast 9 September 2017.

In the wake of Grant's 2017 article, the Cook statue was sprayed with graffiti—in fact, a counter-inscription—declaring 'No pride in genocide' and 'change the date'. British journalist and blogger Reni Eddo-Lodge was in Australia at the time promoting her bestselling book Why I'm No Longer Speaking to White People about Race in which she details the student-led campaign to remove a statue of the imperialist Cecil Rhodes, set in an alcove in the façade of Oxford University's Oriel College. Eddo-Lodge was struck by the idea that any challenge to the story told by the Cook statue constituted an 'edit' of objective history. 'We can have a debate about whether or not graffitiing was the right way to attempt to challenge [the myth of discovery]', Eddo-Lodge told me on Awaye!, 'but let's be real—any suggestion that Australia was discovered by [Cook] is not true'.[13]

I would describe the original Cook inscription as an alternative fact, to use the Trumpian term.[14] Although regarded as a statement of historical truth, it is clearly a fabrication—or, at best, a concealment. As truth itself is now a matter of ideological dispute, and lawful ballots are cast as fraudulent, we should be alert to the manipulation of facts. Historical truth is the same: we may not like it, but we cannot

13 Reni Eddo-Lodge with Daniel Browning, Awaye!, ABC Radio National, broadcast 9 September 2017.

14 Aaron Blake, 'Kellyanne Conway Says Donald Trump's Team Has "Alternative Facts." Which Pretty Much Says It All.', Washington Post, 22 January 2017, https://www.washingtonpost.com/news/the-fix/wp/2017/01/22/kellyanne-conway-says-donald-trumps-team-has-alternate-facts-which-pretty-much-says-it-all/.

change it. However, history is not just a set of facts—it is negotiable. The events described in public history, or in monuments for that matter, are often the subject of interpretation and review. In this sense, history can be revised; it can literally be rewritten. If history were incontrovertible and sacrosanct, then we would have no need for historians.

There is a tension between the public history told by monuments and the suppressed, outlier version of events. In fact, monuments are often deployed as propaganda—the Soviet Union industrialised monument-making and the former satellites of central and eastern Europe are littered with examples of this identity construction, particularly the former Yugoslavia. Monuments are symbols infused with political and strategic power rather than objects weighted by standards of proof or historical evidence. It is worth restating here that in and of themselves, monuments and statues are not history. They can be repudiated, and they can be dismantled. Indeed, they often are. Such is their symbolic power that they can often become flashpoints in revolutions and political crises. The overthrow of the monument can echo the intangible shift in power or a reckoning with the past—recall the destruction of the statue of Saddam Hussein in Baghdad's Firdos Square in 2003 or the toppling of the monument to slave trader Edward Colston in a Bristol canal at the height of the Black Lives Matter demonstrations in 2020. But I would suggest that as long as they remain unchallenged, as they oxidise or otherwise age or weather, monuments and statues relay their version of events at an almost subliminal level.

As the historian Bruce Buchan noted in a review of the British Library's exhibition marking the

250th anniversary of Cook's departure from Plymouth in 1768: 'Symbols are never just symbolic; they tremble with a latent power'.[15] The same could be said of colonial monuments. Buchan's remarks pertain to E. Phillips Fox's triumphal 1902 history painting that represents Cook's landing at Botany Bay and its reimagining by the Kudjila, Gangulu and South Sea Islander artist Daniel Boyd in We Call Them Pirates Out Here, 2006, both of which were exhibited at the British Library. Boyd's painting recasts Cook as a pirate, while the fluttering Union Jack is transfigured into a set of red crossbones superimposed with a black skull. Boyd goes further too, showing the boatmen who raise the alarm about the presence of the Aboriginal men over the embankment to in fact be tilting at shadows, mistaking the spear-like Xanthorrhoea—the magnificent grass trees known colloquially as 'black boys'—for men. Another of Boyd's paintings, in his pointillist style, represents the obelisk erected near the site where Cook was killed on the shore of Hawai'i's Kealakekua Bay in 1779. Untitled (CM), 2016, depicts the overgrown and unvisited monument to Cook's victimhood—his 'assassination', according to one description on the National Portrait Gallery's website.[16] In bringing renewed attention to this monument, Boyd also brings into focus its blinkered and one-sided version of the story, when you discover that seventeen Hawaiians also died at the scene.

15 Bruce Buchan, 'Cooking the Books', Inside Story, 14 June 2018, https://insidestory.org.au/cooking-the-books/.

16 National Portrait Gallery, The Death of Captain Cook, 2021, https://www.portrait.gov.au/portraits/2007.28/the-death-of-captain-cook.

There is an empowered reclamation of public history taking place. Indigenous artists such as Boyd, Reko Rennie, Yhonnie Scarce, Nicholas Galanin and Jacob Nash are leading the way in this reclamation and their work represents a new tangent in the way we interpret the meaning of colonial monuments and statues as artefacts of that history. Galanin, a native Alaskan artist of Tlingit and Unangax̂ ancestry, was commissioned to create a new work for NIRIN, the 2020 Biennale of Sydney curated by Wiradjuri artist Brook Garru Andrew. According to the artist, his installation Shadow on the Land, an Excavation and Bush Burial, 2020, uses 'archaeology as a medium'.[17] Conceived in 2019, the work was to have been installed in the shadow of the Cook statue in Hyde Park but was moved for practical reasons to the former shipyards of Cockatoo Island in Sydney Harbour. Galanin excavated a site in the precise dimensions of the statue, creating both a void and a resting place for the monument. Galanin's own cultural history is touched by Cook, who surveyed the coastline of Alaska and is monumentalised in a public statue in the state capital of Anchorage. Galanin draws a parallel between the monuments and the brutal legacies of settler colonialism in North America, including the mass internment of Native populations on reservations, the deeply disturbing phenomenon of missing and murdered Indigenous women, and the extra-judicial killings of both Indigenous people and African Americans. 'These are all extensions of

17 Nicholas Galanin, 'NIRIN Artist Interview: Nicholas Galanin', YouTube video, Biennale of Sydney, 29 April 2020, https://www.biennaleofsydney.art/artists/nicholas-galanin/.

settler colonial violence', Galanin says.[18] Monuments are not empty vessels.

> These narratives and representations of who tells or holds history are important—they're important to all of us. You're not living in reality when you choose to tell one partial form of that narrative, and a discovery monument in Hyde Park is that. What's erased from that? How much history has been actively, purposely removed to tell that narrative.[19]

A contemporary artist working primarily in glass, Kokatha and Nukunu woman Yhonnie Scarce has embarked on a study of memorials, including monuments to war and acts of genocide throughout central and eastern Europe, erected in the Soviet era in the aftermath of the Second World War. Although impressive and vaulting in their day, most are now decaying and unloved. In 2019, Scarce visited the abandoned Memorial House of the Bulgarian Communist Party on a peak in the Balkan Mountains which, despite its altitude, is often defaced and vandalised with anti-Communist graffiti. In the course of her research for a collaborative project with artist Lisa Radford, Scarce has visited memorials and monuments to nuclear disasters at Chernobyl and Fukushima, as well as those to the nearly three hundred Lakota who were massacred by the United States Army at Wounded Knee and to those at the former internment and mass extermination camp at

18 Nicholas Galanin, interview with Daniel Browning, Awaye!, ABC Radio National, broadcast 11 July 2020, https://www.abc.net.au/radionational/programs/awaye/burying-the-colonial-past/12982198.

19 Ibid.

Auschwitz in what was Nazi-occupied Poland. Much of Scarce's previous work has exposed the conspiratorial silence over the British nuclear tests at Maralinga—and the toxic effects of fallout that rained across her Kokatha country in the west of South Australia. Scarce was herself born at Woomera, declared a prohibited area in 1947 for the testing of long-range weapons. Her monumental installation Death Zephyr, 2017, in the collection of the Art Gallery of New South Wales, recreates the plume of a nuclear explosion—the first ever conducted on the Australian mainland—at Emu Field in October 1953. In a catalogue essay for The National, I wrote that:

> In the suspended, wraith-like clouds . . . we are temporarily blinded to the lingering effects of the British nuclear tests on Aboriginal land across much of inland South Australia in the 1950s. On close inspection, the beauty of the work is subsumed by a deeper sense of national unease, on the excesses of blind ethno-nationalism, the flagrant disregard for human life and indifference to environmental destruction of which nations are capable.[20]

Recently, Scarce collaborated with the Melbourne architecture studio Edition Office to create a temporary monument for the National Gallery of Victoria's Architecture Commission at least partly inspired by the impossibly vaulting lines of the spomenik[21] and other futuristic Soviet-era

20 The National 2017: New Australian Art, Art Gallery of New South Wales, Carriageworks and Museum of Contemporary Art Australia, Sydney, 2017.

21 The term spomenik is the Serbo-Croatian word for 'monument'.

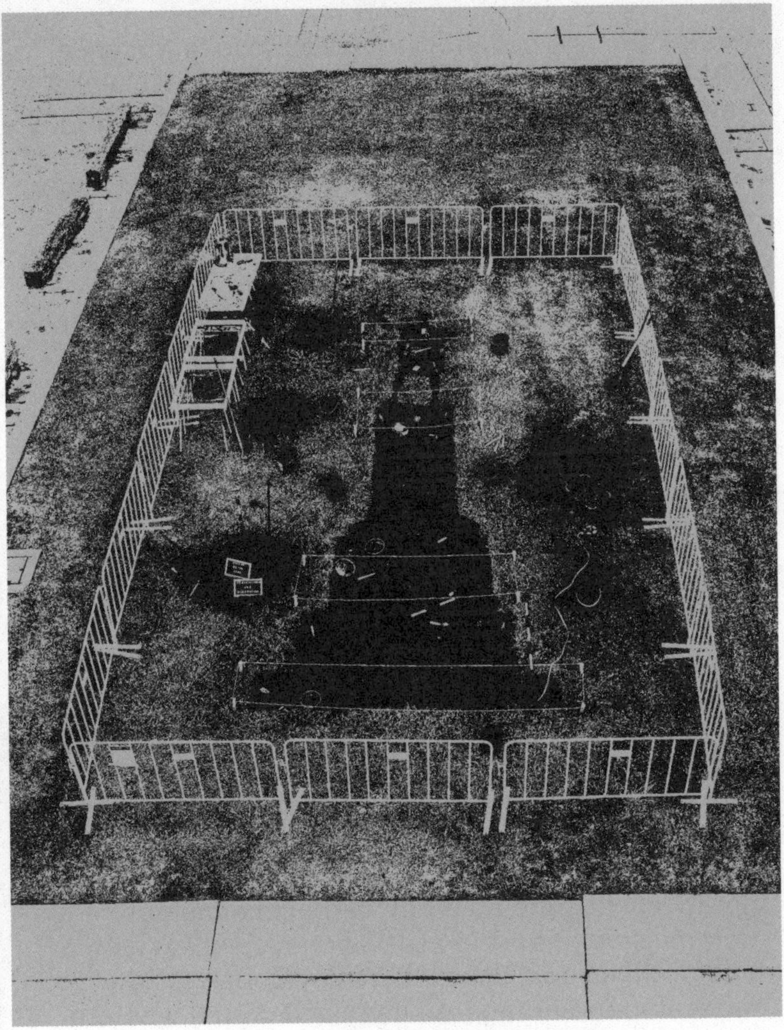

Nicholas Galanin, Shadow on the Land, an Excavation and Bush Burial 2020. Commissioned for the 22nd Biennale of Sydney and courtesy of the artist. Installation view, Cockatoo Island, Sydney, 2020. Photo: Alex Robinson

monoliths. The collaboration produced *In Absence*, 2019, a contemplative space made from blackened Tasmanian hardwood oak, lined with basalt and hung with hundreds of Scarce's signature handblown glass forms evoking the murnong (yam), like teardrops dotting the interior of the building. Although temporary, the building memorialised the erasure of permanent stone dwellings, encampments and villages, the economies and systems of food production that existed before 1788—the Indigenous built environment—and the false declaration of *terra nullius*. The inner semicircular chambers of the building also formed an acoustic space, open to the sky like the oculus of the Pantheon.

Set designer, artist-in-residence with Sydney Festival and current head of design at the Indigenous dance company Bangarra, Jacob Nash has made one of the most evocative yet simple interventions in the debate over public history. His counter-artwork *Always*, 2019, is not on permanent exhibition—like Galanin's excavation on Cockatoo Island and the collaborative work of Scarce and Edition Office, it is a temporary installation that can be dismantled like a set piece. But unlike the other works cited here, *Always* does move around iteratively despite its monumental dimensions. Commissioned for the 2019 Sydney Festival with a brief from artistic director Wesley Enoch for the redeveloped Barangaroo headland on the western foreshore of Sydney Harbour, the artwork is composed of a thirty-two ton steel panel which stands over five metres high and which extends over twenty-eight metres. Asked to think about the term 'always' in the context of the festival's theme, Nash created an elegantly simple rendering of the word punched out of the steel panel that clearly stakes a claim to historical truth, ownership and sustained Aboriginal presence which echoes in the chant 'always was, always will be, Aboriginal land'—a counter to the Cook statue and its blunt inscription. The installation is also the backdrop to a festival event held on the day before the increasingly contested Australia Day—otherwise known as Invasion Day—during which a vigil takes place to remember and honour ancestors and family. On one side, the exposed panel weathers and rusts, while on the other the surface is mirrored, reflecting the morphing skyline as construction of a high-roller casino, luxury residential apartments and a bustling new financial district completely transforms what was a working port (known during the Great Depression as the Hungry Mile). The headland has itself been entirely rebuilt over a cavernous void—described to me by a Dharawal educator Shannon Foster as a wound and a carbuncle—regenerated with plants indigenous to the area before 1788 and fortified with gleaming local Sydney sandstone largely mined from the site. Nash told journalist Josh Dye that 'I've never really seen [this work] . . . as confrontational. I see it as a proclamation of truth . . . We're struggling with identity as a nation and how we deal with the past. The amazing thing about art is it gives people a way to talk about it.'[22]

Kamilaroi artist Reko Rennie also based a public artwork around the same idea when asked to

22 Josh Dye, 'Giant Outdoor Sculpture Aims to be a Powerful Conversation Starter', Sydney Morning Herald, 24 January 2019, https://www.smh.com.au/entertainment/art-and-design/giant-outdoor-sculpture-aims-to-be-a-powerful-conversation-starter-20190124-p50taz.html.

create a temporary design for a highly visible junction in the inner-city suburb of Darlinghurst. Rennie, a former Fairfax journalist who grew up in the outer suburbs of Melbourne, has a background in street art—and his practice often features short declarative statements, gestures or iconic signatures by which the artist is clearly identified just as if he were tagging. In 2012, Rennie was commissioned by the City of Sydney to create a work for the exterior of a disused former bank building in Taylor Square, erected in 1910 near the intersection of bustling Oxford and Flinders Streets. Over a geometric design drawn from Kamilaroi iconography on carved trees, neon text declared 'Always was always will be'. The artwork was a focal point for visitors and local residents but when the council-owned building was sold in 2017, Rennie advocated that the work be painted over if municipal authorities could not guarantee the future commercial use of the site would be complementary to the spirit of the work. Rennie said at the time that the City of Sydney gave him no choice in the matter than to have the work removed. 'There's no way I want my artwork to be associated with a gaming venue or any licensed establishment', he told the ABC. 'I'd rather have the work taken down rather than glorifying some misappropriated venue'.[23] In 2020, Rennie was commissioned to create another temporary work for the exterior of the

23 Nadia Daly, '"Always Was, Always Will Be" Artwork on Taylor Square Building to be Painted Over as Council Sells Icon', ABC News (online), 21 November 2017, https://www.abc.net.au/news/2017-11-21/taylor-square-pink-and-blue-artwork-removed-from-building/9171672.

Carriageworks performing arts hub in the former Eveleigh railyards in the inner Sydney suburb of Darlington. The date of the commission was significant—2020 was the 250th anniversary of Cook's landing at Botany Bay and his journey along the coast towards his florid, theatrical taking of Possession Island on the northern tip of the continent. Again, illuminated text makes a short declarative statement: 'REMEMBER ME'. The first iteration of this work is no less impressive. On a bicycle trail in the inner Melbourne suburb of Fitzroy in 2005, Rennie painted an Aboriginal flag with the same words stencilled in the yellow disc at the centre of the mural. An early work in much smaller dimensions in a much less visible spot, this mural has outlived Rennie's other grand designs.

Just like carved trees, monuments and public artworks do have a mnemonic function. As Scarce has suggested, memorials can serve to deepen our knowledge of history and the erasures and falsehoods upon which the metanarrative of 'Australian achievement' is based. They can often drive ideological struggles in memory politics and may become the archaeology of propaganda as in the former Communist states of eastern Europe. Historian Gary Foley has suggested that Australia's colonial era monuments, and those erected ever since to the unreconstructed version of colonial history articulated by politicians such as Howard, be sequestered in a theme park, for which he might conduct corrective guided tours. Just as archaeology, these statues do not stand for history but our relationship to it. Although criminalised as vandalism, the act of defacement—which I regard to be a form of counter-inscription—can be as instructive, in archaeological terms, as the monument itself. Amid the reckoning of Black Lives Matter and the sinking of the Colston statue in Bristol, archaeologists Hilary Gopnik and Jessie Birkett-Rees opined:

> Let the statues topple. We'll dig them up one day, or retrieve them from the long-forgotten storage vaults of a museum, and derive more meaning from the fact of their felling than we ever would from the fact that they once stood. The Black Lives Matter tags and broken plinths will write the history.[24]

If we consider colonial monuments and statues to be archaeology—markers that project a certain kind of history, or material objects to aid public memory or the construction of identity—rather than history itself, then they lose some of their symbolic power. The human instinct towards iconoclasm—which is precisely what we are talking about when we dismantle, deface or counter-inscribe statues and monuments—has been practised for millennia. It is nothing new. Speaking of iconoclasm and the fate of unloved colonial statues, I am particularly struck by the evocative work of the New Delhi-based Raqs Media Collective, which I first saw in the Giardini at the 56th Venice Biennale in 2015. Their installation Coronation Park included nine fibreglass sculptures raised on high wooden plinths coated with bitumen. The title relates to Coronation Park in Delhi, the site of several statues of King George V and other

24 Hilary Gopnik and Jessie Birkett-Rees, 'The Toppling of Statues Is a Moment in History, Not Its Erasure', Lens, Monash University, 25 June 2020, https://lens.monash.edu/@politics-society/2020/06/25/1380735/the-toppling-of-statues-is-a-moment-in-history-not-its-erasure.

colonial dignitaries of the British Raj that were moved to the park in the 1960s from across India. The collective—Jeebesh Bagchi, Monica Narula and Shuddhabrata Sengupta—recast several of the statues and busts but reimagined them as defaced; in some cases, entire limbs and bodies are missing, while in another just imperial robes are present. In an interview for an online magazine, Narula described the actual Coronation Park as 'a derelict quasi-ceremonial space, where relics of the British Raj are kept for the consideration of an absent public'.[25] Indeed, some of the monuments in Coronation Park have no inscription left visible and only a student of the Raj could identify them. However, their provenance is clear; these are artefacts, part of the archaeology of a brutal, imperialist colonial administration now fallen. As they prepared to make their truncated version of the park, Raqs came to a deeper realisation about the nature of power—that the statues have always been empty.

It was here, amongst the dilapidated and near-forgotten official commemorations, that Raqs experienced an epiphany, 'about the hollow interiority of all constituted authority; the constant panic at the heart of power considering its fraught, frayed and often fraudulent claims to legitimacy'. This moment of revelation, Narula tells me, provided the initial impetus for the Coronation Park work, which they consider as 'a provocation to think

25 Monica Narula quoted in Amelia Groom, 'Raqs Media Collective: Epiphany and Escape', Neue Luxury, no. 5, https://www.neueluxury.com/feature/raqs-media-collective/.

> about the inner life of power, and its deepest anxiety: the inevitability of abdication'.[26]

As artefacts, the Coronation Park monuments are markers of time, and of the obsolescence of power. But I would suggest that their second life (and their reimagining in the work of Raqs) is even more compelling: these are hollow monuments to the hubris, cruelty, and futility of a fallen empire.

26 Ibid.

Responsibilities to Time
Callum McGrath*

* Callum McGrath is an artist and researcher based in Narrm/Melbourne. His photographic and video works take interest in reimagining institutionalised aesthetics of historiography, memorials and archiving. Among his recent exhibitions and writing are To Resound, Unbound, Centre for Contemporary Photography, Melbourne (2021); 'Metabolism', un Magazine, no. 15.2 (2021); Deviations, Brisbane Art and Design Festival (2021); and The Weatherman, Metro Arts, Brisbane (2021). McGrath is also a contributor to Kink, a collective researching queer Australian art. McGrath is currently undertaking a Master of Fine Art at Monash University.

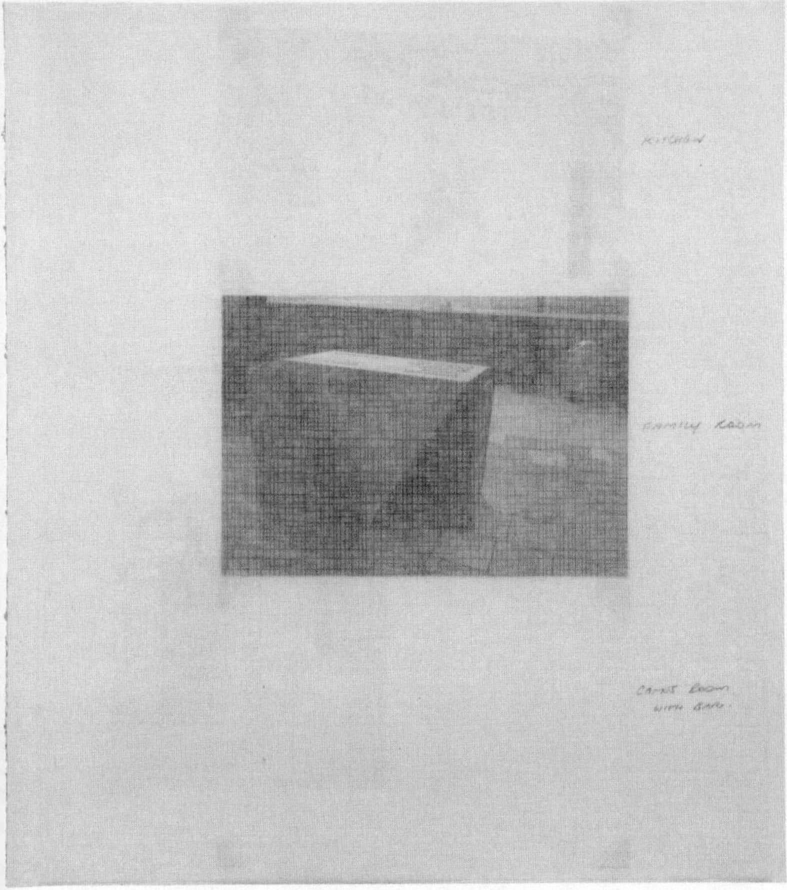
KITCHEN
FAMILY ROOM
GAMES ROOM
WITH BAR.

NIKKI, JALENA & I
PRESENT AT UNI!

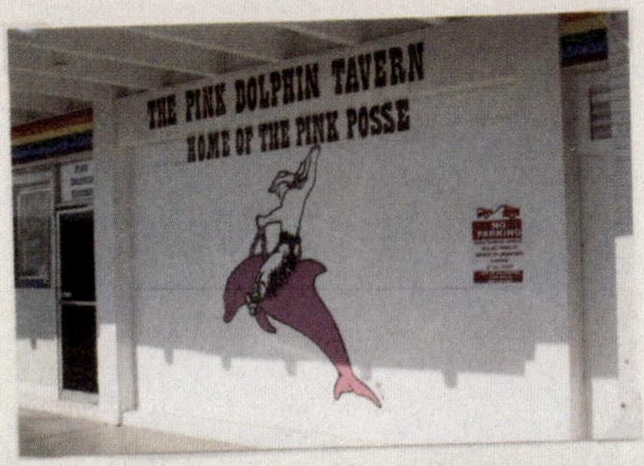

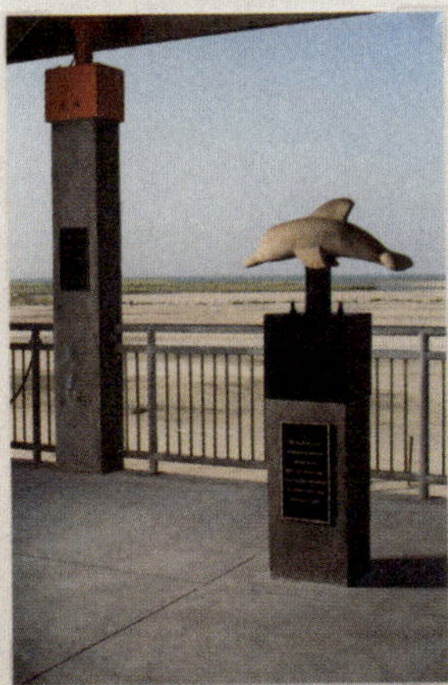

FAMILY GRADUATION - APRIL '92.

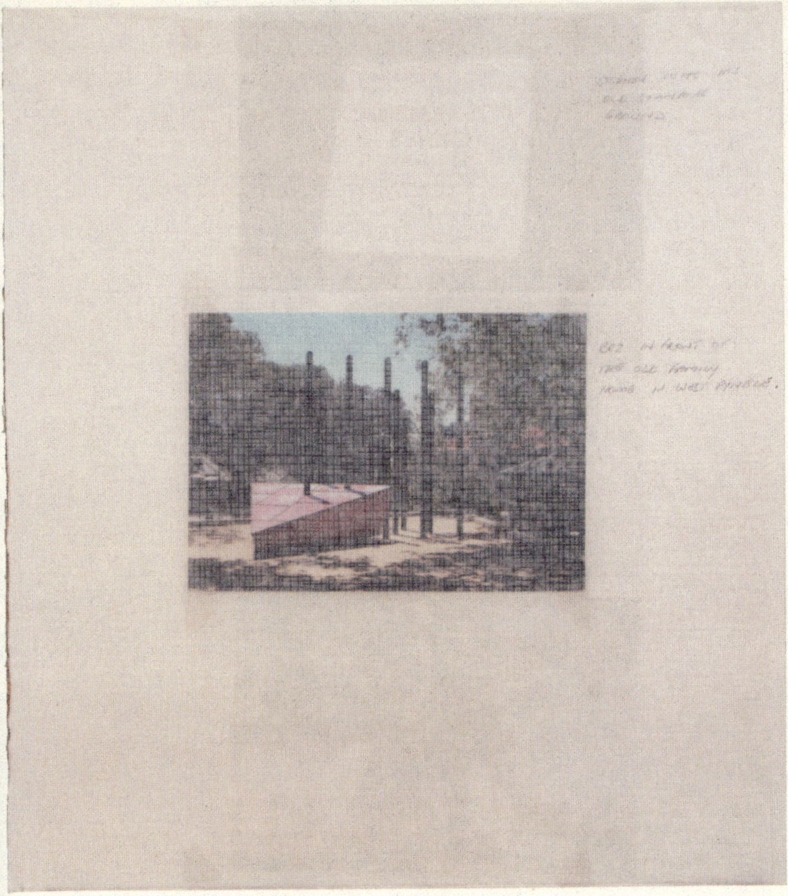

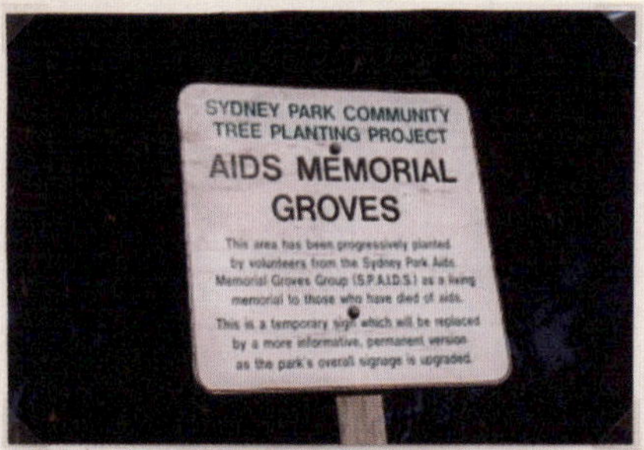

MICHAEL + LIBBY'S
WEDDING –
MELBOURNE
APRIL '93

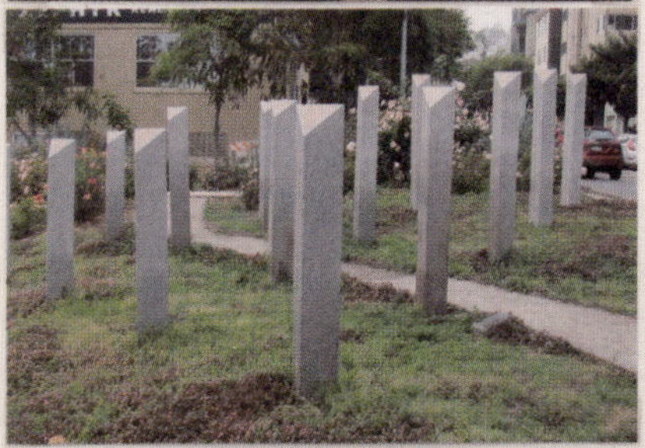

4-SOME SHOT – NOT
BAD FOR 6HRS AFTER
THE START!!

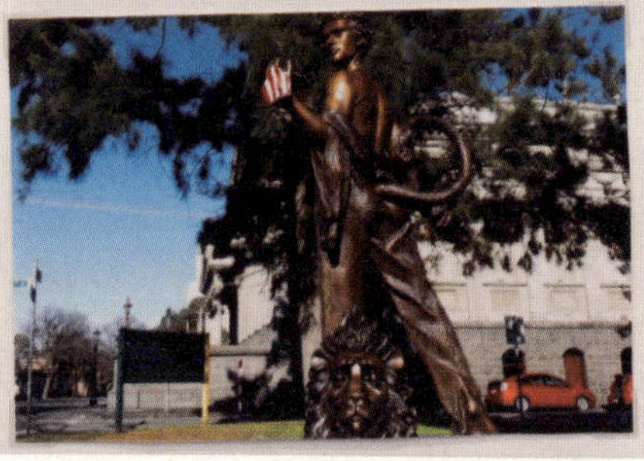

VERITY + BRIAN AT
THE JONES' WEDDING

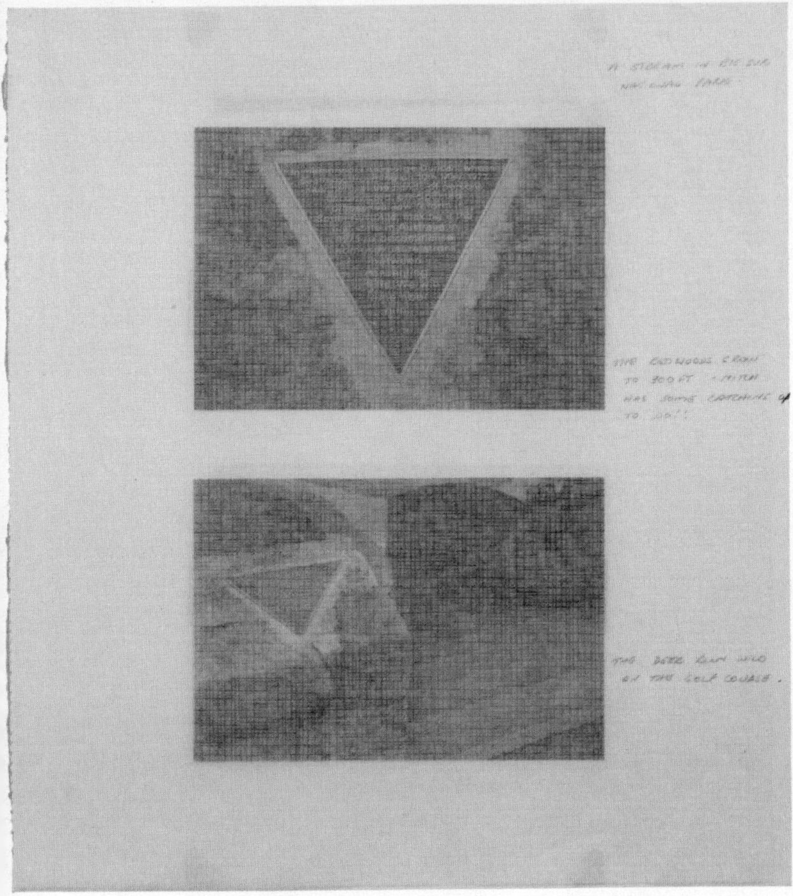
THE DEER RUN WILD
ON THE GOLF COURSE.

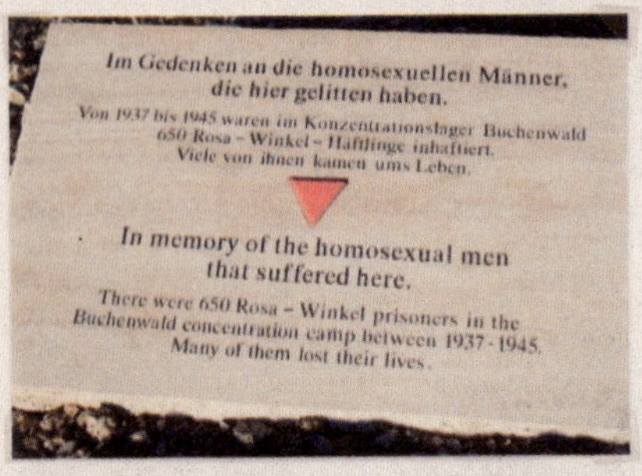

ANGUS SHOWS HIS TONSILS.

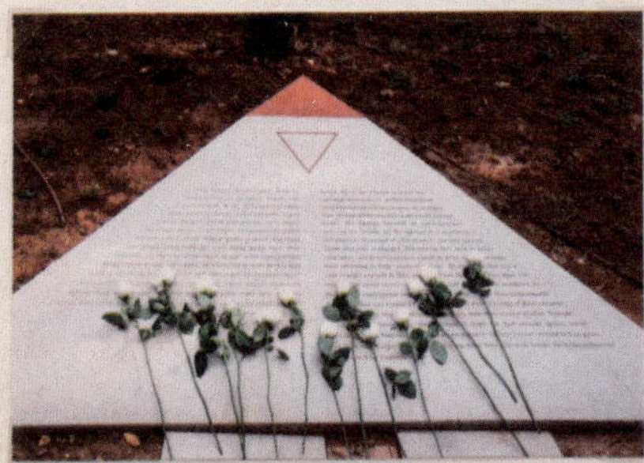

GRAEME + CHRIS TRY TO GET CONTROL OF THE 22 LITTLE DARLINGS.

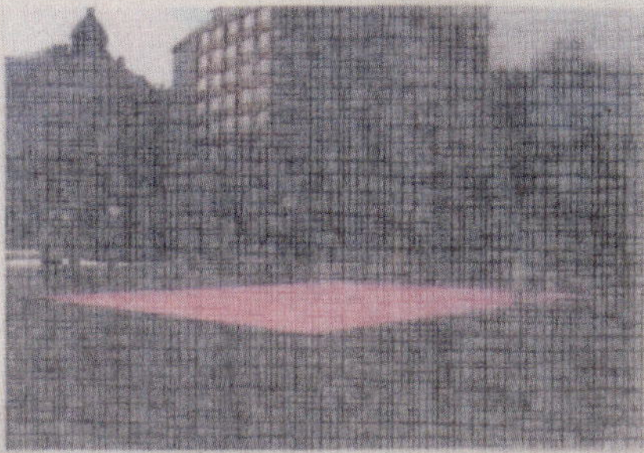

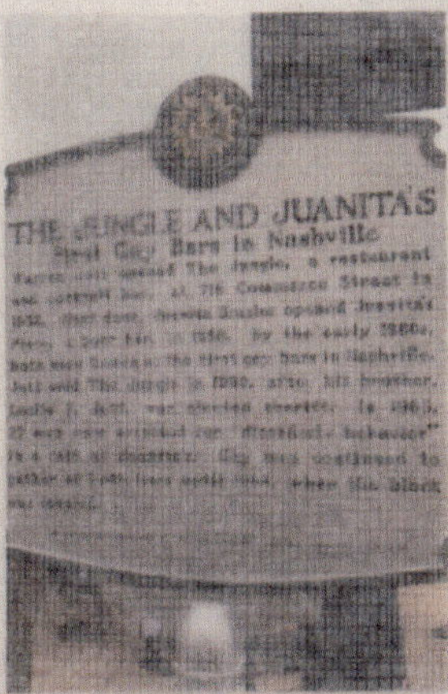

AND JUANITA'S
Bars in Nashville

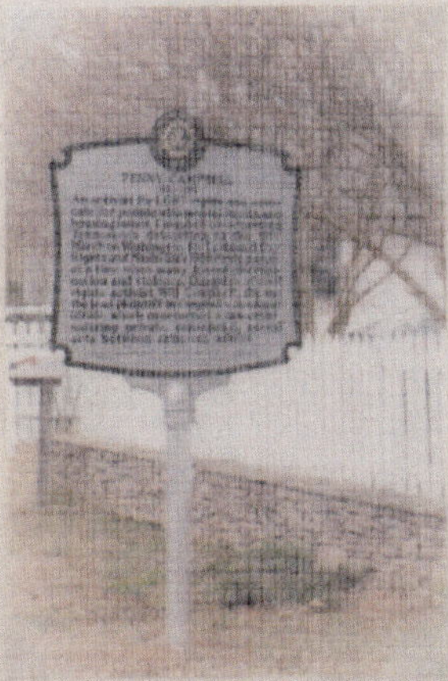

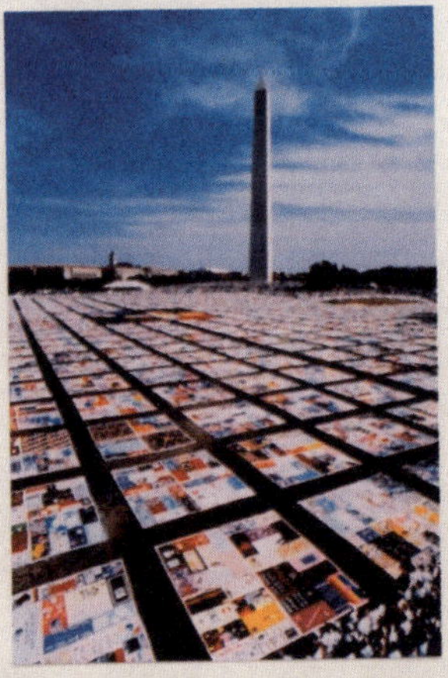

TWO LIVING DOLLS - CAITLYN + ELOISE

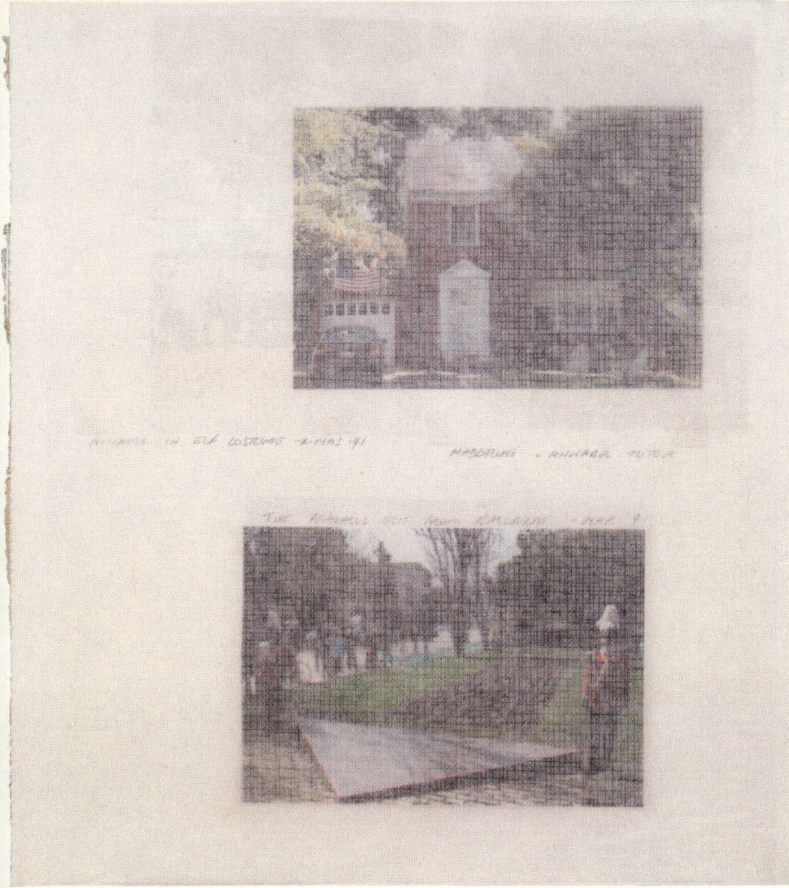

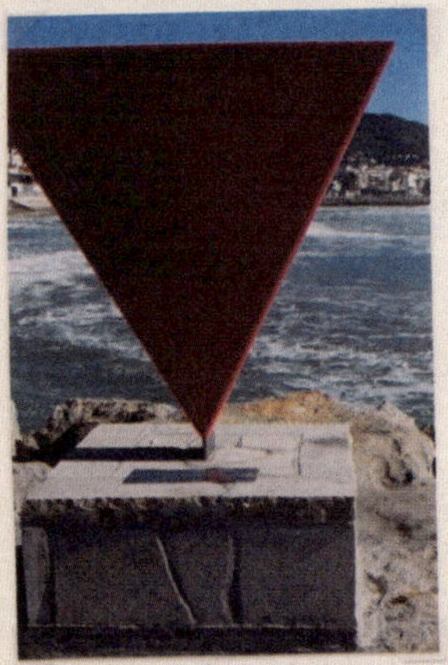

MITCH'S FIRST PANTOMIME · DEC '90

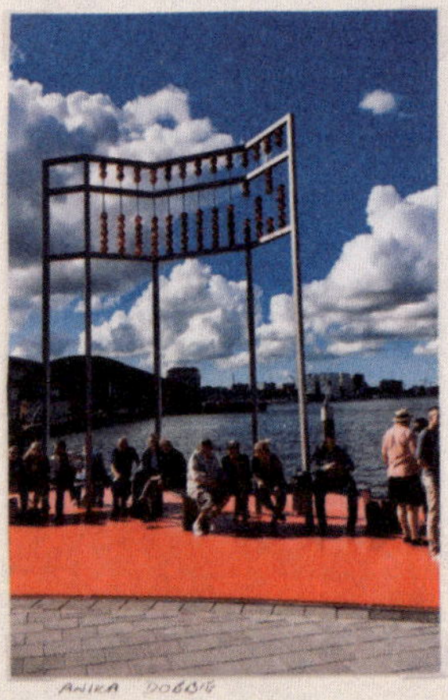

ANIKA DOBBIE

LONE PINE

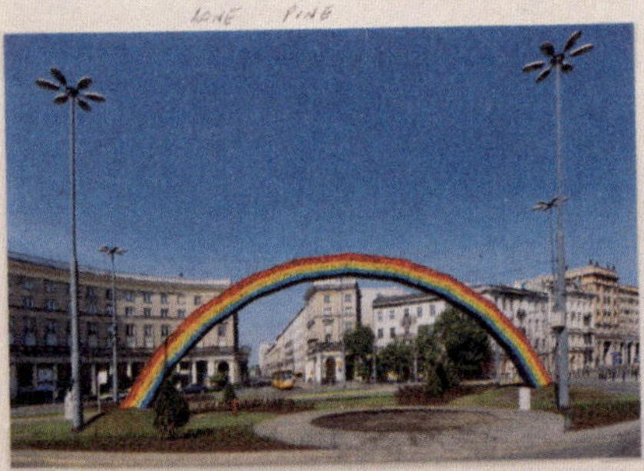

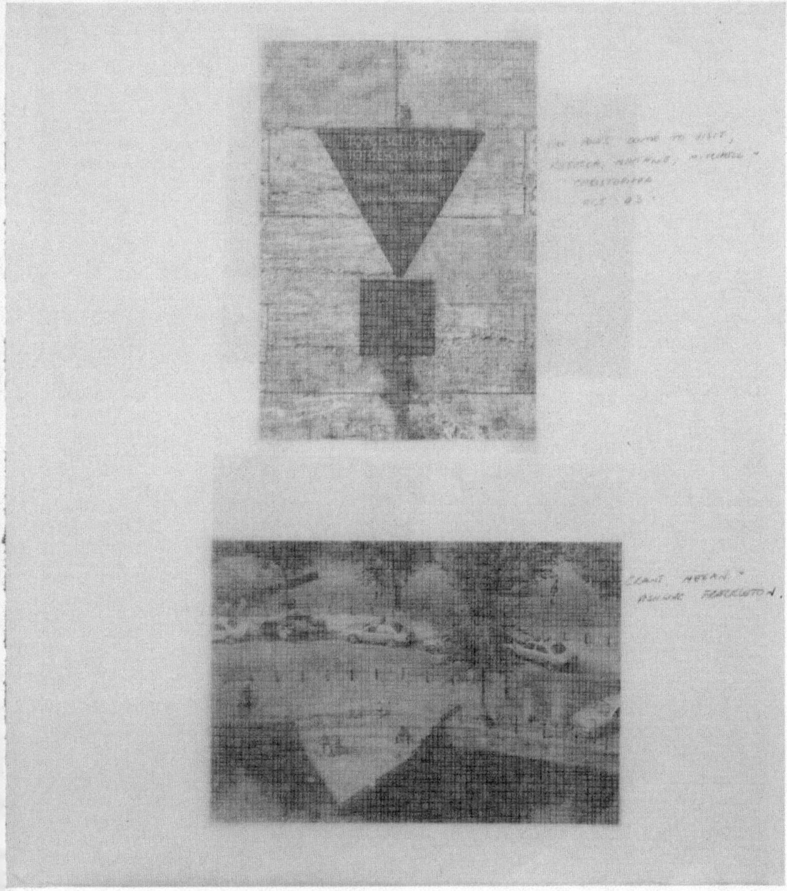

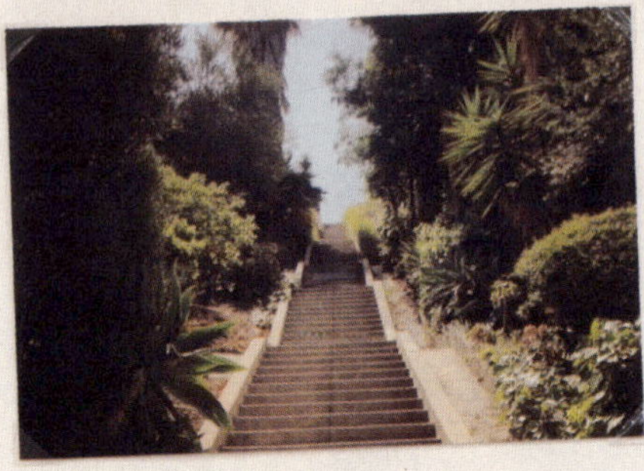

SUNSET IN CAMBRIA
- TRUELY WONDERFUL.

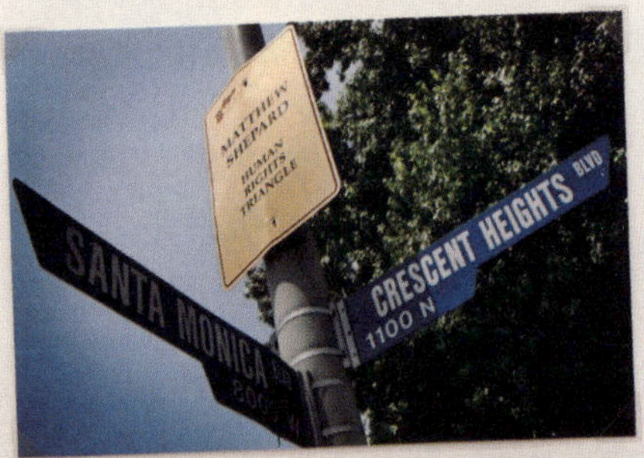

DINING OUT ON THE MOST WESTERN EDGE OF CALIFORNIA - 'ROCKY'S RESTURANT!

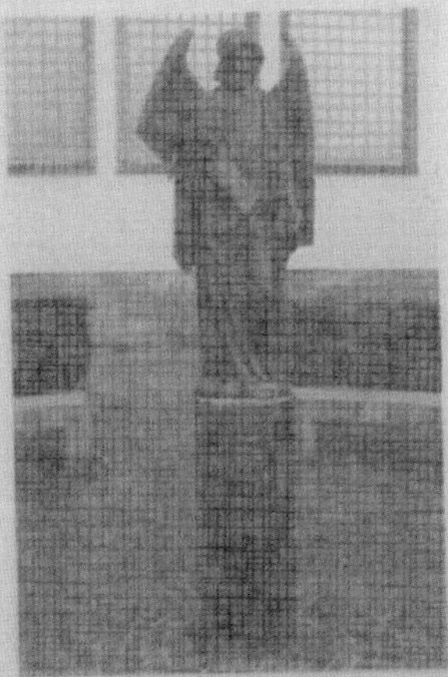

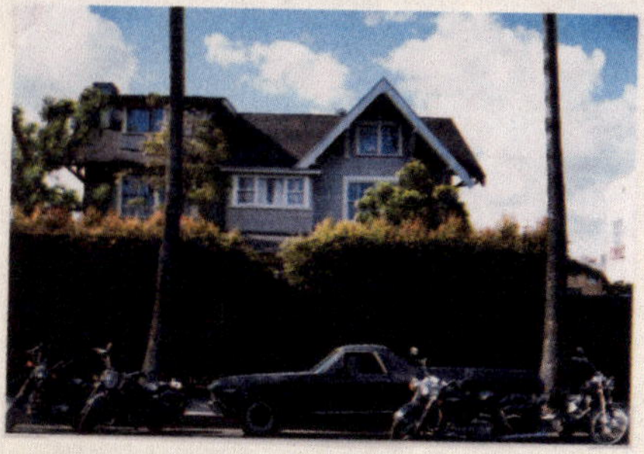

ULBA TEAM .

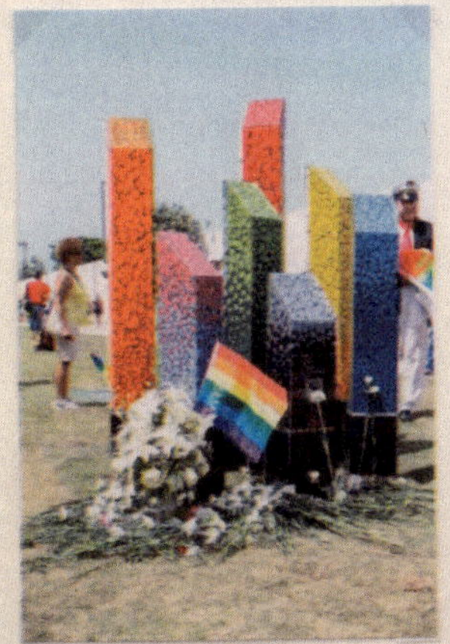

CAROLYN + MICHAEL'S WEDDING - NODGEE CHAPEL
JULY '92 .

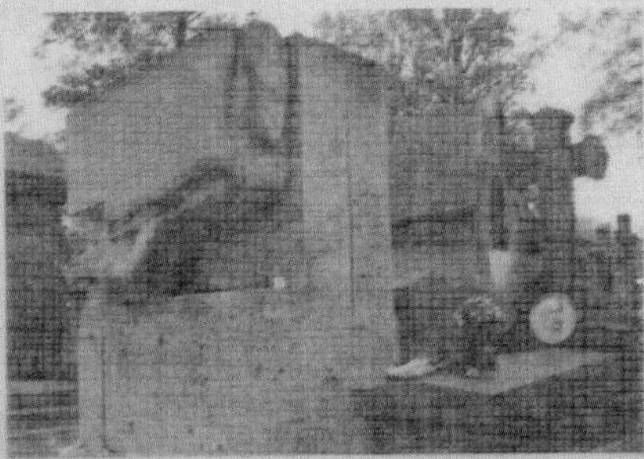

X-MAS '90

Selected album pages from Callum McGrath, Responsibilities to Time 2021, digital photographic prints on found photo album pages, 24 parts, each 29 × 32 cm. Courtesy of the artist

p. 121 Memorial to Gay and Lesbian Victims of National Socialism, installed 1995, Rheingarten Embankment, near Hohenzollern Bridge, Cologne, Germany. Design by Achim Zinkann. Proposed by community group Dykes and Queers and officially commissioned by the Federation of German Trade Unions' Cologne chapter.

p. 122 The now-closed Pink Dolphin Tavern on Galveston Island, TX, United States: inspiration for the Pink Dolphin Monument, installed 2014 on the promenade in R.A. Apffel Park/East Beach on Galveston Island. Created by artist Joe Joe Orangias in collaboration with writer Sarah Sloane and scientist Frank Prega with support by Galveston Artist Residency, Galveston Commission on the Arts and Galveston Park Board of Trustees.

p. 123 Gay and Lesbian Holocaust Memorial, installed 2001, Green Park, Sydney. Designed by Russell Rodrigo and Jennifer Gamble, commissioned by The Gay and Lesbian Holocaust Memorial Project and supported by South Sydney City Council.

p. 124 SPAIDS Memorial Grove, first planting 1994, reflection area added 2001, Sydney Park, Sydney. Commissioned by the Sydney Park AIDS Memorial Groves Group (SPAIDS) and supported by South Sydney City Council.
Pink Triangle Park, dedicated 2001, San Francisco, CA, United States. Designed by artists Robert Bruce and Susan Martin. Commissioned and maintained by the Eureka Valley Promotion Association with support from local individuals, businesses and city agencies and major funding by the Mayor of the City and County of San Francisco.
Courage, installed 2014, Whitlam Place, Melbourne. Designed by artist William Eicholtz. Commissioned by the City of Yarra with funds also raised by the artist.

p. 125 Dr George Duncan Memorial, installed 2002, updated 2020, Kintore Ave on the banks of the River Torrens, Adelaide. Initiated by the Pride Club, University of Adelaide and maintained by the City of Adelaide and Adelaide Park Lands.

p. 126 Commemorative Stone for Homosexual Men, installed 2006, Buchenwald Memorial, Weimar, Germany. An initiative of the Evangelischen Studentengemeinde Leipzig (Community of Protestant Students Leipzig), realised with the support of AIDS-Hilfe Weimar.
Memorial to Gay Holocaust Victims, installed 2014, Gan Meir (Meir Park), Tel Aviv, Israel. Designed by landscape architect Yael Moriah and organised by Eran Lev with support from Tel Aviv City Mayor Ron Huldai and the Tel Aviv Municipal LGBT Community Center.

p. 127 Rosa Platz, conceived 2006, unrealised project proposed for Morzinplatz, Vienna, Austria. The design by artist Hans Kupelwieser was chosen in a competition process initiated by the City of Vienna and organised by Kunst im öffentlichen Raum Wien (Art in Public Space Vienna) and Wissenschaftszentrum Wien, but could not go ahead for stated technical reasons.
The Jungle and Juanita's Historical Marker, erected 2018, Commerce Street, Nashville, TN, United States. Commissioned by The Historical Commission of Metropolitan Nashville and Davidson Country.
Penny Campbell Historical Marker, erected 2017, McEwen Avenue, Nashville, TN, United States. Commissioned by The Historical Commission of Metropolitan Nashville and Davidson Country.

p. 128 AIDS Memorial Quilt, first displayed 1987, this display 1992, National Mall, Washington, DC, United States. Conceived by activist Cleve Jones, organised for three decades by the NAMES Project Foundation and realised by tens of thousands of individuals. Now based at the National AIDS Memorial, San Francisco, CA, United States.

p. 129 Dr Franklin E. Kameny Residence, first designated a historic landmark in 2009, Cathedral Ave NW, Washington, DC, United States. Listed on the United States National Register of Historic Places in 2011 and managed by the National Park Service.
Monumento en Memoria de los Gais, Lesbianas y Personas Transexuales Represaliadas (Monument in Memory of Gay, Lesbian and Transexual Victims of Persecution and Repression), installed 2011, Ciutadela Park, Barcelona, Spain. Commissioned by the City of Barcelona.

p. 130 Monument Against Homophobia, installed 2006, fourth jetty between Bassa Rodona and Estanyo beaches, Sitges, Spain; restored and relocated 2013, Passeig Marítim Promenade. Commissioned by the City Town Hall led by Mayor Jordi Baijet.
Living by Numbers, installed 2006, south bank of the river IJ, Amsterdam, the Netherlands. Designed by artist Jean-Michel Othoniel. Initiated by the NAMES Project Netherland Foundation with support from Aidsfonds, the OLVG hospital of Amsterdam, RELX Group and ViiV Healthcare.
Tęcza (The Rainbow), installed 2012, permanently removed 2015, Plac Zbawiciela (Savior Square), Warsaw, Poland. Designed by Julita Wójcik. Commissioned by the Adam Mickiewicz Institute and maintained by the Warsaw City Council until 2015, when it entered the collection of Warsaw's Centre for Contemporary Art.

p. 131 Rosa Winkel Memorial Plaque, installed 1989, updated 1993, Nollendorfplatz, Berlin, Germany. Initiated by the AHA (Allgemeine Homosexuelle Arbeitsgemeinschaft / General Homosexual Working Group) and HuK Berlin (Ökumenische Arbeitsgruppe Homosexuelle und Kirche / Ecumenical Working Group Homosexuality and Church).
Homomonument, installed 1987, Keizersgracht Canal, Amsterdam, the Netherlands. Designed by Karin Daan. Initiated by the Homomonument Foundation and realised through a fundraising campaign matched with funds from the Dutch Parliament, City of Amsterdam and Province of North Holland.

p. 132 Mattachine Steps, dedicated 2012, Cove Avenue, Silver Lake, Los Angeles, CA, United States. Organised by the Los Angeles City Council following a campaign led by Wes Joe. Matthew Shepard Human Rights Triangle, dedicated 1999, corner of Santa Monica and Crescent Heights Boulevards, West Hollywood, Los Angeles, CA, United States. Initiated by former West Hollywood City Council member Steve Martin.

p. 133 Frankfurter Engel, installed 1994, intersection of Stephanstrasse and Schaefergasse, Frankfurt, Germany. Designed by artist Rosemarie Trockel. An initiative of the association Initiative Mahnmal Homosexuellenverfolgung (Homosexual Persecution Memorial Initiative), realised with support from the City of Frankfurt am Main, the Hessian Cultural Foundation, the Hannchen-Mehr Zweck-Stiftung and private donations.

p. 134 Tom of Finland House (TOM House), designated as a Historic-Cultural Monument in 2006, 1421 Laveta Terrace, Echo Park, Los Angeles, CA, United States. Established by Durk Dehner and maintained as the base of the Tom of Finland Foundation since 1984. LGBT Memorial, installed 2016, Third Millennium Park, San Juan, Puerto Rico. Designed by Alberto de la Cruz and commissioned by the Autonomous Municipality of San Juan.

p. 135 Oscar Wilde's Tomb, constructed 1912, Père Lachaise Cemetery, Paris, France. Designed by sculptor Jacob Epstein. Commissioned by an anonymous donor, later revealed as Wilde's friend Helen Carew.

These artist pages are from Callum McGrath's ongoing project Responsibilities to Time, 2019–, which researches public memorials dedicated to queer subjects and communities. McGrath arranges photographic documentation of these sculptures and sites into anonymous, pre-used family photo albums—retaining their original captions—to consider queer memory and the heteronormative archive.

Art and the City
Mel Dodd*

* Mel Dodd is an architect, academic and head of architecture at Monash University, Melbourne. She has led architectural studies and spatial practice programs at London Metropolitan University; RMIT University, Melbourne; and Central Saint Martins, University of the Arts London, where she served as Associate Dean. Dodd has been a collaborator with muf architecture/art and has produced public realm projects in both London and Melbourne, working with local government on social policy initiatives for public space. Her interest in contested urban regeneration contexts has been explored in the books Live Projects: Designing with People (RMIT Press, 2012) and Spatial Practices: Modes of Action and Engagement with the City (Routledge, 2019).

> While it is possible . . . to separate the production of culture from the urban, it is very difficult to separate the production of the urban from culture.[1]

Urbanists and planners are increasingly aware that they need to engage with broader and messier practices if they are to nurture culture and identity in the contemporary city. Arts and cultural activities can produce discursive and intermediary spaces in the midst of larger urban metamorphoses, contributing more freely to the creation of new stories and narratives. A new genre of public art has increasingly found traction within urban-regeneration policy and practice, with commissions allowing for a space of risk and uncertainty in what otherwise tends to be a controlled and rigid redevelopment and construction regime. Not surprisingly, the commissioning of public art for urban projects has led to a burgeoning set of interdisciplinary practices in its own right, where artists, urbanists, landscape architects and curators formulate ways in which commissions might unfold as part of festivals, temporary events and regeneration initiatives. These arts and culture-driven urban-regeneration initiatives are also underpinned by cultural policies informed by the economic value of cultural consumption, at the same time that local manufacturing has declined and emptied out urban centres.[2] Contemporary city

1 Kate Oakley, Creating Space: A Re-evaluation of the Role of Culture in Regeneration, Arts and Humanities Research Council UK, 2015, https://eprints.whiterose.ac.uk/88559/3/AHRC_Cultural_Value_KO%20Final.pdf.

2 Sharon Zukin, The Cultures of Cities,

commissioners now adopt terms such as 'placemaking' to refer to the way in which arts and cultural programming can contribute to the enhancement of social life, catalysing activity in the public realm. Another term that is increasingly used within the Australian context, 'Indigenous placemaking' refers to the participation of Indigenous peoples in place-based design and urban renewal according to their own knowledge and methods. Under the banner of 'placemaking', arts and cultural strategies have become overlapping instruments feeding into city-making practices.

While there is much to celebrate in the way that public art has been co-opted into placemaking practices by both government and private development, there are also reasons to be cautious. Identities of place arise from the complex interactions between multiple stakeholders, citizens and residents over time. Specific physical contexts and geographies exist, but histories and embedded meanings are often latent, contested and invisible. Artists, creative practitioners and cultural organisations are well suited to uncover and reveal these identities as part of new site-based practices and are invaluable in building new constituencies in sites of regeneration and flux. But the cultural identity of a place cannot be applied cosmetically from the top down as if an urban-regeneration site was a clean slate to be constructed anew. This is a

Wiley-Blackwell, Hoboken, NJ, 1995, pp. 1–2; Charles Landry, Lesley Greene, Francois Matarasso and Franco Bianchini, The Art of Regeneration: Urban Renewal through Cultural Activity, Comedia, London, 1996.

lesson that has already been learnt in the previous century, with the ideology of the planned city conceived by architects and planners now largely discredited. Commissioning public art as a way to create an identity for new city precincts is, unfortunately, unlikely to be a panacea. But it is also true that creative approaches to city-making can challenge the conventions of urban development, regeneration and placemaking. Public art practice has a grounding in social engagement, collaboration and participation—practices that consider the production of space as a social and political process, not just a physical one. Public art practitioners navigate complex and dynamic urban scenarios using alternative approaches that embrace diversity, cross-cultural social experiences, chance encounters and risk.

In light of this, how do public art strategies in urban regeneration play out in practice, and what factors determine their success? And perhaps more importantly, given the contribution of art to urban public space, how can we assess its impact and value in relation to city-making?

King's Cross is often celebrated as one of London's regeneration success stories, located behind King's Cross Railway Station on railway goods lands disused since the 1970s. In 2001, the site developers Argent St George composed a set of 'Principles for a Human City', emphasising long-term stewardship, high quality, inclusive design, accessible public realm, diversity, and engagement.[3] These principles were envisaged as part of a

3 Argent St George, Principles of a Human City, edition 3, July 2001, https://www.kingscross.co.uk/media/Principles_for_a_Human_City.pdf.

'flexible' masterplan that had placemaking at its heart. The intention was that King's Cross should be an accessible place throughout the development period. Central to the placemaking effort was the delivery of over seventy thousand square metres of public realm, providing space for a diverse range of uses, from major events and community group meet-ups to art installations and creative and cultural 'meanwhile uses'. Meanwhile use, otherwise known as 'temporary' or 'interim' use, is a term used to denote activities that occupy empty urban space while it is waiting for another activity on site. It's an increasingly popular practice in urban regeneration and renewal because it activates vacant or dormant space, creating social, economic and cultural value which would otherwise not exist. At King's Cross, active estate management was used to establish the construction site as a destination in the interim period through a range of programming and activation initiatives. In particular, the role of art was identified in the King's Cross Central Public Realm Strategy where it was proposed that 'art would be integrated throughout the public realm, as a means of enrichment and animation' via an Art Commissioning Strategy.[4] As Peter Bishop, Head of Planning at the London Borough of Camden, observed, 'Argent recognised the importance of establishing a "place" or destination early in the development process. The introduction of new activities, the management of public spaces, and

4 EDAW, Townshend Landscape Architects, General Public Agency, and Access Design Consultants, King's Cross Central Public Realm Strategy, April 2004, p. 53, https://www.kingscross.co.uk/media/35-Public-Realm-Strat.pdf.

encouragement of temporary art installations and activities all formed part of their strategy.'[5]

The emerging public realm unfolded over the fourteen years of the development from 2006 to 2020, hosting simultaneous public art interventions so that the production of art and of public space were often in synergy. Although some initiatives were led by others and hosted at King's Cross (e.g. High Wire, 2008, a video installation by Catherine Yass, commissioned by Artangel and installed at the German Gymnasium, Pancras Road; and Scattered Crowd, 2009, a balloon installation by William Forsythe, commissioned by Sadlers Wells and installed at The Midland Goods Shed), most were initiated by the developer via the King's Cross Central Limited Partnership. Michael Pinsky and Stéphanie Delcroix were appointed by Argent as the curators for the first three years, and their program RELAY was inspired by the active transformation of King's Cross into a new piece of city. As Pinsky writes: 'The commissions reflect the dynamism of the construction of King's Cross. Since the development will take a generation to complete, the planners need to be acutely aware, not just of the final scheme, but how King's Cross comes into being.'[6]

Individual commissions were both significant in scale and experimental in format. Black Maria, 2013,

5 Peter Bishop and Lesley Williams, Planning, Politics and City-making: A Case Study of Kings Cross, RIBA Publishing, London, 2016.

6 Michael Pinsky, 'Kings, Swings, Pings, Wings and Rings', Urban Design Group Journal, vol. 128, Autumn 2013, https://www.udg.org.uk/sites/default/files/publications/UD128_magazine.pdf.

by artist Richard Wentworth and architects GRUPPE, was a temporary installation that functioned as an auditorium located in 'The Crossing'—the atrium in front of Central Saint Martins College of Art and Design. Named after Thomas Edison's first movie production studio, Black Maria was a large and ambiguous timber infrastructure which served as a venue for hosted events as well as more informal gatherings. Tiered seating, staircases and bridges within the structure created the effect of an 'inhabitable billboard', where performance and audience relationships were in flexible relationships to one another. The construction's provisional physical quality and the programming of the space enhanced the potential for appropriation and informal use. As Pinsky has since reflected: 'The nature of this installation probed every complexity of the site: Where can you make things? How much noise can you make? Who insures the space?'[7] Like other commissions in the RELAY program, Black Maria tested the flexibility of the public realm both in terms of the hard infrastructures of its architecture and the soft infrastructures of its management, use and programming. By committing to an active public realm throughout the construction period and investing in the commissioning of significant pieces of temporary public art, this venture opened up questions about the ownership, use and identity of public space, and how it is managed and maintained.

Of Soil and Water: King's Cross Pond Club, 2015–16, by Ooze (Eva Pfannes and Sylvain Hartenberg) and Marjetica Potrč, was another remarkable example of how the King's Cross public art program engaged in the transformation of the

7 Ibid.

development site. Located on a cleared construction site of rubble and hardcore, to the rear of King's Cross, Pond Club created a micro-ecological environment with a natural swimming pond at its centre. Free of chemicals, its water was purified by natural processes using plants, nutrient mineralisation and a set of filters to supplement natural filtration in a closed-loop cycle. The pond was open to exactly 163 visitors each day, for nine months, a limit set by the capacity of the plants to filter the water. Although urban development is not readily open to spontaneous 'co-building', the pond became a focus point of the development; it was something on a human scale that local residents could fight for. As part of a campaign to save the pond, 5,289 individuals signed an online petition for the temporary art commission to become permanent. As Ooze reflect, the project itself became a 'pioneer', testing and rehearsing new constituencies with multiple stakeholders.[8] Pond Club provides a visceral reminder that the construction sites of urban regeneration are not empty tabula rasa but contested locales holding historic tensions of use and access.[9] Policy- and planning-orientated discussions about development tend to emphasise glossy, new visions of sanitised futures and in so doing they often obliterate histories that don't fit this new narrative. In the 1980s and 1990s, King's Cross was a focus of counterculture, with a reputation for drugs, raves,

8 Eva Pfannes and Sylvain Hartenberg, 'Of Soil and Water: The Kings Cross Pond Club', in Mel Dodd (ed.), Spatial Practices: Modes of Action and Engagement with the City, Routledge, London, 2020, pp. 113–20.

9 Ibid.

sex work and homelessness. Though undoubtedly insalubrious, it had an active culture and identity that has now been displaced. For Ooze, the unexpected constituency of pool users became a new 'engine' for stakeholders and residents to re-assert ownership. In this sense, the commission was open-ended, and the precise outcome was unknown. When the pool was duly removed on schedule after nine months, it received a host of negative press coverage.[10] However, this example demonstrates ways in which the imbalance toward control and over-management in urban redevelopment can be shifted positively through progressive public art commissioning, which arguably gave the Pond Club—and the RELAY program as a whole—greater long-term traction and a stronger legacy with broader audiences.

The 'formal' art program by Argent was also complemented by 'informal' activities by early tenant Central Saint Martins. As the College occupied the semi-complete regeneration site, it was not surprising that creative work by staff and students responded to questions of transformation, displacement and erasure. Anna Hart and Tilly Fowler founded AiR at Central Saint Martins in 2007, and over four years, they tested alternatives to privatised public space through interactions with the surrounding communities of Cally, Somers Town and Maiden Lane. AiR's King's Cross interventions

10 Oliver Wainwright, 'King's Cross Pond Club: Is This the End for City-Centre Wild Swimming?', The Guardian, 8 October 2016, https://www.theguardian.com/lifeandstyle/the-swimming-blog/2016/oct/07/kings-cross-pond-club-is-this-the-end-for-city-centre-wild-swimming.

included ten 'Unannounced Acts of Publicness'—a series of artworks installed over a month in Granary Square in 2015, in which the audience was anyone present who encountered the works as part of everyday life. 'Unannounced Act of Publicness' probed the meaning of 'public' in privately owned public spaces, introducing elements of the unexpected, the reflective, the local, and the fleeting. Challenging the emerging dominance of programmed spectacle, these works explored, among other things, the amplitude of trust, invitation and conversation with those beyond the development's red line, and the formal art commissioning process.[11] Unofficial and informal public art interventions such as AiR's deliver alternative commentaries on civic space, and are a necessary contribution to making cities energetic and productive.

When art intervenes in the public realm, issues of impact and value are foregrounded. Like architecture and urbanism, public realm design answers to a range of policy and planning objectives, including the promotion of civic engagement and well-being. The art commissioning at King's Cross was most effective where it framed the city as a civic space, mobilising and engaging communities. In this way, public art has been evidenced to have an impact on people's social and civic attitudes, and even their political engagement: 'arts based practice does indeed make a very significant and positive contribution to the development of the attributes of civil society'.[12]

11 AiR Studio, https://airstudio.org/places/kings-cross/.

12 Hilary Ramsden, Jane Milling, Jenny Phillimore, Angus McCabe, Hamish Fyfe, and Robin Simpson, <u>The Role of</u>

These evaluations of arts and culture initiatives have uncovered feedback from developers, professionals, local authority officers and others that their understanding and approach have been significantly shifted by the presence of an artist. Artists' involvement in urban projects introduces creativity and challenge, which 'either makes teams work differently or leads to different design possibilities: often both; involving communities in consultation and co-design on the one hand or re-imagining a site and how the public and private realms might be reconfigured, on the other'.[13] The strengthening of the connections between people is arguably the more interesting impact for arts and cultural organisations, rather than the direct economic impact associated with culture-led regeneration.

The discussion above gives an insight into an example of large-scale urban regeneration which has co-opted public arts programming and activation as a key tool in its development transformation. At the other end of the spectrum, the Melbourne Arts Precinct Blueprint, a collaboration between Creative Victoria, City of Melbourne and The University of Melbourne, has recently proposed a planning vision overlaid onto an existing arts precinct. The overall ambition—to

<u>Grassroots Arts Activities in Communities: A Scoping Study</u>, Third Sector Research Centre, Birmingham, 2011, https://www.artshealthresources.org.uk/wp-content/uploads/2018/10/2011-Grassroots-Arts-Activities-in-Communities.pdf.

13 Geoffrey Crossick and Patrycja Kaszynska, <u>Understanding the Value of Arts & Culture: The AHRC Cultural Value Project</u>, Arts and Humanities Research Council UK, 2016, p. 72.

create a vibrant and active destination—is similar to that of King's Cross Central, although this time in a very different and already well-established cultural context (indeed, it has one of the highest concentrations of arts, cultural and creative organisations in the world).

The cluster of arts organisations that exists on the southern bank of the Yarra River in Melbourne, bordering on St Kilda Road, include the National Gallery of Victoria (NGV), Australian Centre of Contemporary Art (ACCA), the Arts Centre, Recital Centre, Malthouse Theatre, Buxton Contemporary and Victorian College of the Arts. The people of the Kulin Nation gathered on the site for thousands of years, and following European colonisation, this area became host to an increasingly permanent entertainment district. In 1946, the land was set aside for arts and cultural uses by a post-war government reconstruction committee, and from 1968 onwards, a series of formal arts institutions were constructed, including the NGV, a performing arts centre and other concerts halls and venues. The 2014 'Melbourne Arts Precinct Blueprint'[14] was initiated by the Victorian government as a guide for future development. It identifies key issues with the Precinct, including urban barriers and vacant sites ripe for future development; perhaps most importantly, it reveals a deeper concern about the Precinct's original 'formal' planning approach, which has created an enclave of 'high art'

14 Melbourne City Council, Melbourne Arts Precinct Blueprint, 2014, https://www.melbourne.vic.gov.au/about-council/committees-meetings/meeting-archive/MeetingAgendaItemAttachments/639/11308/Agenda%20Item%206.2%20Melbourne%20Arts%20Precinct%20Blueprint.pdf.

institutions and inward-looking buildings that have minimal programming or interaction with the public realm. While the co-location of arts venues has provided a critical mass of cultural venues, it is questionable what impact these buildings have in relation to social and economic consequences for broader public and popular audiences. It's more often the case that really successful creative quarters are based on clusters of much smaller-scale cultural assets—studios, live-music venues, small galleries, small creative industries and so on—which generate associated trade and industry. These endeavours are far more significant in supporting healthier and more balanced cultural communities, including added benefits such as local employment.

At the Melbourne Arts Precinct, this concern has been supported by feedback from over one thousand residents, students and visitors to the Southbank, which revealed the desire for an inclusive, accessible, affordable and active neighbourhood—one that is less highbrow and that has more opportunities for independent artists and creative activities.[15] The Blueprint therefore proposes a fully integrated and activated precinct with the desire to bring life into the streets—and this vision is framed in two architectural and urban design framework reports established by the Melbourne Arts Precinct Working Group in 2013 (Peter Elliott Architecture Southbank Arts Precinct Architectural Design Blueprint and John Wardle Architects Southbank Arts Precinct Urban Design Framework).[16]

15 Ibid.
16 Ibid.

The question is how can public art and creative spatial practice form part of this urban transformation in such a way that it supports diversity and a breadth of cultural uses and doesn't just perpetuate a 'high art' ghetto? With a hiatus since 2014, the Precinct has had a recent commitment to its transformation with a $1.46 billion investment promised by the Victorian government. This may mean that a significantly resourced arts and cultural programming strategy would be a possibility for the Melbourne Arts Precinct in a similar way to that developed at King's Cross. An integrated arts and cultural programming strategy could provide the opportunity to co-create the public realm through incremental and unfolding projects that explore culture and identity in situ.

In fact, exemplar projects already exist across the city, supported and led by Creative Victoria and the City of Melbourne, as well as other independent arts and commissioning organisations. For example, in 2016, Public Art Melbourne's Biennial Lab, 'What Happens Now?'[17] initiated a curatorial framework for the Queen Victoria Market, offering independent artists development and production support for site-based works, which were intended to develop new encounters within the municipality via open-ended enquiry and the prospect of imagining new possibilities.[18] The program deliberately questioned the role that public art plays in bringing existing and new communities together within a changing urban environment of rapid redevelopment; in this case, it

17 City of Melbourne, Public Art Melbourne, 'What Happens Now?', accessed May 2021, http://www.biennallab.com/.

18 Ibid.

was the potential redevelopment of Melbourne's historic market hall that opened in 1978 and remains a major landmark in the CBD. A curatorial group including Natalie King, David Cross and Claire Doherty (Director of Situations, the UK-based arts commissioning and production organisation) worked with the commissioned artists to develop 'The Melbourne Principles: New Rules of Public Art'.[19] The first of these principles reinforces art's role in the transformation of urban places: 'Address what is urgent. Public art has the capacity to effect change. Seek out what demands to be addressed right now without fearing failure. Ask "what happens now?"'

In illustration of this, one project commissioned from the collaborative practice Sibling and entitled Over Obelisk, constructed a physical framing structure, or folly, around the John Batman obelisk, originally erected in 1881. The folly functions as a socially engaged mobile device to facilitate public conversations that can reframe the politics of contested histories on the site. The folly actively corrects inaccuracies in the monuments inscriptions that state that Melbourne was 'unoccupied' before 1835 and foregrounds Indigenous knowledges by asking passersby in English and in Woiwurrung: 'Do you acknowledge that the events referred to by this monument are inaccurate?' In this sense, the folly draws attention to site contexts that require reconsideration in advance of redevelopment.

19 City of Melbourne, Public Art Melbourne, 'The Melbourne Principles: New Rules of Public Art', accessed May 2021, http://www.bienniallab.com/melbourne-principles.

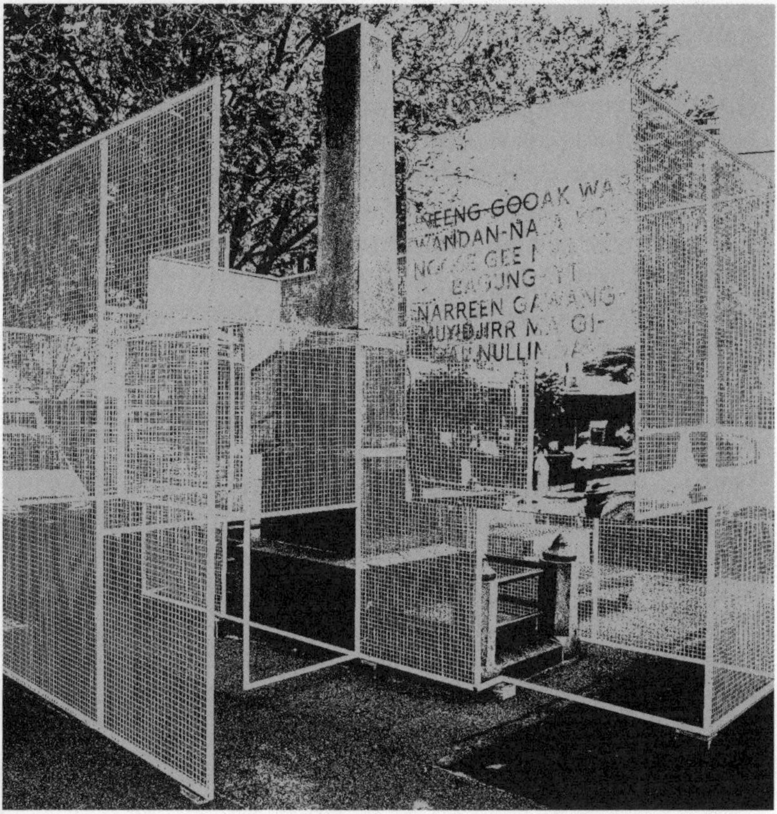

Sibling, Over Obelisk 2016. Temporary architectural installation presented as part of Public Art Melbourne's Biennial Lab, Queen Victoria Markets, Melbourne, during the 2016 Melbourne Festival, 17–23 October 2016. The Biennial Lab was convened by the City of Melbourne and curated by Natalie King with co-convenors Claire Doherty and David Cross. Photo: Bryony Jackson

Another example of experimental art commissioning ahead of redevelopment in Melbourne is 'Testing Grounds', located within the area designated as the Melbourne Arts Precinct. Testing Grounds is a temporary infrastructure for creative practice sited at 1 City Road, and it provides further direction for the way in which public art and city-making might collaborate productively. Originally a site made vacant through demolition, the land was then acquired by the State of Victoria as Crown Land and reserved for arts purposes. Initially independently proposed for interim uses by 'The Projects',[20] Testing Grounds has developed into a creative infrastructure and urban-renewal project hosted by Creative Victoria and The Projects as an interim use or meanwhile space for creative and alternative arts. In activating an otherwise vacant development site in the Precinct, it has provided a successful and tangible form of experimentation or 'testing' that has complemented the more traditional art venues. The space essentially provides a supportive physical and programming infrastructure for artists, students, producers and directors to create short-term projects and to make connections with new audiences. Testing Grounds's organisational and physical infrastructure is arguably in itself a piece of public art, because it provides an equitable social framework for cultural creativity and expression and in so doing actively positions itself as an alternative to a gallery, museum or institution. Importantly for the Precinct, the Testing Ground Manifesto, available on the These Are the Projects We Do Together website, states 'It is different from

20 These Are the Projects We Do Together, 'About', https://www.theprojects.com.au/about/.

the monolithic objects that are art museums and art centres.'[21]

In both these cases, public art practice has provided and can continue to provide a mechanism for temporary, interim and permanent uses that activate and enliven the public realm—but that also offer a catalyst for new forms of city-making. As Peter Bishop, Head of Planning at Camden, says, these new forms of city-making are 'a recognition of the difficulties of end-state planning' and require a more radical commitment from planners, developers' authorities and city commissioners to produce more 'flexible' masterplans. In respect of this, it's useful to reference Jane Jacobs's distinction between 'cataclysmic money'—the large-scale capital investment for new developments and large urban buildings—and 'gradual money', or the operating expenditure that builds the social and cultural capital between people and sustains ongoing activity.[22] Conventional planning and development often relies on the cataclysmic money, which can fail to integrate sufficiently with the ongoing operating expenditure that supports the active maintenance of public spaces. Charles Landry puts it another way:

> [The Creative City] requires infrastructures beyond the hardware—buildings, roads or sewage. Creative infrastructure is a combination of the hard and the soft including too the mental infrastructure, the way a city

21 These Are the Projects We Do Together, 'Testing Grounds Programming Methodology', https://www.theprojects.com.au/testing-grounds-programming-methodology.

22 Jane Jacobs, The Death and Life of Great American Cities, Random House, New York, 1961.

> approaches opportunities and problems; the environmental conditions it creates to generate an atmosphere and the enabling devices it fosters generated through its incentives and regulatory structures.[23]

A balance needs to be struck between the investment in facilities (hardware) and investment in activities (software). The challenge is to develop new forms of city-making that accommodate integrated visions for both hard and soft urban infrastructures, with the necessary financial instruments that can support and program art and cultural events and activities, at a range of scales. Contemporary public art practice is well placed to operate as the 'software' of the city, and its potential interaction with traditional urban planning offers a new opportunity for creative city-making.

Powerful discourses and practices have emerged in recent decades linking cultural activity not simply to understanding the city but to changing it. This has been seen as one of the most powerful arguments for the instrumental benefits of the arts, pointing to the impact of major cultural buildings and the emergence of vibrant creative and cultural quarters. It was observed in 2005 that 'within the space of little more than two decades, the initiation of culture-driven urban (re)generation has come to occupy a pivotal position in the new urban entrepreneurialism'.[24] Emergent city-making

23 Charles Landry, 'Lineages of the Creative City', in Creativity and the City, Netherlands Architecture Institute, Amsterdam, 2005, p. 3, http://charleslandry.com/panel/wp-content/uploads/downloads/2013/03/Lineages-of-the-Creative-City.pdf.

24 Steven Miles and Ronan Paddison, 'The

practices that co-opt forms of public art and cultural programming bring both opportunities and challenges. As Oakley states, 'the spectacular, the newly built and high art have been seen as the drivers of regeneration', while how everyday cultural practices fit into the narrative is far less clear.[25] The provocation for Melbourne is obvious. Its rich history of artist-led activity needs to be actively co-opted into larger-scale infrastructural renewal to enable everyday cultural practices to be strategically connected into the hardware of urban redevelopment; otherwise, our new city precincts will remain lifeless. Large urban and engineering infrastructure projects continue to be delivered across Melbourne as part of state and city government initiatives. They will be increasingly seen as pathways to recovery post-COVID, and it's imperative that culture and creative activity are conceived as the critical software for such developments. They will need to be firmly integrated into urban redevelopments, not as window dressing or cosmetic add-ons but as operational ingredients from the start, and supported for the onward life of the precinct as a rich public realm.

Rise and Rise of Culture-Led Regeneration', Urban Studies, vol. 42, no. 5–6, pp. 833–39.

25 Dave O'Brian and Kate Oakley, Cultural Value and Inequality, A Critical Literature Review, Arts and Humanities Research Council UK, 2015, https://ahrc.ukri.org/documents/project-reports-and-reviews/cultural-value-and-inequality-a-critical-literature-review/.

Women as Storytellers: Public Art in Sydney

Felicity Fenner*

* Felicity Fenner is a curator of contemporary and public art, and author of books such as Running the City: Why Public Art Matters (NewSouth, 2017) and Curating in a Time of Ecological Crisis (Routledge, 2022). Chair of the City of Sydney's Public Art Advisory Panel, she was the inaugural Director of UNSW Galleries (2010–18) and visual arts co-curator for the Perth Festival (2017–19). Other curatorial projects include City Dialogue: Public Art Interventions + the Biennale of Sydney (Customs House, 2020), Making Change (National Museum of China, 2012), Australia's group exhibition for the 2009 Venice Biennale, and the 2008 Adelaide Biennial of Australian Art.

The cultural enunciation of public spaces in our cities is largely determined by town planners and architects, with only occasional input from artists, despite the fact that even the most subtly integrated public art has the capacity to elevate the best-designed city spaces from being generic and anonymous to being meaningful to the site and its communities of users. In recent years, Australian women artists working in the public domain have demonstrated particularly empathic, curious and creative responses to place. Yet, their contribution has historically been limited: up until the end of the twentieth century, the only notable artworks by women in Australia's first city of Sydney were Margel Hinder's 1964 abstract sculpture outside the Reserve Bank of Australia in Martin Place and Janet Laurence and Fiona Foley's Edge of the Trees, 1995, in the nearby Museum of Sydney forecourt. In the three decades that passed between the installation of these two works, numerous major sculptural commissions were awarded in Sydney, but very few to women artists.

Until relatively recently, public art was mostly conceived as icing on the cake of city place-making, with non-site-specific 'plonk' art prevailing over design-integrated and location-relevant projects. It was not until the late 1990s, propelled by the need for an overdue makeover ahead of the 2000 Summer Olympic Games, that the potential for public art to not just beautify city spaces and memorialise prominent colonists and civic leaders, but also to provide insight into and define the character of place, was fully embraced by Sydney. At that time, leading curator and former Artspace director Sally Couacaud (1947–2020) was appointed to commission and deliver a series of ambitious outdoor sculptural installations by Australian and international artists, which established the foundation for the city's subsequent and ongoing public art program. The Sydney Sculpture Walk stretches from the Domain and Royal Botanic Gardens, through East Circular Quay to Macquarie Street. Nine of the ten works delivered by Couacaud were by women artists, and major permanent installations by contemporary women artists have recently been added to this collection. They include Australian artist Lindy Lee's *Garden of Cloud and Stone*, 2015–20, in Chinatown, and British artist Tracey Emin's tiny bronze birds, *The Distance of Your Heart*, 2018, around the northern CBD.

Part of the Sculpture Walk, Anne Graham's *Passage*, 2000, serves as a gently invocative gateway to the pedestrianised zone at the top of Martin Place. Other original works commissioned by Couacaud in 1999–2000 that still enjoy prominence today include Laurence's *Veil of Trees* on Art Gallery Road; Fiona Hall's *Folly for Mrs Macquarie*; Bronwyn Oliver's pod-like *Magnolia* and *Palm* sculptures nestled into garden beds of the Botanic Gardens; and Brenda L. Croft's nearby *Wuganmgulya* terrazzo ground plane work along the foreshore at Farm Cove. Located at the site of the first colonial farm, the latter tells the stories of that significant place from an Aboriginal viewpoint.

Like Croft, many women artists working in the public domain of Sydney tend to be drawn to storytelling, specifically works that evoke the Indigenous, colonial or more recent history of a site. And like the Sculpture Walk, some of the more impactful works are initiated by major cultural events and realised in partnership with the City of Sydney, such as Janet Cardiff and George Bures Miller's *City of Forking*

Paths, 2014, a speculative app-based tour of the Rocks precinct made for Juliana Engberg's 19th Biennale of Sydney and Agatha Gothe-Snape's textual laneway installation Here, An Echo, 2016–17, another Biennale legacy project.

Over the first two decades of the twenty-first century, women leaders in Sydney have played a particularly influential role in shaping the city—for better and for worse. The mostly unsightly legacy of environmentally damaging infrastructure projects imposed by the Government of NSW are thankfully countered by the 'green, global, connected' projects advanced by Lord Mayor Clover Moore. Since 2004, Moore has articulated discrete inner-city 'villages' that are culturally layered, environmentally sustainable, user-friendly and aesthetically pleasing. Establishing the city's first Public Art Advisory Panel in 2007—complemented by a Design Advisory Panel and Aboriginal and Torres Strait Islander Advisory Panel—Moore has presided over the commissioning of dozens of public artworks, temporary and permanent, minor and major. At the same time, curator Barbara Flynn has advanced an impressive catalogue of authentically site-specific permanent public artworks by leading international artists, both in her capacity as curatorial advisor for the City of Sydney and as an independent advisor. In Greater Sydney, Anne Loxley, the former Senior Curator of the Museum of Contemporary Art Australia (MCA), redefined the role of public art with playful and creative, community-based art projects across Western Sydney, delivered through the MCA's C3West program.

In the context of First Nations art, curator Hetti Perkins is one of Australia's leading advocates for Aboriginal and Torres Strait Islander artists. An original member of the City of Sydney's Public Art Advisory Panel, Perkins now leads the Eora Journey, a cultural program of which a key pillar is seven major public art projects foregrounding the culture of Australia's First Nations peoples. Works completed thus far include those by Reko Rennie (*Welcome to Redfern*, 2013), Tony Albert (*YININMADYEMI Thou Didst Let Fall*, 2014) and Nicole Foreshew (*born in darkness before dawn*, 2013–14). The scale and iconic siting of the most recent artwork in the series, Judy Watson's *bara*, 2021, signifies the importance also vested in the Eora Journey program by the City of Sydney.

Occupying the elevated grassy headland known as the Tarpeian Precinct Lawn adjacent to Government House, above Dubbagullee (Bennelong Point) where the Sydney Opera House stands, *bara* is visible from the city's Circular Quay and Rocks districts, the northern side of the Harbour from North Sydney to Kirribilli, the Harbour Bridge, and from the Harbour waters. The work's commanding presence celebrates the First Peoples of Sydney, the traditional custodians of Gadigal Country, and honours clans of the Eora Nation and Elders.

Modelled on the crescent-shaped traditional fish hooks made by Gadigal women, Watson's sculpture pays homage to the vital role played by women as the primary food providers. According to historian Grace Karskens, the bara symbolised women's identity, power and status in the community. Aboriginal fisherwomen—including Bennelong's strong-willed wife Barangaroo—were commonly seen around Port Jackson until the late 1820s, fishing from their bark canoes ('nowie' or 'nawi') in all weather, while the men stood along the shoreline fishing with spears. On land, the women sometimes wore the bara on fishing twine like necklaces: though beautiful, pearly objects in their own right, they were not worn as decoration but carried as essential working implements.[1]

With a gleaming white finish reminiscent of local seashells, the form of bara also suggests a crescent moon and the coves of the harbour, and in relation to modern additions to the landscape, Watson cites the sails of the Sydney Opera House and arch of the Harbour Bridge as influences. A grand sculpture about strong women by an esteemed woman artist, Watson's bara occupies a more high-profile site in the public arena than any other work by a First Nations artist in Australia, if not the world.

In a very different way, one of the first public domain installations realised for the Sydney Sculpture Walk over twenty years earlier, Graham's Passage summons through its form and location a historical aspect of Sydney of which too little is appreciated by its modern inhabitants and visitors. Sited just along the road from bara, among the commanding sandstone buildings of Macquarie Street traditionally associated with colonial power and supremacy—from the State Library, Sydney Hospital, State Parliament, numerous churches, legal chambers and medical specialists—Passage traces the footprint of the modest Georgian houses that once occupied the site.

Set into the granite ground plane, Passage sits at the top, eastern end of Martin Place. Its three

1 Grace Karskens, 'Barangaroo and the Eora Fisherwomen', Dictionary of Sydney, 2014, https://dictionaryofsydney.org/entry/barangaroo_and_the_eora_fisherwomen.

bronze bowls, reflection pools and fountains represent washrooms. The house plan is marked out by polished black granite paving and metal grilles lit from below, through which a light mist rises periodically, evoking ghost-like walls. In Georgian times, washrooms were placed at the back of the house, and water would have been carried up from the nearby Tank Stream for use in the ablution area, kitchen and laundry of the original house.

Women artists as storytellers are often compelled not to commemorate well-known, public figures and their achievements, but the unsung communities and people who weave the cultural thread of places and social fabric. Unlike Watson's bara, and despite also being sited in a very high-profile part of the city, Graham's reference to the past conjures rather than celebrates the work of women. It is a gently invocative work, subtle to the point of near invisibility when pedestrian traffic is at a peak, yet literally holding its ground, whispering from the past of Martin Place, the CBD's civic spine since colonisation.

Graham is interested in the workings of the city as a metaphor for the living body, portrayed here by the water elements and mist that rise and fall like breath. Indeed, being bodily immersed in a place—through walking, listening and empirical observation—can reveal its essential and somatic qualities. This was the chosen mode of preparation for Here, an Echo, a public artwork developed by Gothe-Snape during the 20th Biennale of Sydney.[2] According to the artist, walking was her key research

2 The 2016 Biennale of Sydney, The Future Is Already Here—It's Just Not Evenly Distributed, was curated by Stephanie Rosenthal.

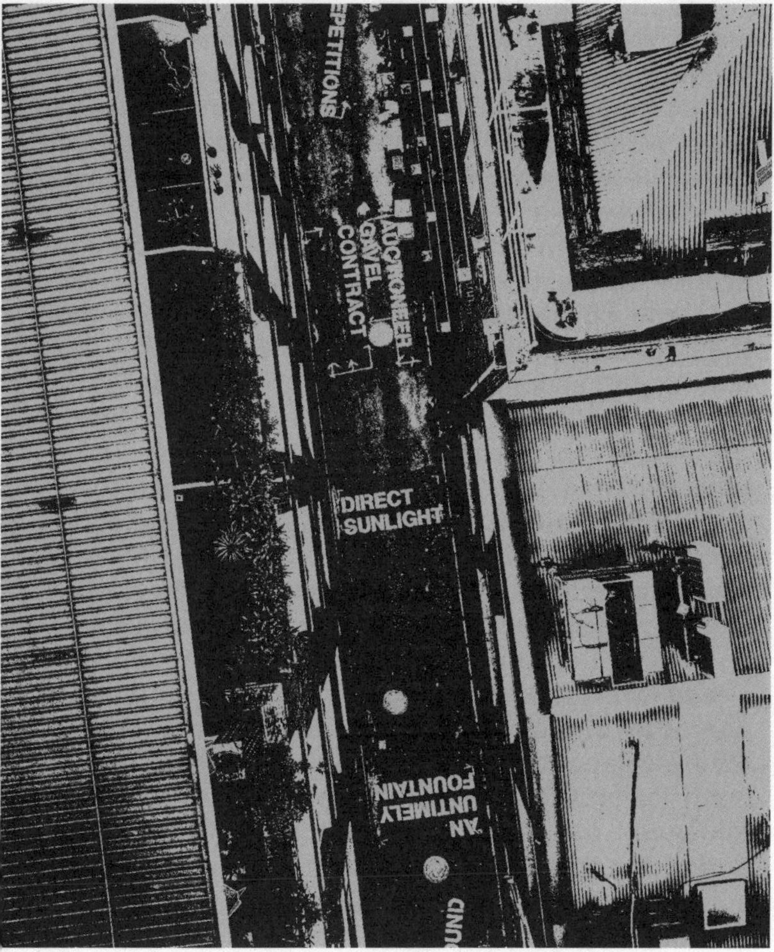

Agatha Gothe-Snape, Here, an Echo 2016–17. Permanent public artwork; retro-reflective road paint, approx. 180 metres of laneway road surface (including some walls of adjacent buildings). Co-commissioned by the Biennale of Sydney and City of Sydney for the Second Biennale Legacy Artwork, City of Sydney Art Collection. Aerial installation view, Wemyss Lane, Surry Hills, Sydney. Photo: Yanni Kronenberg, courtesy of the artist and The Commercial, Sydney

methodology in the quest to glean a sense of place: 'Even though Sydney is where I live and grew up, it has so many stories, hidden histories and layers. We found walking a great way to try and tune into these . . . to use the body, how it moves through space, as a way to research.'[3]

Created in collaboration with choreographer Brooke Stamp, the first stage of the project involved research, conversations, performances and walks in the CBD during the Biennale in 2016. The permanent, second iteration of the work was installed in 2017 as a series of words and phrases that appear for perpetuity in the ground plane of Wemyss Lane, Surry Hills, on the south-western side of the CBD towards Central Station. The long and narrow laneway was once a crowded residential strip, a precursor to the nearby modern Chinatown district, before being turned into a manufacturing and commercial hub during the First World War. These layers of history, including the pre-colonial character of the naturally inclined site, prompted Gothe-Snape to offer possible rather than historically factual interpretations. The open-ended texts were intuitively arrived upon by the artist during the first stage of research. Like whispers emitted from the tall brick warehouse walls that frame the narrow laneway, the capitalised texts written in white road line-marking paint include phrases such as 'Below the threshold of audibility', 'Inclusions and misprints' and 'Not predictability but inevitability'.

3 Nicholas Carolan, 'Agatha Gothe-Snape: Here an Echo' (interview), Grazie, 2017, https://graziamagazine.com/articles/agatha-gothe-snape-here-an-echo-interview/.

Gothe-Snape is a poetic, conceptual artist; offering a literal interpretation of the texts would defeat her mission to foster imaginative and new understandings of the laneway. This imperative to take the viewer on a journey of discovery is also the motivating concept underpinning a public sculpture in central Sydney that commemorates the centenary of the Boy Scouts movement in Australia. The work was commissioned from artists Jennifer Turpin and Michaelie Crawford by philanthropist Dick Smith, who believes that he benefitted enormously from his childhood experience as a Cub and Boy Scout in terms of it engendering a sense of self-confidence and appetite for responsible risk-taking. As a patron of the Scouts, Smith wanted to promote the continuing relevance of the Boy Scouts in the twenty-first century: 'It is hard as a parent and grandparent but we have to stop "helicoptering" (hovering over) our children and grandchildren and allow them to have adventure in their lives, expanding their horizons by accepting an element of risk.'[4]

While the original vision of Dick and Pip Smith was for a more traditional, probably figurative statue representing the Scout movement, with the encouragement and guidance of the City of Sydney's design and public art teams to explore less conservative approaches, a more contemporary path was embraced by the commissioners. The result was <u>Windlines: The Scout Compass of</u>

4 Dick Smith AO (2009), quoted in 'Windlines, the Scout Compass of Discovery', City of Sydney website, last updated 2021, https://www.cityartsydney.com.au/artwork/windlines-the-scout-compass-of-discovery/.

Discovery, an 8.8-metre-high steel and stone sculpture, resembling the form of an orienteering compass, installed in 2011 at Scout Place in the very busy Circular Quay precinct.

In the spirit of scouting adventure, Turpin and Crawford sought to harness the ever-changing nature of the wind to inspire fanciful and actual journeys of discovery. On the ground plane, a twelve-metre-wide bronze map of Greater Sydney is inscribed with lyrical place names imagined from stories, some of them folklore, about each place. In their artist statement, they explain:

> Windlines seeks to remind us of the adventure inherent in our city and its surrounds. The ground compass includes near and far, urban and natural, past and present. 'Snapper Watches Spectacle As Camping Cockatoos Lasso A Lonely Goat, 14km WNW' for example, refers to the inner harbour islands of Snapper, Spectacle, Cockatoo and Goat and is accompanied by a distance and direction from Scout Place.[5]

Most of the destinations are of significance to the Scouts, including little-known places dotted around Sydney's waterways and off the beaten track of inland urban centres. Extending out from the map are encircling lines of text embedded in the ground. The distance and direction for each of the sixteen points of the compass are noted, while above ground, a weathervane turns with the wind, inviting curious passersby to discover the places referred to in the acrostics.

5 Turpin Crawford Studio, 'Windlines', artists' statement, https://turpincrawfordstudio.com.au/work/windlines.

In our green-deprived cities, the discovery and appreciation of the life-giving ecosystems of the natural world form a recurring theme in the work of many artists. The strategy of re-planting urban environments that have been de-greened by industrial and commercial development has gained traction internationally since Agnes Denes planted, nurtured and harvested a two-acre field of wheat in downtown Manhattan in 1982.[6] Other famous international examples—each of which are ongoing projects—include Joseph Beuys's 7,000 Oaks: City Forestation Instead of City Administration, 1982, in the German city of Kassel; the High Line in Manhattan, 2009; and numerous environmental projects initiated by the Echigo-Tsumari Triennial in the rice-growing Niigata prefecture of Japan, 2000.

These are all permanent works of public art, yet temporary projects such as Denes's Wheatfield can also have immediate impact as catalysts for change. For example, an instant native forest planted by artists in central Sydney just a year after the devastating 'Black Summer' bushfires and on the cusp of a return to normal life during the COVID-19 pandemic was immediately embraced by the city's communities of workers, residents and visitors.

Barlow Street Forest, 2021, was created by the Dirt Witches, a cross-disciplinary collective of female environmental and climate activists including well-known artists such as Janet Laurence and Caroline Rothwell. A micro-forest measuring eight by thirteen metres, it created the layers of a natural ecosystem, incorporating over thirty species belonging to the critically endangered Eastern

6 Agnes Denes, Wheatfield—A Confrontation, 1982.

Suburbs Banksia Scrub, as well as beehives containing sugarbag stingless native bees (Tetragonula carbonaria). It served as a poetic reminder of the 5,300 hectares of scrub that once stretched between Botany Bay and North Head, and aimed to shift the aesthetic appreciation and understanding of Banksia Scrub by recontextualising it within the city. The artists asserted:

> As Dirt Witch artist activists we have the opportunity to bring our individual practices and networks together to create the micro forest installation. This aligns with local and international movements to establish fast growing, dense and biodiverse plantings. Complex ecosystems and nature conservation are fundamental to this moment.[7]

Maintenance of the garden was undertaken by Dirt Witch community volunteers and also engaged the local city community. It was accompanied by a program of talks and workshops and heralded on the street by a message chalkboard where the artists and visitors shared knowledge and information on environmental statistics, plant varieties and maintenance tips. The Barlow Street Forest connects with the City of Sydney's vision to create green corridors as part of a liveable green network.

Unlike the other, permanent public art projects discussed here, Forest was commissioned as a temporary artwork, intended to remain in place for just six months. Yet, within days of its installation, it

7 Lara Merrett, Caroline Rothwell, Rena Shein and Floria Tosca, 'Barlow Street Forest', City of Sydney website, last updated 2021, https://www.cityartsydney.com.au/artwork/barlow-street-forest/.

had gained not only substantial media coverage, but also calls to Council from the public to make it permanent. This was not the first time in Sydney that a temporary artwork bringing wild nature into the city prompted members of the public to petition for it to become a permanent feature: in 2012, the City of Sydney made permanent a very popular installation featuring the songs of fifty different bird species displaced by urbanisation, originally commissioned as a temporary work in 2009.[8]

The same happened in response to public demand to Rothwell's Youngsters, 2012, commissioned as a temporary work and subsequently acquired by the City of Sydney for permanent installation. Some years later, Youngsters inspired further action by an unknown person who used two of the sculptures of children to make a point about the appalling treatment of child refugees by the then government, illegally affixing on the nearby wall an engraved plaque close to one of the figures.[9] The City allowed the plaque to stay, where it remains to this day. These actions are testament to the power of public art as an effective vehicle of knowledge transfer and public discourse, even as a catalyst for change. They recall the impact of Turner Prize-winning Rachel Whiteread's House, 1993–94, which stirred the local community to spontaneously adopt the work as a symbol of unwanted

8 This was Michael Thomas Hill and Richard Major's Forgotten Songs, 2009–12, located in Angel Place, Sydney.

9 The plaque reads: 'Children seeking asylum in Australia are kept in detention as part of a government policy which inflicts harm on refugees fleeing violence and persecution'.

development in the neighbourhood, and to use it as a canvas to which they affixed petition posters opposing the M11 road extension in Wanstead.[10]

Urbanist Jane Jose believes that women are particularly well placed to address the needs of city spaces, because 'women take a long view, acting as intergeneration custodians for their children, tomorrow's children, and they care what happens to strangers'.[11] Indeed, since the earliest postcolonial involvement in the planning of our cities by women of prominence, such as Elizabeth Macquarie and Marion Mahony Griffin, women have exerted enormous influence on the design, character and identity of our city spaces. The public domain is a shared environment that should offer a sense of inclusivity and belonging for all users. Drawing on investigative and knowledge transfer skills as archivists and narrators, women artists in Sydney have been motivated to reveal layers of history, to offer alternative understandings of place and to provide inclusive spaces. While the responsibility for city-making has historically fallen to men, it is the contribution of women planners, urban designers and, as argued here, artists, that often establishes compelling connections to places and people, past and present.

10 Malcolm Miles, Art, Space and the City, Routledge, Oxford, 1997, p. 148.

11 Jane Jose, Places Women Make, Wakefield Press, Mile End, South Australia, 2016, p. 22.

Becoming Molecular in Public

Emily Cormack*

* Dr Emily Cormack is a curator and writer with a special interest in how art operates within the public realm. She has curated over thirty exhibitions, including _From Will to Form: The 2018 TarraWarra Biennial_; _Monument to Now: MoreArt 2020_, an exhibition of temporal public art, Melbourne; Primavera 2016, Museum of Contemporary Art Australia, Sydney; and as co-curator, _City Within the City_, Artsonje Center, Seoul (2011); and _Still Vast Reserves_, Magazzino d'Arte Moderna, Rome (2009–10). She is the curator of _BEYOND_ for the 2022 Melbourne Art Fair and was awarded her doctorate from Monash University in 2021. She has an independent curatorial practice that specialises in commissioning permanent artwork for public spaces.

> Art opens us up to the non-human universe that we are part of. And we, as spectators, as representational creatures, are involved in a dance with art, a dance in which through careful manoeuvres the molecular is opened up, the aesthetic is activated, and art does what is its chief modus operandi: it transforms, if only for a moment, our sense of ourselves and our notion of our world.[1]

This quote by Deleuzian commentator Simon O'Sullivan suggests that art has the ability to make us molecular—to break us open—so that we might transform in some way. Molecules are common among all matter—liquid, solid and gas. They are the substance from which all else is comprised and yet they are undifferentiated, and able to shift between states, contingent on the forces of their context. Electrically neutral, they are waiting to be chemically bonded, open and undefined. When art is considered in this way—as a set of shifting molecular forces—the viewer and the art object are subject to the same chemical properties and might become molecular together.

The possibilities presented by Deleuze and Guattari's thinking regarding the transmission of sensation and force has underpinned my approach to working with art in the public sphere. Thinking through art's ability to disturb the calcified cipher through which we filter sensation has encouraged me to try and create contexts within which the everyday encounter with an artwork might become an opportunity to become molecular. I work closely

1 Simon O'Sullivan, 'The Aesthetics of Affect: Thinking Art Beyond Representation', Angelaki, vol. 6, no. 3, December 2001, p. 128.

with architects to develop briefs for public art commissions that attempt to account for the potential forces within a site, imagining how they might be captured within the artwork and transmitted as sensation to the viewer. As well as drawing on Deleuze and Guattari, my curatorial work in the public realm stems from my thinking through of Nietzsche's writing on force[2] and Spinoza's understanding of substance as something that is shared across both humans and the celestial.[3] Informed by these ideas, I try to commission artworks that capture the forces of community and context. In this text, I discuss public artworks by Isadora Vaughan, Jose Dávila and Céleste Bouriser-Mougenot that I have commissioned in Melbourne between 2020 and 2022, all of which I feel express these ideas in different ways.

As Deleuze suggests, art is 'not a matter of reproducing or inventing forms, but of capturing

2 Friedrich Nietzsche describes the world as 'a monster of energy, without beginning, without end . . . as force throughout, as a play of forces and waves of forces . . . a sea of forces flowing and rushing together, eternally changing and eternally flooding back.' Friedrich Nietzsche, _The Will to Power_, trans. Walter Kaufmann, Random House, New York, [1901] 1967, p. 550.

3 The following quote by Spinoza has been fundamental to the thinking through of substance as something that is shared by both God and nature: 'That eternal and infinite being we call God, or Nature, acts from the same necessity from which he exists.' Baruch Spinoza, _The Collected Writings of Spinoza_, trans. Edwin Curley, Princeton University Press, Princeton, 1985, Part IV, Preface.

forces'.[4] An artwork is able to transmit forces in the form of sensation to the viewer, so that the viewer is chemically altered by viewing it. This way of thinking takes on a special significance when the art is placed outside the gallery, within the public realm. After all, the public realm is a highly striated space where the determinations of civic infrastructure are so coded by instructive signage and predetermined usage that 'becoming molecular' in such a space can seem impossible. Conceived by urban planners and landscape designers, the division of public from private space ensures that codes dictating behaviour are evident within these spaces through signage, landscaping and street furniture. There is a silent, civilised compliance with these codes dictating what is prohibited and what is permitted in these spaces. However, while these 'diagrammatic' spaces, as Deleuze would refer to them, are mapped and planned with great precision, art's ability to break apart the map persists, encouraging the viewer to drop through its cartographic certainty into the level of the molecular.

The non-human molecular universe of forces that O'Sullivan describes is pre-subjective, able to affect and be effected in an endless unknowing dance of sensation. This idea stems from Deleuze's writing, where he presents the possibility that art has the ability to emit or transmit sensation directly into the body of the viewer.[5] According to Deleuze and his commentators, understanding art according to a 'logic of sensation', rather than an orthodox logic

4 Gilles Deleuze, Francis Bacon: The Logic of Sensation, trans. Daniel W. Smith, Continuum, New York, 2003, p. 56.

5 Ibid.

of figuration and representation, means that art can be understood via the sensations it emits and the activity it generates, rather than the perceptions projected onto it. This philosophy establishes a way of thinking whereby the 'meaning' of an artwork is generated by forces that are 'internal to its own activity'.[6] Deleuzian commentator John Rajchman explains that 'Artworks are composed of sensations, prelinguistic and presubjective, brought together in an expressive material.'[7] The public realm is particularly rich in these sensations and forces, as opposed to the relatively closed space of the gallery, because it invites the compositional and energetic forces of architecture, the dynamic and purposeful movement of humans, and the amorphous vagaries of weather and climate. Each of these might be captured within the artwork itself.

Working with Moreland City Council in 2020, I commissioned Melbourne-based artist Isadora Vaughan to create a large rammed-earth artwork for the Glenroy Community Hub in Melbourne's north, which incorporates these forces, and combines them with the immanent energetics of the earth. Designed by Design Inc., the Glenroy Community Hub is an innovative local government initiative that was designed to address disadvantage within the Glenroy region. As this region had been identified by Moreland City Council as a locale with low literacy, education and income outcomes, Council used infrastructure to act as a strategic intervention in the cycle of generational disadvantage, so that it might

6 Reidar Due, Deleuze, Polity Press, Cambridge, UK, 2007, p. 30.

7 John Rajchman, The Deleuze Connections, MIT Press, Cambridge, MA, 2000, p. 138.

become a catalyst for social transformation. The hub incorporates a Kindergarten, a Community Centre and a Maternal Child Health Centre along with the Glenroy Library. In this way, the centre's aim is to embed literacy and learning within everyday experience, ensuring that they are positioned alongside health and wellbeing. The building itself has a strong emphasis on the social benefits of biophilic design,[8] and the architecture adheres to high standards of sustainability and occupant health, having gained certification under the Living Building Challenge.[9] As such, it was imperative that the artworks selected for this site should share and enhance these outcomes.

8 Biophilic design is an approach to architecture that seeks to connect building occupants more closely to nature. Biophilic-designed buildings incorporate elements that create a more productive and healthy built environment for people, such as natural lighting, better ventilation and natural landscape features. One key text exploring this approach is Stephen R. Kellert, Judith H. Heerwagen and Martin L. Mador, <u>Biophilic Design: The Theory, Science and Practice of Bringing Buildings to Life</u>, John Wiley & Sons, Hoboken, NJ, 2008.

9 The Living Building Challenge is an international sustainable building certification program created in 2006 by the non-profit International Living Future Institute. It is described as a philosophy, advocacy tool and certification program that promotes the most advanced measurement of sustainability in the built environment. Its end goal is to encourage the creation of a regenerative built environment. See https://living-future.org/lbc/basics4-0/.

After a targeted EOI process where short-listed artists were invited to propose works in response to the brief, Vaughan was selected. Her practice is typified by an engagement with the energetic activity within her materials, and for Glenroy she proposed a work drawing attention to the continual transformation of the land and its communities. Her approach highlighted our interdependent connections with the earth, and the shared molecular materiality between humans and the land. Entitled Terra Pneumatics, the intention of the work is to evoke a sense of time and collectivity in these visibly human-made yet organic forms. The rammed earth and bluestone used in these sculptural forms were both sourced locally, and they reveal the shifting tonal variations from yellow to grey and beige. In doing so, they embrace and recognise the continual transformation of the terrain synonymous with the changing Glenroy communities. As Vaughan describes, they are 'indicative of the real amassing of phenomena beneath the ground that is occurring in our cities and suburbs, with this cross section of earth becoming a dynamic way to comprehend time and place'.[10]

The City of Moreland and Glenroy lie on the Western Basalt plains of Victoria, where the predominant soil is derived from ancient volcanic lava flows. Evident in the sediments is the changing use of the land with the introduction of various soils and rocks, sand and gypsum from more coastal areas of Victoria. The basalt has been quarried to build roads and buildings far away from its origin. In addition to these sediments and colour variants,

10 Isadora Vaughan, Glenroy Community Hub proposal, March 2021, p. 3.

each of Vaughan's soft curving rammed-earth forms is interspersed with what the artist refers to as the 'tongues' and 'lips' of individually selected bluestone sections chosen for the prominence of their holes and marks, which are testament to its life as a molten liquid. Vaughan arrests these materials by bringing them above ground and stilling their gradual passage from volcanic deposit to clay substrate and crumbling riverbank. As Vaughan explains, the materials draw attention to

> the water flowing in rivulets into the drains and tunnels of the Merri and Merlynston Creeks, matter too is passed from one place to another, silt and soil floats from embankments, leaves and industrial waste drift into these waterways and from there flows of energy, silt and water travel out through the port into the bay, eventually leading out to the sea. Layers of mulch, plastic and animal waste compact and slowly, over time, the geology of the area continues to grow and change.[11]

Glenroy Community Hub is an epicentre of community activity, and it acts as a monument to the small, individual forces that comprise a community. Through the imposition of human and industrial waste, the earth persists as part of us, recording our habitation and adjusting with us—for better or worse. Vaughan's sedimentary structures bring to the surface the molecular fact of our existence. Her sculptural forms are evidence of our occupation over time, further highlighting our interdependent relationship with the land, and how the communities we live in and the land we live on comprise a shared substance, and that we are part of the same cycle.

11 Ibid.

Being both in and of the land, Vaughan's sculptures not only display our habitation but also enable it. The forms hold the body, as they are shaped to enable sitting, leaning, steadying and a gathering for the community. They hold the sediments of this site—both human and terrestrial—and invite the community to become part of a molecular monument of place.

Similarly, a collection of public artworks that I have commissioned for the lobby in 101 Collins Street were selected for the manner in which they direct attention to the energetics of their material context. Each of the six commissions, selected through a competitive RFP (Request for Proposal) process, attends to the flow of forces that move through the building and the way materials inform space in different ways. 101 Collins Street is a high-end office building designed by Denton Corker Marshall with an acclaimed/maligned postmodern interior designed by American architect John Burgee. The expansive, vaulted lobby spaces feature internal reflecting pools, and elaborate, veined marble and gold-leaf walls. I was invited to curate a new suite of permanent public artworks for 101 Collins as part of a major refurbishment by Bates Smart Architects in 2021. I was struck by the opposing compositional forces present, which are determined by a strong emphasis on thick square marble forms, complemented with circular patterning and details. The sphere and cube volumes are contrasted with ephemeral qualities of liquid and reflection in a unique play of densities across the spaces, and it was these affecting material qualities that I highlighted in the briefing process.

As artist Daniel Buren attested in 1972, 'Every place radically imbues (formally, architecturally, sociologically, politically) with its meaning, the object (work/creation) shown there.'[12] Similarly, each artwork that was commissioned for 101 Collins necessarily addresses the fact that art making and its exhibition are porous activities, giving form to and being influenced by often-incorporeal forces in the world. This process of forming is always at the mercy of variables—of the effects of space, of subjectivity, of perception, of ineffable responses—each of which lays claim to our influence over the art object in a process of enfolding, with varying intensities. In my curatorial approach to the commission process, I highlighted how the lobby of 101 Collins traverses from the elegance of Collin Street's 'Paris end' to the dynamic vibrancy of Flinders Lane—a centre for art galleries, dining and street art. This passage from light, rarefied affluence to an edgy, dynamism passes through a centre of gravity. The building's lift core is heavy, weighted with the import of dark grey marble engendering the hushed tones of conservative, neo-liberal wealth acquisition. As such, in the briefing process for the art commissions, each area of the lobby was broken into zones that spoke to the material energies that I felt were specific to that location, as well as to the contextual energetics. The briefs requested that artists think through specific qualities of material, activity and essence. In particular, the works for the Collins Street entrance responded to the qualities of 'Transparency, Reflection, Immersion and Liquid'; the central core of the lobby to 'Tranquil, Pure,

12 Daniel Buren quoted in Reesa Greenberg, Bruce W. Ferguson and Sandy Nairne (eds), Thinking About Exhibitions, Routledge, London and New York, 1996, p. 223.

Matte, Solid, Deforming and Reforming'; and the Flinders Lane entrance to 'Metallic, Active, Electric and Dynamic'. In this way, the commissioned works would highlight the molecular forces within the materials, as well as the activities that flow through the building. If these forces were captured in the artwork, then, the proposition was, they would more effectively be transmitted to the viewer, enabling a momentary transformation—a becoming[13] molecular within their workday.

Work by Mexican artist Jose Dávila was selected to occupy the central zone of the 101 Collins lobby. In this space, artists were invited to think through the contrast between the weight of

13 Becoming, in a Deleuzian sense, is a way of being that is not determined by imitation or analogy but is instead generative and immanent with the forces that it describes/assembles. In a moment of becoming, one piece of the assemblage is drawn into the territory of another piece, changing its value as an element and bringing about a new unity. Deleuze and Guattari give the example of the way that atoms are drawn into an assemblage with nearby atoms through affinities rather than an organisational function. The term is discussed in particular detail in the following texts: Gilles Deleuze and Felix Guattari, A Thousand Plateaus: Capitalism and Schizophrenia, The University of Minnesota Press, Minneapolis, 1987; Gilles Deleuze and Felix Guattari, What Is Philosophy?, Columbia University Press, New York, 1991; Gilles Deleuze, Pure Immanence. Essays on a Life, trans. Anne Boyman, Zone Books, New York, 2001; Gilles Deleuze, Francis Bacon: The Logic of Sensation, trans. Daniel W. Smith, Continuum, New York, 2003.

marble, the light-reflective nature of the gold leaf in the Collins Street entrance, and the reflective pool that it sits within. The artwork brief suggested the art might reflect on ideas of being in formation, with the central core being a dark space where ideas are discussed and conversation occurs. Dávila's sculpture is typified by this process of formation—with found objects arranged in ways that draw attention to qualities of balance, equilibrium and tension, and the process of formation held in stasis. Dávila's work is informed by his previous practice as an architect, with the assemblages embodying the metaphorical qualities of his materials as much as the formal ones.

For 101 Collins, Dávila created two sculptural compositions, incorporating travertine, reflective stainless-steel orbs and volcanic rock. As Dávila states, 'These works intend to function as equations written with sculptural language, they render the invisible physical procedures that enable the works to maintain a specific shape. Forces are exchanged, weight is distributed, gravity is confronted.'[14] The sculptures also mirror the structural intuition found in the buildings and surrounding environment, so that each work is able to emulate the interactions between the viewers and the internal dynamics of the city. The sculptures incorporate materials from their immediate architectural context—the rigidity of the marble, and the qualities of reflection, the sphere and the cube. As with Vaughan's work for Glenroy, Dávila's inclusion of volcanic rocks speaks to the role of sculpture as a representation of energetic forces, a capturing of the perpetual

14 Jose Dávila, 101 Collins Street proposal, November 2020, p. 3.

movement of the world, that is held in stasis, for the viewer to contemplate and become with it. As Dávila explains, 'I always want my work to touch and move people. I like to view my work as an artistic tool rooted in the capacity to trigger people's minds and open all sorts of questions.'[15]

Dávila's desire to 'touch' and 'trigger' people's minds also speaks to art's ability to break the viewer down to the molecular level of sensation. Art transmits sensation in such a way that it penetrates our body, breaking us apart—it deterritorialises us—and in so doing, it alters us. Deleuze suggests that 'sensation' was a term first applied to painting by Paul Cézanne, who used it in reference to paintings of the figure. To Cézanne, something in these figures acts directly on the nervous system; as Deleuze explains, 'What is painted on the canvas is the body, not insofar as it is represented as an object, but insofar as it is experienced as sustaining this sensation.'[16] In this way, according to Deleuze, Cézanne establishes a viewing mode that dissolves the divide between our viewing bodies and those bodies depicted on the canvas, inviting us to consider ourselves as porous, having incomplete boundaries between an artwork and ourselves, an idea that resonates in the public realm.

Elizabeth Grosz expands on this idea, attesting to the theory that not only does art capture and embody the forces of sensation of that which it depicts, but it also conveys this force into the body

15 Ryan Waddoups, 'Jose Dávila's Eternal Pursuit of Equilibrium', Surface, 7 March 2021, https://www.surfacemag.com/articles/jose-davila-studio-visit/.

16 Deleuze, Francis Bacon, p. 35.

of the viewer, where it then opens the viewer to the realm of sensation, and deepens the experience of the work.[17] As Grosz clarifies:

> Sensation impacts the body, not through the brain, or representations, signs, images or fantasies, but directly, on the body's own internal forces, on cells, organs, the nervous system. Sensation requires no mediation or translation. It is not representation, sign, symbol, but force, energy, rhythm. Sensation lives, not in the body of perceivers but in the body of the art-work.[18]

When considered in this way, the artwork becomes a body, like any other body proprioceptively connecting in space, transmitting sensation. It is open to the same bodily conditions of porosity and transmission. French artist Céleste Boursier-Mougenot's kinetic installation that was selected for a series of reflecting pools at the entrance to 101 Collins demonstrates this embodied dynamism and its capacity to transmit forces and sensation across the public realm. Duplex, 2021, is located in the Collins Street entrance's famous gold-leaf reflecting pools and is part of Boursier-Mougenot's corps

17 Ronald Bogue discusses this in relation to what D. H. Lawrence calls 'the appleyness of the apple'. He goes on to describe 'the body of sensation rendering visible the invisible forces that play through our visible bodies'. Ronald Bogue, Deleuze on Music, Painting, and the Arts, Routledge, New York, 2003, p. 125.

18 Elizabeth Grosz, 'Sensation: The Earth, a People, Art', in Daniel W. Smith, Eugene W. Holland and Charles J. Stivale (eds), Gilles Deleuze: Image and Text, Continuum International, New York, 2009, p. 86.

sonore (sonic body) series. This artist, who is a classically trained composer and musician who later practiced as a dancer for ten years, has a unique understanding of how sound manifests in the body as movement, and he carries this knowledge into his kinetic sound installations. Duplex consists of a collection of white ceramic bowls suspended onto the surface of one of the two pools. A gentle current is introduced to the pool, which activates the water's surface and encourages the bowls to quietly clink together, making audible the invisible forces within the water, and amplifying the reflective quality of the gold-leaf walls. On the opposite wall, above the second reflecting pool, Boursier-Mougenot establishes a synaesthetic connection across the lobby space by projecting a video featuring white circular forms that gently orbit each other in ways that emulate the movement of the bowls in the pool opposite. This work, in many respects, approaches the entire site as an instrument for multi-sensory connection. The building becomes Boursier-Mougenot's artwork, with its molecular forces made visible and audible. The clinking ceramic bowls sound out the acoustic properties of the hard marble lobby spaces, making audible the gentle physics of solid and liquid. The vast, shimmering projection of choreographed circles then emulate the reflective dance between an artwork's movement and how it lands in the body, ensuring that this movement is felt within the body of the viewer, the unknowing commuter en route to work.

Isadora Vaughan's entropic gathering of community forces, Jose Dávila's understanding of the energetic forces in his materials, and Boursier-Mougenot's embodied architecture each have the effect of connecting the public with an essence that is outside of their prescribed daily activity. Rather than being engaged in commercial or industrial activity, these public artworks are instead concerned with connecting the public to our very human ability to create and to wonder outside of function. These works connect us with wonder, transmitting sensation into our bodies and opening our perceptive capacity to what Deleuze refers to as the molecular world of forces. This molecular world is precognitive and occurs prior to text. It is the generative force inside architecture, human movement, temperature, sociohistorical connotations, weather, affective impulses, physical sensation, memory, the bird-sound above, or the idling truck nearby. Rather than serving as a distraction, each of these forces maintains a molecular power to generate connections and assemblages that influence the encounter. I propose that art in public spaces can capture these generative forces of affect and intensity, this human need for wonder. Art's connective transmissions, its peculiar functionless meanderings, can open us to these forces. It can dissolve the barriers that divide us and crack open the diagrammatic overlay that proscribes function onto our behaviour, ensuring that we are free to become molecular in public.

Public Art: A View from New York
Claire Bishop*

* Dr Claire Bishop is a critic and professor in the PhD program in art history at the Graduate Center, City University of New York. Her seminal books include _Artificial Hells: Participatory Art and the Politics of Spectatorship_ (Verso, 2012) and _Radical Museology, or, What's Contemporary in Museums of Contemporary Art?_ (Walther König, 2013). She is a contributing editor of _Artforum_, and her essays and books have been translated into twenty languages. She is currently working on two books: a short publication about Merce Cunningham's Events, and a collection of essays about contemporary art and attention. Her most recent publication is a book of conversations with Cuban artist Tania Bruguera (Cisneros, 2020).

Like so many other industries, the art world ground to a halt in 2020 as a result of the COVID-19 pandemic. Museums and galleries across the US closed in mid-March and didn't re-open until August, and only then on a limited basis. You might have thought, then, that 2020 was a prime moment for public art. In fact, in New York, it kind of was a good year—but not for the kind of public art that typically gets commissioned by the city's arts organisations. The best public art wasn't big-budget spectacle commissioned by the usual institutional suspects, but self-initiated and produced on a shoestring. This isn't surprising. New York's high-profile public art projects tend to be showy and shallow: think monumental sculpture, massive video screens, and pigeons with lights.[1] Such efforts require permission from municipal agencies and collaboration with corporate sponsors—the two culprits responsible for purging public art of any personality.

The city's public art scene is largely dominated by Creative Time, which was founded in 1974, and Public Art Fund, which started in 1977. Both have a long track record in which a handful of highlights rise above many mediocre duds. Public Art Fund, the more conservative of the two organisations, specialises in old-school, large-scale sculpture plonked around the city. The two projects that opened late in summer 2020 (and remained on view for a year) are typical. Sam Moyer's Doors for Doris sat near the southeast entrance to Central Park on Doris C. Freedman Plaza, named after Public Art Fund's founder. Stonehenge-style arches,

1 In 2016, artist Duke Reilly attached LED lights to a flock of trained pigeons for Fly by Night (Creative Time).

bricolaged in concrete, marble and bluestone, provided a snapshot-perfect frame for tourists on their way to Central Park Zoo. Reverberation by Davina Semo comprised five bronze bells, which were installed along the waterfront of Brooklyn Bridge Park. Painted bright orange, the bells could be rung by park visitors; a sign gently reminded participants to sanitise their hands before and after.

While the above works were undoubtedly the result of many months, if not years, of planning, Public Art Fund attempted to be nimbler and more responsive with Art on the Grid. Brace yourself for the stats: fifty emerging artists—all based in New York but representing eighteen different nationalities—created posters that were mounted on five hundred bus shelters and 1,700 WiFi kiosks across the five boroughs. Although the artists were asked to reflect on the pandemic, the results were oblique, with only a few alluding to the current moment. Photographs by D'Angelo Lovell Williams and Andre D. Wagner depicted Black men wearing masks, while Wong Kit Yi's poster advertised a 'jet lag inducing patch' for those 'feeling stuck in the same time zone' (the product promised '24 hours of circadian rhythm disruption'). While the organisers claimed the project was intended to 'create new art viewing itineraries'—providing a map of locations so that art lovers could make the grand tour—they also acknowledged that the posters might function simply 'to enliven the days' of passersby. Art on the Grid's primary audience was unquestionably essential workers: by the time of its June 2020 launch, the richest residents of the city had long moved out to their country houses, while those capable of working from home avoided public transit as much as possible.

Two-dimensional commissions seem to have been the default position. Art on the Grid bears comparison to another billboard project, 2020 Awakening, by the artist-run organisation For Freedoms, founded by Hank Willis Thomas and Eric Gottesman. (The organisation's name is an allusion to Roosevelt's 'Four Freedoms' wartime address in 1941, while the project title refers to the Wide Awakes of 1860 movement that helped elect Abraham Lincoln.) Founded in 2016, For Freedoms has a substantial—and at times controversial—track record of placing artist billboards around the country. For example, in the run up to Trump's election, they erected one in Mississippi with a Civil Rights-era photograph of state troopers facing protestors shortly before attacking them with tear gas; the image was caustically overlaid with Trump's nostalgic slogan 'Make America Great Again'.

By contrast, 2020 Awakening invited one hundred artists to design billboards for display in all fifty states, including Hawaii, with a view to engaging the public in the upcoming presidential election in November. Artists ranging from the emerging to the established (Ai Weiwei, Guerilla Girls, Edgar Heap of Birds, Alfredo Jaar) were asked to approach the issues of voter engagement and civic consciousness through the new 'four freedoms' of justice, awakening, listening, and healing. The one billboard on display in New York was somewhat muted and missable—a dour Audre Lorde quote, courtesy of artist Carlos Motta. Elsewhere in the country, posters were more likely to allude to indigenous rights (Did You Forget About the Earth? asked Josué Rivas in Wyoming), the election (Mutale Nkonde in Vermont: Have You Mailed in Your Ballot?) and Black Lives Matter

(Zoe Buckman's Breonna Was Sleeping and Phenomenal's Say Her Name).

As a model of public art, For Freedoms is more outspoken than Public Art Fund or Creative Time, in part because it doesn't have to pander to billionaires such as Michael Bloomberg. Instead, their projects are crowdfunded, while their archive of posters is (in theory) available for anyone to mount in their own region.[2] It's striking, however, that few of these 2D poster projects, by any of the commissioning agencies, pack the memorable punch of AIDS-era billboards (such as those by Gran Fury). The billboard format arguably works best with an explicitly activist imperative (e.g. the Guerilla Girls); without this, most don't live up to the space and visibility they are granted.

*

Creative Time, which bills itself as presenting 'the most innovative art in the public realm', embarked on three projects in 2020. The last of these, a film installation by recent Columbia graduate Allison Janae Hamilton, dislocated watery footage of her native Florida (in the wake of a tropical storm) onto an arc of five screens in Brooklyn Bridge Park. It was due to open in December, but on a day when a massive snowstorm hit the city; the ensuing urban standstill perhaps explains the relative lack of media coverage. Had the artist envisaged this seasonal disconnect—a juxtaposition of flickering tropical colour against the biting cold of a New York winter? I'm not sure. Either way, the audience's capacity to stand still, be socially distanced, and watch non-narrative moving-image work was surely tested to

2 See The Infinite Playbook on the For Freedoms website, https://forfreedoms.org/.

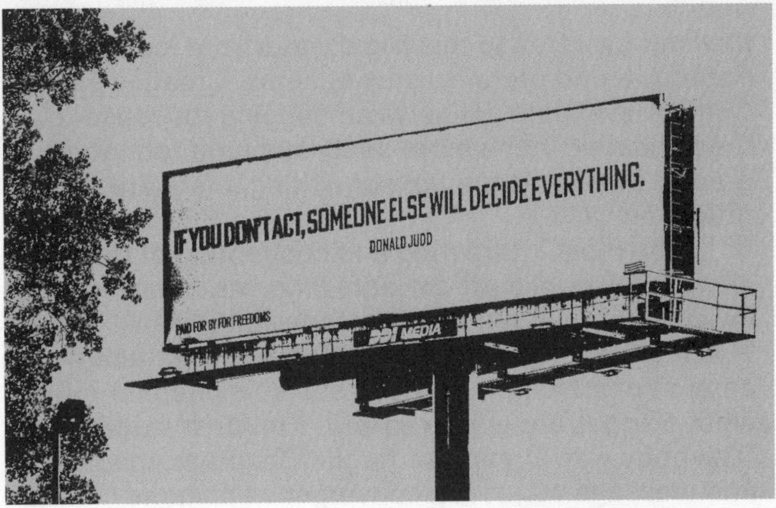

Donald Judd/Judd Foundation, The Artist and Politics: A Statement (1970) 2020. St. Louis, MO, United States. Billboard from For Freedoms' 2020 Awakening Campaign. Photo: Alyssa Meadows

the limit by a trek to this frigid waterfront location. For those who prefer to stay at home, Creative Time Comics (available online) is an ongoing response to the pandemic in the more feisty and lurid format of graphic novels. At the time of writing, there are fifteen on view.

The most interesting and conceptual of the city's many public art projects flirts with near invisibility, while remaining utterly material. Jill Magid's Tender comprises 120,000 pennies (the amount of a Trump-endorsed stimulus cheque) whose edges are engraved with a modest slogan: 'The body was already so fragile'. Together, the title and message suggest a convergence of money (legal tender) and physical vulnerability, the economy and care. All of this came to a head during the onset of the pandemic, when we saw the health of the stock market pitted against that of the population, with ensuing vast disparities in the mortality rate between Black and white, rich and poor. Magid's pennies have circulated across the five boroughs of the city, with the point of dispersal being bodegas: corner stores largely staffed by immigrants and workers of colour. Bodegas, which remained open throughout the lockdown, vend the type of items bought with small change (gum, coffee, newspapers). Magid's project ultimately functions more as an idea or gesture than as a traceable object. With its melancholy message, it could be considered a dispersed memorial to the hundreds of thousands of Americans who have died.

*

The 1970s' veterans Creative Time and Public Art Fund have recently experienced some competition from the High Line, an elevated urban park on a former viaduct running some twenty blocks from

Chelsea up to Hudson Yards. Since it opened in 2009, the High Line has been accompanied by a somewhat hit-and-miss art program (High Line Art) that inserts screenings, sculpture, billboards, and the occasional performance alongside this windswept and tourist-rammed ribbon of manicured shrubbery. In 2020, it simply extended one of its most popular projects, Simone Leigh's Brick House, a sixteen-foot-tall bust of a Black woman. This was the organisation's first commission for the Plinth, located on a piazza-style gathering spot that juts prominently over Tenth Avenue. For most of the year, High Line Art chose to solicit public feedback on contenders for the third and fourth commissions, drawn from a longlist of eighty proposals.[3] The High Line Plinth was undoubtedly inspired by London's Fourth Plinth, a longstanding public art commission for the empty plinth in Trafalgar Square, located closest to the National Gallery. While Trafalgar Square has a host of pompous civic, military and colonial references for artists to riff against, the High Line is synonymous with conspicuous consumption and unbridled gentrification—and the unappealing complicity of the art world in both, which makes it harder for artists to gain critical traction.

Times Square Arts (founded in 2012), another site-specific commissioning organisation, carves out pockets of pedestrianised space between Forty-Second and Forty-Seventh Street for sculpture and the occasional sixty seconds of electronic billboard time to show artists' videos (in the series Midnight Moment). As an actively inhospitable environment

3 See the High Line website, https://www.thehighline.org/plinth-proposals/.

for art, already overloaded with visual and sonic noise, Times Square is rivalled only perhaps by Disneyland and the Mall of America. But Times Square Arts has been relatively active throughout the pandemic, putting artists' projects on billboards, digital displays, and even recycling bins. One series in the runup to the November 2020 election, Vote Your Future, was explicitly tied to voter engagement. With strong graphics and messages geared especially to Black and brown constituents, the posters looked more suitable for a protest march than as discreet adornments for trash cans.

Throughout 2020, Times Square Arts worked in collaboration with local arts organisations, including the Queens Museum of Art (digital signage from artist Mierle Laderman Ukeles), For Freedoms (a group show/poster project on recycling bins, Messages for the City), and New Jersey-based Pomegranate Arts. The last of these helped realise the only 3D project by Times Square Arts, an installation called The Plastic Bag Store, by playwright and puppet designer Robin Frohart. The bulk of the work was an installation-as-grocery store with products created from vibrantly coloured plastic bags (a citywide ban on plastic bags was introduced in October); it also contained a filmed puppet play, screened four times a day. Delayed from its planned opening in March, the work had to be adjusted; instead of an audience of fifty, only socially distanced groups of twelve were allowed at a time.

*

What the proliferation of 2D public art projects confirms is the sheer quantity of advertising space in New York—and how little of it has been used to mobilise a co-ordinated public health response.

Everything has been fragmented and ad hoc. The same can be said for the pandemic memorials that have sprung up not only in New York but also around the country. The most visually powerful is probably that of artist Suzanne Brennan Firstenberg in Washington, DC, who took over a parade ground near the Robert F. Kennedy Stadium. On this belt of grass, the artist has planted a white flag for every life lost to the virus in the US. Titled <u>In America How Could This Happen . . .</u>, the installation has required extensive public participation to keep up with the death toll, which reached 3,800 a day at the end of December 2020.[4] This outdoor installation packs an emotional punch on a par with First World War cemeteries in northern France, while the title is a bitter indictment of the Trump administration's immoral inaction.

In Detroit, Michigan, the Belle Isle Park in the middle of the Detroit River became a community memorial. For families who could not be with their loved ones when they died nor hold a funeral gathering, finding a place to grieve has become an important emotional outlet. Large-scale colour photos of 907 Coronavirus victims were installed by the side of the road that loops Belle Isle, creating a 'Detroit Memorial Drive'. As in Washington, DC, the pace of bereavement vastly outstrips the honouring that can take place; at the end of 2020, Michigan's daily death toll approached two hundred.

In New York, city organisations—tellingly, none of them specifically associated with visual art—have produced other forms of community monuments, often in collaboration with artists and inviting the

4 Artist Shane Reilly has been filling his yard with similarly sized flags to honour the dead in Texas.

participation of the public. Notable are the Morris-Jumel Mansion (CoVIDA, by Andrea Arroyo), the Bronx Documentary Center (Día de los Muertos: Covid Memorial), an outdoor children's exhibition at Flushing Town Hall, and even the MTA subway system (honouring deceased employees on its digital information boards). A proposal is underway, put forth by City Council member Mark Levine, to create a COVID-19 memorial on Hart Island, in the Bronx. Currently inaccessible to the public, Hart Island is where unclaimed bodies are buried, including those of hundreds of victims whose families could not be located or afford funeral expenses during the pandemic. Drone footage from last spring showed chilling images of unadorned wooden coffins lined up in the ground for mass burial.

A public art roundup would not be complete without mention of the public visual culture of Black Lives Matter. Following the murder of George Floyd by Minneapolis police in late May, a national outpouring of anger and indignation led to a life-affirming swell of protest. In New York, this ranged from physical gestures—wearing white for a Black Trans Lives Matter rally; taking a knee at key sites around the city; thousands taking over the streets in bicycle protests—to painting the phrase 'Black Lives Matter' in vast yellow letters on Fifth Avenue in front of Trump Tower. But the most powerful intervention by far has been the repurposing of Confederate-era monuments, a prominent feature of urban space in the South. If public art in 2020 could be captured in a single image, it has to be that of the General Robert Lee memorial in Richmond, Virginia (eventually removed in 2021). Its imposing stone plinth was smothered in brightly coloured graffiti, civil rights slogans, affirmations of Black love and mourning, candles, projected images (George Floyd, Breonna Taylor), and abuzz with life—music, basketball, dancing, food, a radical library. It was a place for collective grief while also being a vital incubator for an empowered Black future. Everything else in 2020 looked defanged and optional by comparison.

Solidarity Grid
Blair French*

* Dr Blair French is a curator, writer and arts administrator. He is currently CEO of Carriageworks in Sydney and was previously Director, Curatorial and Digital at Museum of Contemporary Art Australia and Executive Director of Artspace, Sydney. He was curatorial convenor and curator of the 6th (2011–12) and 7th (2013) SCAPE Public Art: Christchurch Biennials in which capacity he was commissioning curator of Mischa Kuball's permanent public artwork Solidarity Grid, 2013–16.

Between 2013 and 2016, a set of disparate streetlamps incrementally grew along a key section of public path and cycleway tracing the meandering line of Ōtākaro (Avon River) and boundary between the CBD and the greenbelt parklands of Hagley Park in the city of Ōtautahi (Christchurch) in Te Wai Pounamu o Aotearoa (the South Island of New Zealand). In its final form, Solidarity Grid, by Düsseldorf artist Mischa Kuball, comprises twenty-one streetlamps of vastly differing forms and styles, each gifted and permanently relocated to Ōtautahi by different municipalities from around the world as a contribution to a dual act of rebuilding and remembering.[1]

The differentiation between the streetlamps' appearance is the first sign the work is an interruption to the general homogeneity of urban infrastructural services. The designs of some signify the relationship of their originating cities to their own cultural history. Others point to that respective city's sense of a dynamic present, or technologically intelligent future. Small plates attached to each provide contextual information regarding the origin of the streetlamp as well as record the occasion of its gift from its original city to Ōtautahi.[2] The

1 Participating municipalities were Adelaide, Belgrade, Boston, Christchurch (UK), Düsseldorf, Gansu, Graz, Ieper, Kurashiki, La Rochelle, Mexico City, Montreal, Seattle, Sendai, Singapore, Sofia, Songpa, Sopot, St. Moritz, Sydney and Wuhan.

2 Early artist outlines for the project included proposals to build a website to comprehensively document the acts of streetlamp gifting, including surrounding discussions and ceremonial moments of unveiling with civic

resulting complete work is at once a major public artwork; the fulcrum for an extended set of international cultural interactions; a practical contribution to the urban infrastructure of a city in recovery and rebuild mode; and a memorial to the loss suffered by the people of Ōtautahi in the major earthquake of 22 February 2011.

Solidarity Grid emerged out of discussions I had with the artist in my capacity as curator of the 7th SCAPE Public Art Christchurch Biennial (2013). The work developed as a highly place-sensitive extension of Kuball's longstanding practice of deploying both the material and symbolic properties of light in public, propositional and fundamentally connective modes within built environments, civic spaces and wider community settings.[3]

representatives, as well as live GPS tracking of the transit of the streetlamps across the globe. However, this ultimately proved to be beyond the financial and logistical scope of SCAPE Public Art and their project partners.

3 See in particular the following books on Mischa Kuball: Andreas Beitin, Holger Broeker and Fritz Emslander, Mischa Kuball: ReferenzRäume, Verlag der Buchhandlung Walther und Franz König, Cologne, 2021; Gregor H. Lersch and Léontine Meijer-van Mensch (eds), Mischa Kuball: res.o.nant, Sternberg Press, Berlin, 2019; Vanessa Joan Müller (ed.), Mischa Kuball: Public Preposition, Distance Verlag, Berlin, 2015; Andreas Beitin, Leonhard Emmerling and Blair French (eds), Plato's Mirror and the Actuality of the Cave Allegory Inspired by Projections of Mischa Kuball, Verlag der Buchhandlung Walther König, Cologne, 2012; and Florian Matzner (ed.), Mischa Kuball ... in Progress,

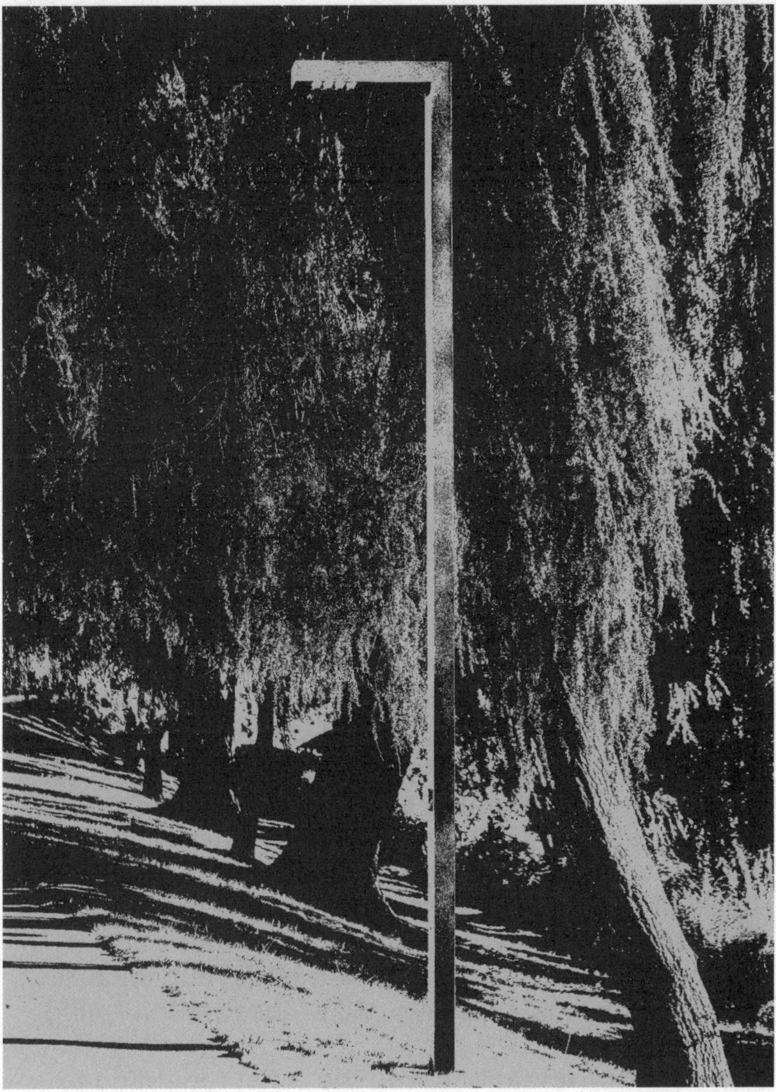

Mischa Kuball, Solidarity Grid 2013–16.
Twenty-one streetlights and brass plates commissioned by Christchurch City Council and SCAPE Public Art, Ōtautahi/Christchurch.
Photo: Duncan Shaw-Brown

Solidarity Grid acutely demonstrates the generosity that shapes Kuball's practice. Although not overtly signalled in its final form, the work's realisation depended on the underlying drive of the artist as an agent of international connection and community building. The artist initiated and nurtured relationships that gave rise to the genuine desire to be part of this exchange, a desire manifested also in the very many practical supporters of the project through its various stages: from private individuals through to civic officials, engineers, planners and community groups.

Solidarity Grid did not evolve out of any initial tender invitation or project scope. It grew out of Kuball's personal response to a particular crisis in a city he had previously visited and had developed relationships with. For a project that required such official support in its realisation, this sense of an immediate, intimate response to experiences of loss still lingers, barely tangible, in the idiosyncratic form of the work and its modest realisation as now a constituent part of, rather than an addition to, its immediate environment of city and parklands.

The apparently straightforward structure of the in-situ work, aligned with both the natural ecological form of its immediate environment (the river) and its human-scaped features (public parklands and plantings, pathway, road and street layout), also belies the complex issues and processes informing its realisation.

My conversations with the artist regarding te initial idea for this work began in the months following the February 2011 earthquake. Within

Projekte/Projects 1980–2007, Hatje Cantz, Ostfildern, 2007.

hours of that quake, the city centre was cordoned off and access restricted. Administered by government authorities and the army, this cordon was rapidly formalised, marking a closed 'no-go' area—the central city red zone—with the only entrants allowed in being rescue, then assessment, and finally demolition teams. The heart of the city was shut down and emptied out. Although the cordon contracted inwards over the months and then years that followed, ever shrinking the exclusion zone, residents and visitors alike were effectively excluded from the urban core of the city. This was the location Kuball initially planned for his project, proposing the work would mark out a section of the CBD grid. But this location was subject to many uncertainties. It was likely to be a changing development site for many years, and night-time pedestrian use of the CBD was clearly going to remain minimal through early rebuilding phases.

Government agency planning for the city also began to produce a polite, campus-like model of a CBD. This ran counter to Kuball's project. From the outset, Solidarity Grid was pitched against any slide towards homogenisation and insularity that disaster might bring in its aftermath. While taking a permanent, and in many ways highly conventional, form, it shared an impulse to unsettle formality and uniformity in its planning with other unexpected temporary interventions in the built environment, from pop-up shopping centres, cafes and community centres housed in shipping containers, a range of extraordinary art activities and projects,[4]

4 For example, the work of new collectives and agencies such as Gap Filler, Greening the Rubble, and the

through to a cardboard cathedral.[5]

Critically, in both process and form, Solidarity Grid exemplified an attitude of openness to context and locality. Following extensive consultation with local partners and interlocutors—in particular, city planners—Kuball agreed that the work should shift from its initial proposed position at the heart of the CBD street grid to its final location bordering Hagley Park. This agreement was not simply in response to complications noted above, but came out of recognition of the importance of locating the work where it would be of most use to the people of Ōtautahi. At Hagley Park, it provides lighting for a popular pathway. Its growth over a three-year period along the riverbank commanded attention and served as symbol of the city's own new growth and its growing connections to communities globally.

This speaks to the mesh of relationships, interests and determining factors at play in developing a public artwork for a city. Working to create a permanent intervention—a 'preposition'—within public space is always a challenging exercise, not just logistically and financially but also in terms of negotiating civic and community desires and impediments. The intensely fraught context of a city in disaster-recovery mode further complicates this

Festival of Transitional Architecture, as well as new models of 'off-site' projects by art organisations exiled from their former buildings, from the contemporary art space Physics Room through to the city's major public institution, Christchurch Art Gallery Te Puna o Waiwhetū.

5 This temporary cathedral was designed by Japanese architect Shigeru Ban. See http://www.shigerubanarchitects.com/works/2013_cardboard-cathedral/.

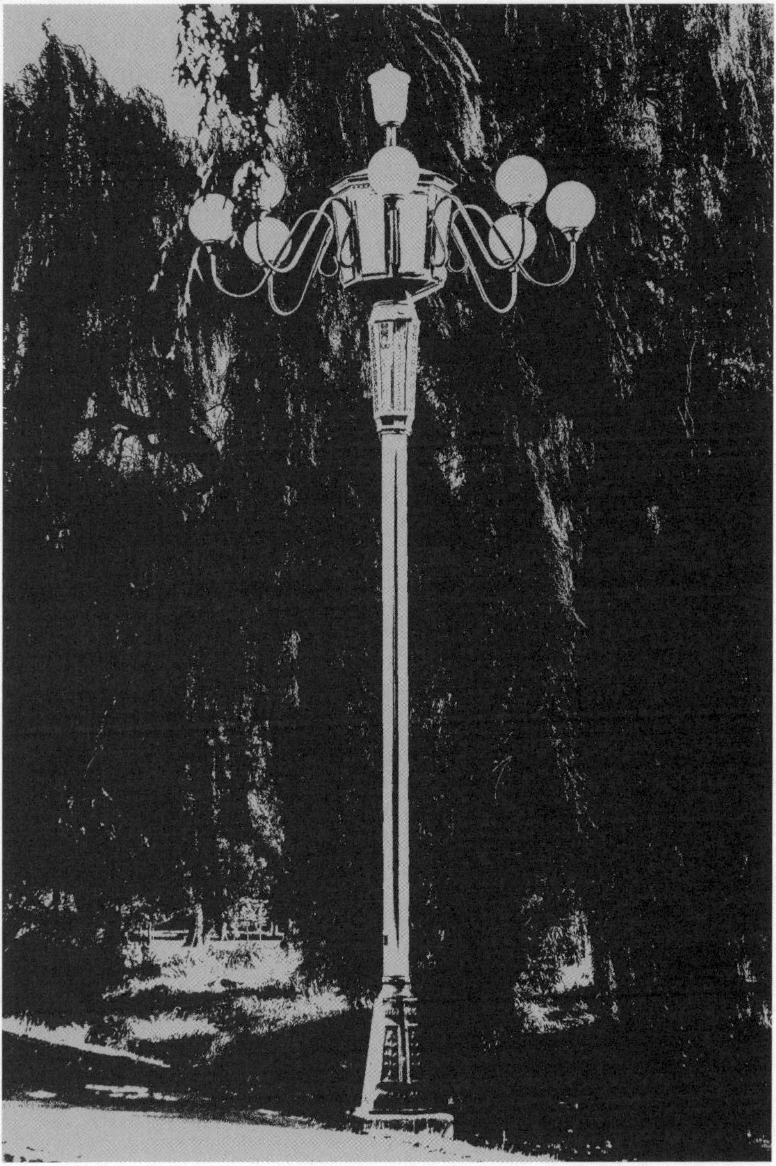

Mischa Kuball, Solidarity Grid 2013–16. Photo: Duncan Shaw-Brown

challenge. Here the situation necessitated dynamic modification of an initial concept through dialogue with, and responsiveness to, local community, all the time holding onto the core idea and impetus at the heart of the work.

Solidarity Grid provides functionality in its final location. It is identifiable as a permanent addition to the city scape; it marks a zone of transition and exit out of the city; it rides the border of and thus simultaneously links and delineates CBD and natural environment; and it recalls the community experience of the 2011 earthquake. It is a communal work in the broadest sense, dependent equally on the managerial and financial support and expertise of institutional, business and civic structures and on the generosity and hospitality of communities, most particularly those of its host city. It is temporal in character as much as material, relational as much as sculptural. Most tellingly, as one traverses its length, it could not feel more emphatically of the place that it marks.

Drawn from the longer essay 'Marking Solidarity', in Blair French (ed.), Mischa Kuball: Solidarity Grid, Ōtautahi Christchurch 2013–2016, Koenig Books, London, 2017, pp. 16–23.

The Art of Demonstration: A New Public Art in the City of Hong Kong
Michelle Antoinette* interviews Oscar Ho** and Clara Cheung***

* Dr Michelle Antoinette is a senior lecturer and researcher in art history and theory at Monash University, Melbourne. Her research focuses on modern and contemporary Asian art histories and significant publications include _Reworlding Art History: Encounters with Contemporary Southeast Asian Art after 1990_ (Brill | Rodopi, 2015) and with Caroline Turner, _Contemporary Asian Art and Exhibitions: Connectivities and World-Making_ (ANU Press, 2014). She is the recipient of two prestigious Australian Research Council Fellowships and most recently co-edited a special issue of _World Art_ on 'Contemporary Art Worlds and Art Publics in Southeast Asia' (2020).

** Oscar Ho Hing-kay was formerly exhibition director of the Hong Kong Arts Centre and founding director of the Museum of Contemporary Art, Shanghai. His curatorial projects since the late 1980s have included serving as a guest curator for the 2nd and 3rd Asia Pacific Triennials in Brisbane and curator for the Asian section of _Container 96_ in Copenhagen (1996). He was a member of the advisory group for M+ in Hong Kong's West Kowloon Cultural District and one of the founding directors of Asia Art Archive. He writes regularly for publications such as _Artforum_, _Art Journal_ and _ArtAsiaPacific_, and is the founder of the Hong Kong chapter of the International Art Critics Association. He is an adjunct associate professor at the Chinese University of Hong Kong, where from 2006 to 2020 he was associate professor in practice and director of the master's program in cultural management.

*** Dr Clara Cheung is a member of the non-profit art groups Art Together and Project226, and the founder of C&G Artpartment. Since 2007, she has curated and co-curated more than fifty art exhibitions at C&G Artpartment, located in a 'tong-lau' building apartment in Hong Kong, which critically responds to local social and cultural issues, including the local art ecology. She is currently a member of Wan Chai District Council and holds graduate and postgraduate degrees from Rhodes College, Memphis, TN; the Chinese University of Hong Kong; and Lingnan University, Hong Kong, in the areas of fine arts, computer science, education and cultural studies.

Since the 2014 political street protests known as the Umbrella Movement, public art in Hong Kong has taken on new meaning and significance, becoming an urgent expression of collective empowerment and political activism. For the Umbrella Movement, protesters initially used umbrellas to shield themselves from tear gas and pepper spray used by the police to disrupt pro-democracy protests. Subsequently, the everyday umbrella quickly transformed into a powerful visual icon for the movement, spurring a wave of creative activism in public spaces.

Public art is now arguably a necessity in Hong Kong, given the diminishing opportunities for locals to express themselves in the public sphere. The new public art is often inspired by and forged out of civilian action, and not necessarily premised on artist-led activities or conventional understandings of public art. As with guerrilla tactics, it is rarely assumed to be a lasting display and is instead a changing and organic development that responds strategically to the shifting politics and urgencies of the city-state. While the Umbrella Movement arose as a response to proposed electoral changes, in 2019, Hong Kong people again took to the streets and claimed their urban space in protest to a proposed extradition bill, triggering the Anti-Extradition Movement and another surge of politically motivated public art. Indeed, since the end of British sovereignty in 1997, Hong Kong people have been harnessing public space for communal expressions of Hong Kong identity, as well as to fighting for political autonomy and democratic freedom.

In this context, I invited Hong Kong locals Oscar Ho and Clara Cheung to provide their perspectives on the shifting practices and changed significance of public art in Hong Kong. Our conversation took place online—between Hong Kong and Melbourne—in late November 2020, and an edited version of that conversation follows here.

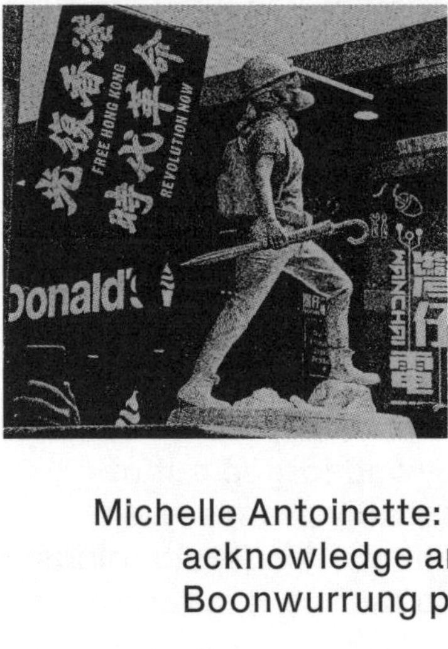

Figure 1: 'Goddess of Democracy/Lady Liberty' Hong Kong statue project, a crowd-funded sculpture project symbolising the pro-democracy movement. Photo: CivilMedia@TW

Michelle Antoinette: Firstly, I want to acknowledge and pay my respects to the Boonwurrung people of the Kulin Nation, the Indigenous Australians who are the traditional owners of the unceded lands on which I live and work. I also want to pay my respects to their Elders, past, present and emerging, as well as to all Aboriginal and Torres Strait Islander people.

To start, please introduce yourselves.

Oscar Ho: I trained as an artist in Canada and the US. I came back to Hong Kong in 1984, and worked as the Exhibition Director at the Hong Kong Art Center between 1988 and 2001. Then I was working in the government for two years, before going to Shanghai to establish the Shanghai Museum of Contemporary Art. Upon my return, I taught at the Chinese University of Hong Kong in the MA Program in Cultural Management, and I just retired earlier this year. I curate and I write a lot. I'm quite active in terms of social activities and actions, so public art, especially that made since the Umbrella Movement, totally fascinates me. I think the art of the Anti-Extradition Movement is even more powerful and more dynamic.

Clara Cheung: I studied in Memphis, Tennessee, between 1998 and 2002, in fine arts and computer science. Back then, I was already quite interested in performance art or art in public sites and in interactions with public audiences. Later on, after I came back to Hong Kong, I taught visual art in primary and secondary schools for ten years. Then in 2007, my husband Gum and I founded

C&G Artpartments in Prince Edward in Kowloon. In that space, to begin with, we mostly curated exhibitions responding directly to social issues in Hong Kong but still mostly within the art space. But after the Umbrella Movement, we had more interest in public sites, believing there was no point in going back to the indoor [art] space to do social critique anymore.

MA There's a growing interest in making and presenting art outside of the conventional gallery context in many places around the world. In Hong Kong, I gather this has been particularly so since the mid-1990s, especially in terms of the development of public art as a self-conscious movement, as I've heard it described by some Hong Kong academics.

CC I'd like to share some images here from 1996 of the Queen Victoria statue, which artist Pan Xinglei poured red paint over (Figure 2). It seems to me that in 1989 after the massacre incident [Tiananmen Square Massacre[1]], more artists in Hong Kong became involved in what you might describe as 'protest art' or even just in making art in public sites in response to the June Fourth incident. Hong Kong

1 On 4 June 1989, there was a student-led demonstration held in Tiananmen Square, Beijing, advocating pro-democracy political reforms. It was violently suppressed by the Chinese government through military force, leading to the mass killing of demonstrators.

artists have been responding to social issues in the public arena and also making art in public for thirty-plus years.

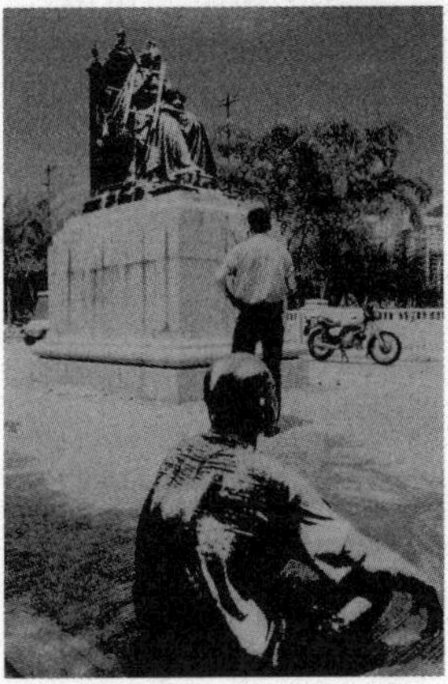

Figure 2: Peformance by artist Pan Xinglei, in which he poured red paint onto the Queen Victoria statue in 1996. Photo: artist's archive, re-photographed and courtesy of Clara Cheung

OH Of course, as Hong Kong was getting more and more political, the artists also became more political. I think before 1989, so-called public art was essentially a big piece of sculpture commissioned by the government that the public could see in a public space and there was no politics involved. I mean, if you're talking about public art involving political expression, I think it was mainly during and after 1989. But relatively speaking it's still very limited because a lot of this political art was made in an art gallery. Only during demonstrations do some of them come out. But since the Umbrella Movement, we see something totally different and I find this is a fantastic development. I see a new definition of public art—art that is made by the public out of their feeling of absolute necessity. Whether it is 'art' or not is not important at all.

One of the most outstanding examples of this kind of public art is the 'Lennon Wall' (Figure 3). The reason I find it outstanding is that it's only a piece of paper with something written by some unknown individual on it. It's just stuck on the wall, and then more and more people add their personal messages. They're not thinking about making art; they want to say something. But one by one, as they gather together, it becomes so powerful. The installation was so impressive. Calling it art or not doesn't matter. It's impressive, it's overwhelming, it passed on the messages strongly. At the same time, it still retained the individuality [of each person's contribution]. You would go through it, and everyone was making a statement. There's no single artist, but a monumental work of public art has been created.

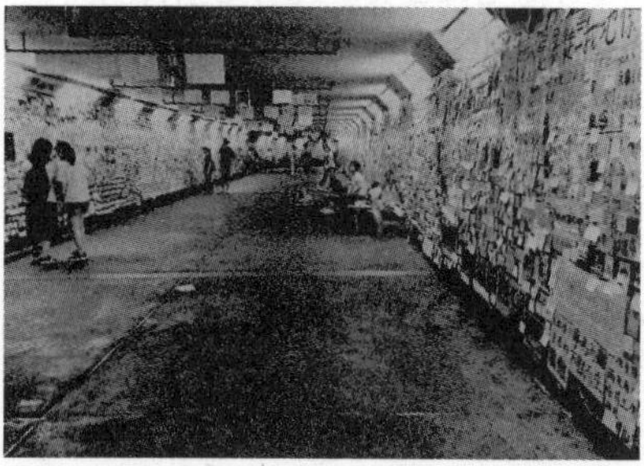

Figure 3: 'Lennon Wall' tunnel, Tai Po District, Hong Kong. Photo: Oscar Ho

MA So one of the things about public art now is that it is not only a permanent installation, but also something that can be ephemeral or transient. Looking at these images, I am just wondering if you can you tell us about the afterlife of these public contributions. What happened to them over the course of time?

OH When the 'Lennon Wall' was created, it occupied a large space, then some other people moved in and destroyed everything.

MA How long did that take?

OH All in one night. But this kind of art is organic—it keeps growing—so a few days later, it all came back. That's the dynamic of this kind of public art. Despite efforts of trying to destroy the walls, new walls were created, frequently in the form of more flexible public spaces. In the most extreme way, people turned their bodies into 'Lennon Walls' (Figure 4). The latest development is that you can buy a jacket and the wall moves around with you wherever you go. Permanence is only for the museum. [By contrast], this is something that keeps growing and developing because it was a struggle where the other side wants to stop you, to eliminate the artwork. This kind of organic role is almost essential in social movements.

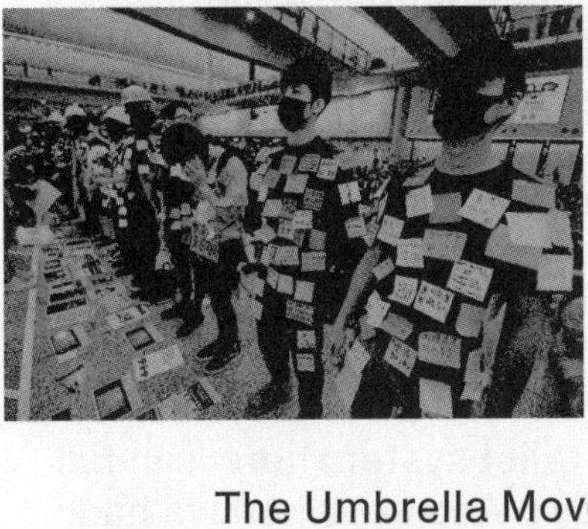

Figure 4: Protestors act as human 'Lennon Walls' during a demonstration at Hong Kong International Airport, 2019. Photo: SOPA Images Limited / Alamy Stock Photo

The Umbrella Movement mainly came from the Occupy zones (namely, the three sites at Admiralty, Mongkok and Causeway Bay), so there was already some fixed sense of space, some stable platforms set up for people to make something. Installations could be slowly developed and people could sit down together, interact and had plenty of time to make more ambitious work. Now it's more mobile, it's like water. Moving around demands flexibility and creativity. As the blocking of any creative expression is getting tighter, so the art-makers need to keep moving around so that they cannot be easily targeted.

We're dealing with a different form of public art. It's not the old style where artists make something, put it in a public space and let the public react to it. The greatest change here comes from giving up the idea of art. Artists are just pissed off. They just want to say something. They want to use the language or image people are familiar with, because they're not making a piece for a museum. They're making a political statement that everybody can understand.

CC I agree with Oscar about how the surprising organicism of the Umbrella Movement was really exciting. I think Oscar had an excellent point about the necessity, the urge from everyone to make something in public sites. I was thinking maybe it is also because most people in this urban space of Hong Kong have been so suppressed by the long working hours. The extremely capitalist system here is in full control of the city. And so, when we had the time during the Umbrella Movement to really occupy a big area, everyone wanted to go there to express themselves.

I want to share some images . . .

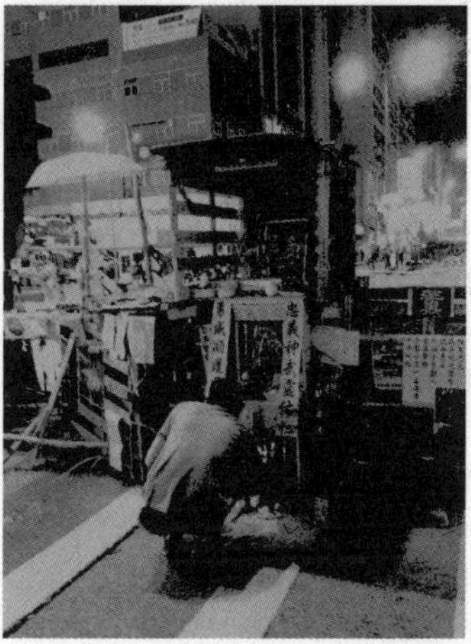

Figure 5: Kwan Tai Temple at the Mongkok Occupy site in Hong Kong during the Umbrella Movement, 2014. Photo: Clara Cheung

Here you can see the Kwan Tai Daoist temple, and then you can see a passerby in front of it (Figure 5). It was a small temple setup, and because of ritual and traditional understanding among the community, some people would just, you know, interact with it, regardless of whether or not they were religious.

And then on the opposite of this Kwan Tai temple, there is also a chapel for Christians. They didn't fight with each other they just coexisted in the same area, and I found that embracing of different religions wonderful.

OH Now over here you see Jesus Christ, and on the right is Saint Michael, who is the patron saint of the police. The presence of the altar is a reminder of the importance of kindness in Christian faith. Interestingly, Kwan Tai is also the Chinese god of the police, as it represents righteousness and justice.

When the policemen cleared the Mongkok-occupied zones, they dismantled the temple of Kwan Tai. There were rumours that after tearing down the temple and destroying most of the altar, they did not dare to touch the Kwan Tai statue, which might lead to punishment from the god.

We heard that in the end, the statue of Kwan Tai was given to a cleaning lady—passing the responsibility to somebody else, with the expectation that somehow she would treat the god of police properly, or if she did something improper, the punishment would go to her. So it's a warfare logic in which you bring in all weapons that might intimidate the other, and you see the creatively dynamic approaches at various levels, including the physical and the spiritual. These religious and political strategies are something that you don't see in the museum.

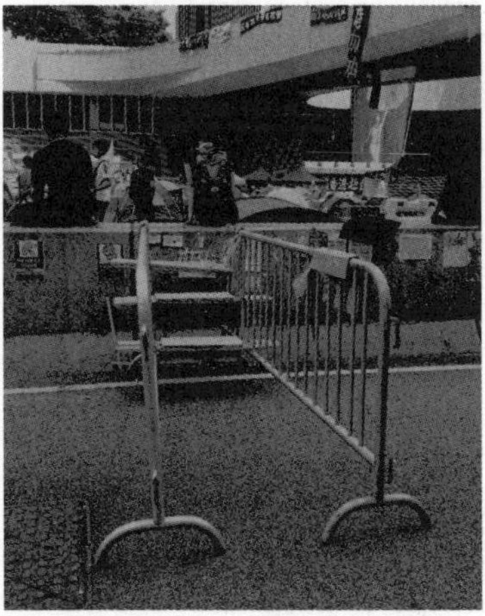

Figure 6: Stairs constructed by volunteers to assist occupiers to cross the highway at the Admiralty Occupy site in Hong Kong during the Umbrella Movement, 2014. Photo: Clara Cheung

CC This image (Figure 6) may also be of interest because it shows a structure to help people to cross the road. This structure is actually set up on a really wide highway. You see, the block here didn't make it easy for people at the Occupy site to go up and down, so people made this structure to help. At that time in the Occupy site in Admiralty, some people also built a lot of big booths for students to study there, with all the [study] equipment, and a lot of those structures were constructed with materials you could find nearby. So it's a really spontaneous kind of response to, and interaction with, the site. I found that quite amazing.

MA In some ways, it's a strange time to be contemplating public art as the world faces a pandemic, and we're confronted with various limits to our engagement with other people and being outside. But the pandemic has also forced us to rethink public space and the significance of art within this. Can you talk a little bit about how public art practice in Hong Kong has been affected by the COVID-19 pandemic?

CC Actually, because of the pandemic, we had a long period of time without a lot of social activities—not even exhibitions. But in the past two months, we have had more. A lot of art shows have started happening again. I can share one example of an event by C&G. It's called 'On Fire'.

On Fire is part of a series called Decongestants for West Kowloonization, a project that we developed after the Umbrella Movement. As I said earlier, we needed some time to consider what else we could do after the Umbrella Movement, after we were moving out to public sites regularly. And On Fire is one of these series of guerrilla events. It takes place every year during the Hungry Ghost Festival[2] evening because, according to the Buddhist and Daoist religions, that's the night when the Gates of Hell open up the widest, so all the spirits are able to come out, especially those spirits who don't usually have any family members to pay tribute to them. So we invited different artists to make paper objects to burn together.

2 The Hungry Ghost Festival is held to coincide with Ghost Month and Ghost Day—the fifteenth night of the seventh month of the Chinese calendar—when Daoists and Buddhists make offerings and perform rituals in honour of the spirits of their deceased ancestors, especially to transmute or absolve their suffering in the afterlife. Traditionally, this includes food offerings and burning incense, joss paper, and papier-mâché replicas of material objects from the realm of the living. It is believed that ghosts and spirits, including those of deceased ancestors, come to visit the living at this time.

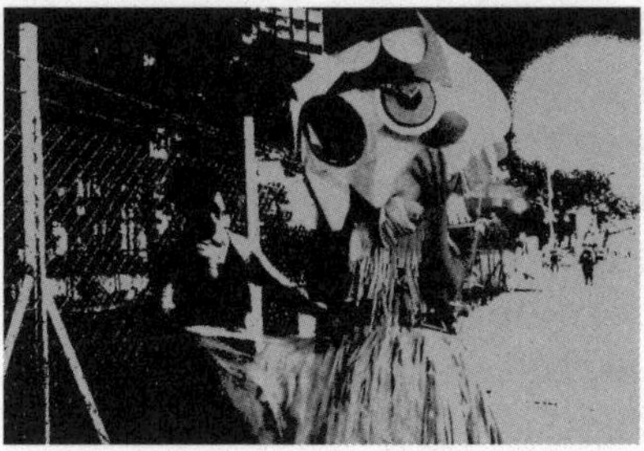

Figure 7: Artist Rik Yu interacting with an audience member during On Fire, 2016, Prince Edward, Hong Kong. Photo: Gum Cheng

This (Figure 7) is a piece by Rik Yu made in 2016. It's a performance with the artist dressed as a fish covered in scales. It's related to the Lo Ting [fish] story.[3] Here, Yu was responding to the goldfish market in the nearby district of Mongkok. Yu invited audience-participants to each pull off a scale from his body, to make a wish with the scale, and then to throw the scale into a fire. At the moment this photo was taken, all the scales had been removed, so Yu's finally taking off his fish hat to throw into the fire. And this was before the Anti-Extradition Law Movement. This work was about 'burning freedom'. As this artist was inviting everyone to put a paper fish-scale into the fire for burning, he was also inviting everyone to contribute to the process of keeping up the fire with their paper scales and the individual wishes contained within them. It is like offering our wishes for the fire, as much as like burning out freedom

3 Lo Ting are the mythical half-human, half-fish creatures said to be the ancestors of indigenous Hong Kong people.

in our hearts. And you can interpret for yourself too, is it an offering for the ghost who doesn't have freedom [in the afterlife] or is this in fact, a comment by the artist on our present-day society losing freedom? We continue to hold the On Fire event every year, but in 2020 we hesitated because of the pandemic. The Hong Kong government has made use of the pandemic as an excuse to control the community and society even more—it's much more like a police state—so before the 2020 On Fire event, we did a small-scale rehearsal. But that was also 31 August, which was the anniversary of one of the very important days in 2019, during the Anti-Extradition Movement.[4] So, because it was the anniversary, more people came out, including a lot of police officers, who surrounded us when we did the rehearsal. Of course, the police officers claimed that they were there just to make sure we were able to maintain social distancing if we were joined by passersby.

4 On the evening of 31 August 2019, police officers went into Prince Edward Subway Station to attack civilians, especially those wearing black outfits, which by then were associated with protesters. The whole station was locked down, and first aiders were refused entry to the station to help the injured. It is suspected that some protesters were actually attacked to death. Following this tragedy, people mourned outside of Prince Edward Station for months, with offerings of white flowers and traditional Chinese ritual materials.

I think with the pandemic, to make art in the public is more difficult. But we still decided that we should make it happen because I think a lot of people longed for some sort of expression at public sites.

OH The use of religious ritual for political warfare is really interesting. During the ceremony for comforting the dead, normally we'll burn gifts to those who are suffering in hell. If the policemen disrupt the act of kindness to those unfortunate ghosts, that would be an unforgivable sin that leads to curses and punishment. Clara was talking about the police behaving with restraint that night; this was precisely because they didn't want to irritate the gods and the ghosts.

CC In 2020, On Fire was very difficult for us to organise. Even at C&G, we did not dare to make any public announcement before the event. We just secretly circulated that information and invited people who knew each other because of the pandemic, but also definitely because of the National Security Law, because we didn't know what to expect. But we successfully launched it, and then we surprisingly got more young artists joining and art students participating, but we didn't know them beforehand—the word just spread.

So we did burn things. Two further examples are a miniature set of all the tools that the protesters used in 2019 (Figure 8), made by artist Kacey Wong, and a ballot box by Peggy Chan (Figure 9).

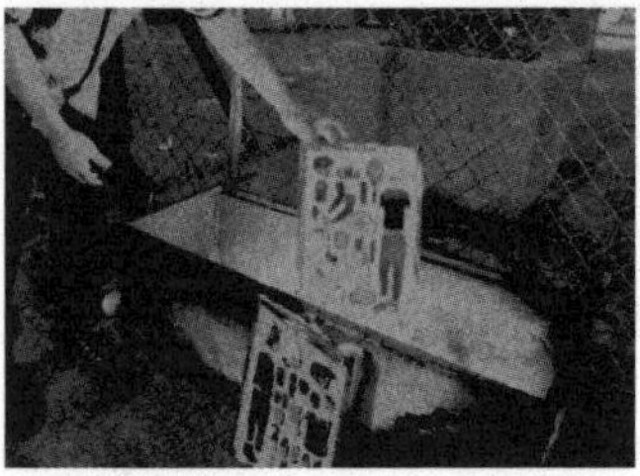

Figure 8: Two miniature sets of protesters' outfits and tools created by artist Kacey Wong for On Fire, 2020, Prince Edward, Hong Kong. Photo: Kacey Wong

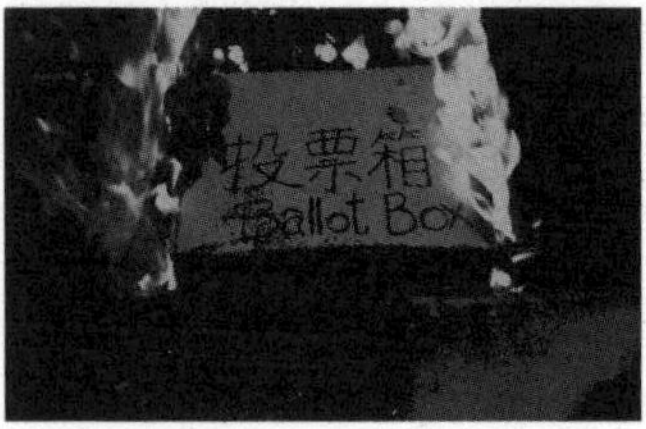

Figure 9: Peggy Chan, There Goes Our Rights To Vote! 2020, paper and bamboo stick installation from On Fire, 2020, Prince Edward, Hong Kong. Photo: Kacey Wong

OH The nice thing about Hong Kong is that people take in any god that can help them. This kind of all-embracing religion is really fantastic. The first time I heard the hymn 'Sing Hallelujah to the Lord' sung in the Buddhist singing format, I thought this kind of combination could only happen in Hong Kong. I mean, they can use Jesus, they can use Wong Tai Sin, Kwan Tai (Guan Gong)—all the gods from all parts of the world come out to help the people. The nice thing about this is that it's really communally accommodative. This co-existence of diversity is a cultural characteristic of Hong Kong. The magic of religion is still very much a powerful part of the everyday life in this modern city. That's why when the Gates of Hell open in July, it is a powerful time to review all the crimes and sins that people have committed during their lives, and to remind people of the punishment in hell.

I want to say something about the new forms of public space. While the web and social media have become extremely effective spaces for the connecting of people, the digital experience in Hong Kong is still limited. In recent years when the annual Hungry Ghost Festival has come around, specific sites have taken on special meaning, such as the Prince Edward Subway Station. These sites have attracted artistic engagement recalling specific meanings and memories that cannot be reproduced digitally: the atmosphere of art located amid an atmosphere of sadness; the slow flowing in of demonstrators with white flowers and the cars driving by; the smell of religious material being burnt. Of course, when you see 'art' on the web, you can still get some of this feeling, but it's not the same.

CC Responding to your earlier question about what's happened during the pandemic, I think even during the 2019 Anti-Extradition Law Movement, more Hong Kong people recognised the strong connection between Hong Kong and the international community. I think that's become even stronger during the pandemic. Now you can say we rely more on the internet, but also recognise more how we can make use of the internet to be connected with others around the world. That may be a positive point.

MA What about international artists who have been invited to Hong Kong to present in public spaces or install public art? What's been the reception to that?

OH It's been difficult for them to display in public spaces because of the pandemic, and before that, the police were really rigid around any use of public space. Actions are taken to block any suspicious people from undertaking activities in public space. It really is a high-risk act for artists or any creative persons to do something in public. It would be very uncomfortable inviting an artist to make work in such a difficult context.

Public art uses public space, and unfortunately most public spaces in Hong Kong are controlled by the government. Unless we have an opening up of government policies, we can never fully utilise public spaces. What people are doing now is engaging in guerrilla warfare. The other side—people hostile to the movement—can come in and destroy anything they find unacceptable. Images in digital space seem to be the most effective means for the moment.

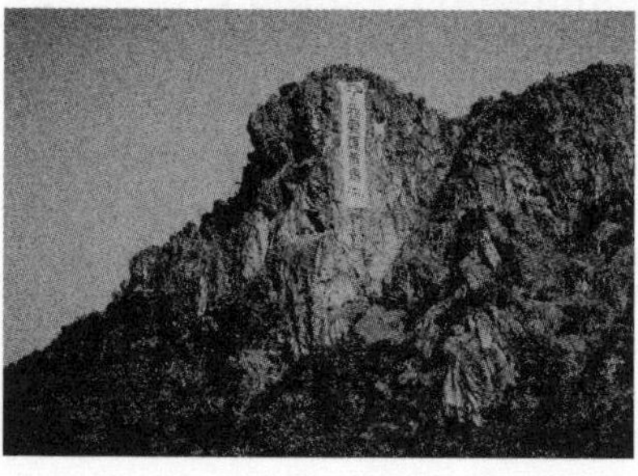

Figure 10: Umbrella Movement protest banner on Lion Rock, Hong Kong, 2014. Photo: Pasu Au Yeung, https://www.flickr.com/photos/29418416@N08/16134715622. Licence at http://creativecommons.org/licenses/by/2.0

One outstanding example of a site-specific artwork using these guerilla tactics is the display of banners on the mountain known as 'Lion Rock' (Figure 10), which is a symbol for the resilient and hardworking nature of Hong Kong people. It has been a popular spot for hanging propaganda banners since the Umbrella Movement. Normally, the government takes banners away the day after they have been put up. The display, subsequently, can only be very short. Sometimes, the demonstrators might even just make a projection at night that lasts for an evening. But that doesn't matter because as long as you have taken a picture and put it on the web, it lasts forever. It can go around the world. That's the distinctive thing about digital media: it can turn something temporal into something permanent and move it all over the world.

I want to talk a little bit about curating as well. It was interesting that when some young people knew the police were going to move into the Occupy zones, they felt that they should collect the artworks before they were cleared. They sought my view as an academic and I pointed out that the artworks were made specifically for those sites but that they could collect them. Before the clearing, these young people moved around the zones and took pictures of the artworks. One by one, they documented them. As soon as the clearing started, they saved them. It is important to save them, but the concept behind the documenting is of course very different.

MA Clara, does it bother you that this kind of activism is not always understood to be capital A 'Art' in the conventional sense?

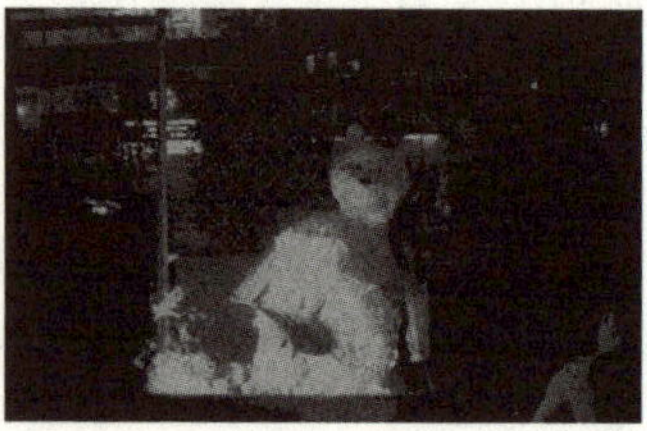

Figure 11: Lai Man Ho, Winnie The Pooh 2020, paper and bamboo stick installation from On Fire, 2020, Prince Edward, Hong Kong. Photo: Kacey Wong

CC Because we didn't announce the On Fire event in 2020 (Figure 11), we didn't promote it as an art event. People or passersby looked, and we heard a shop nearby turn on the music of the protest anthem for Hong Kong. I think the English name for it is 'Glory to Hong Kong'. It's a popular song, played in the recent protests during the Anti-Extradition Movement. I think it doesn't matter whether or not it is capital A 'Art', but I think it depends on the situation and on the context. Maybe at this very moment, if you claim that you're making art, you can escape from some really restrictive controls over freedom of speech.

MA We could talk for a long time on this topic. I think it would probably be appropriate to ask you both about future directions at this point.

CC I'll go first then . . . pessimistic. We can now sense even stronger political censorship everywhere in Hong Kong. That's why I think the outlook for the near future of Hong Kong is pessimistic.

MA And do you think that the kind of public art manifestations of recent times will continue to have a strengthening position in the Hong Kong art scene?

CC I agree with you that there is still possibility for all sorts of creativity. And I think Hong Kong people are very creative and the artists here never want to give up.

OH Life is not always sunny; I mean, there are bright moments and there are also dark moments. I accept that. Yes, things are difficult, so what can you do at a difficult time? Many are looking for new or alternative positions without losing touch with the original ideal. To be optimistic or not, it's up to us and we know what we want.

Living Lumbung: The Shared Spaces of Art and Life A Conversation between Nikos Papastergiadis* and ruangrupa**

* Nikos Papastergiadis is the director of the Research Unit in Public Cultures and a professor in the School of Culture and Communication at the University of Melbourne. He is the founder, with Professor Scott McQuire, of the Spatial Aesthetics research cluster and the project leader and chief investigator of the Australian Research Council Linkage and Discovery Projects, 'Large Screens and the Transnational Public Sphere' and 'Public Screens and the Transformation of Public Space' respectively. Papastergiadis was previously deputy director of the Australia Centre at the University of Melbourne, head of the Centre for Ideas at the Victorian College of Arts, and lecturer in sociology and recipient of the Simon Fellowship at the University of Manchester. A former co-editor of <u>Third Text</u>, he is the author of numerous books, most recently publishing <u>On Art and Friendship</u> (Surpllus) and <u>Museums of the Commons: L'International and the Crisis of Europe</u> (Routledge), both 2020.

** ruangrupa is an art collective and non-profit organisation based in Jakarta that was formed in 2000. The group produces events, workshops, research, publications and exhibitionary projects that are guided by an ethos of resource-sharing and collaboration. ruangrupa work with festivals and exhibitions in Indonesia and around the world, currently serving as artistic director of documenta fifteen in Kassel, Germany (2022). Recent international projects include the Gwangju Biennial (2019); Cosmopolis, Centre Pompidou, Paris (2017); Aichi Triennial (2016); and transACTION: Sonsbeek 2016, Arnhem, the Netherlands. ruangrupa run an art space in the south of Jakarta and in 2018 founded Gudskul together with fellow Jakarta-based collectives Serrum and Grafis Huru Hara.

ruangrupa is an art collective based in Jakarta that was formed in 2000, whose name literally means 'visual space'. Working with festivals in Indonesia and around the world, they produce workshops, publications and events. Their events are loosely structured, and even when they hold an exhibition, it does not usually include work made for the museum. Rather, their exhibitions are complex environments that combine performance, social gatherings, lectures, publications and screenings. The format of these environments resembles a hybrid conjunction of a mini-festival and a mobile art school. ruangrupa's events embed images and experiences inside a complex web of sociality and knowledge production. As people come and go, the formations shift and fold. Speculative conversations on religious and political systems for living with strangers are mixed with workshops and singing sessions. While ruangrupa are fully integrated within the global art discourse, they also draw from traditional concepts and customs. They give emphasis to 'nongkrong' (informal chatting), 'gotong royong' (communal self-help), 'sanggar' (a meeting place for apprentices and masters), 'majelis' (assemblies for leadership debates), and 'lumbung' (a method of distributing surpluses). Their motivation for enabling other ways for people to 'hang out' and 'do stuff' is not simply a consequence of local infrastructure deficits in the Indonesian arts' context; rather, it is a spur for bringing art to the commons.

Nikos Papastergiadis: Where does the concept of lumbung come from?

ruangrupa: Lumbung is a traditional agrarian practice in Indonesia that involves the process of sharing resources. Lumbung literally means 'rice barn', and they are commonly used by villagers to deposit and store their surplus. It has an architecture with space for farmers to store the surplus crops and it also functions as a space to meet, celebrate and share appreciation for the previous harvest. As architecture, it can only be relevant and sustainable if its users continuously renew and refill its resources.

NP How have you adapted it for the context of contemporary society and art?

r If we reflect on the agrarian traditions in many regions of Indonesia, they all have strong communal relations and social interactions. They are operating with the principles of sharing. When it is time to harvest, surplus will

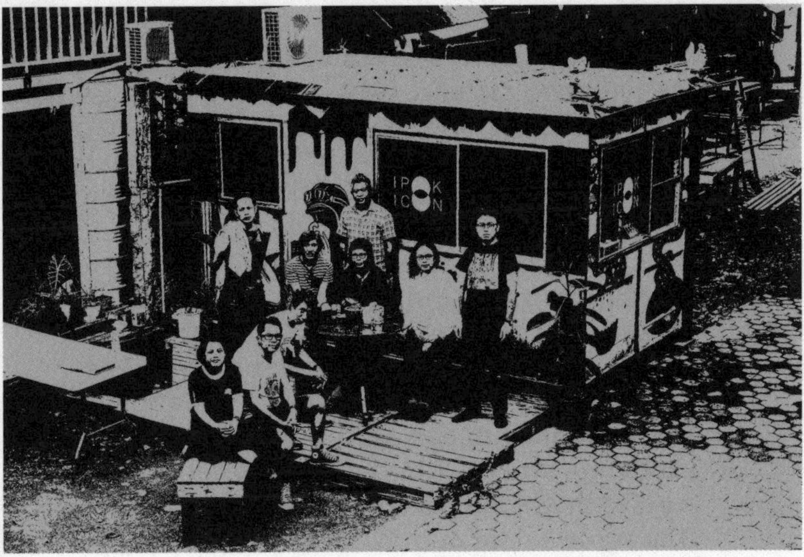

ruangrupa at Gudskul, Jakarta, 2019. Pictured: Ajeng Nurul Aini, Farid Rakun, Iswanto Hartono, Mirwan Andan, Indra Ameng, Ade Darmawan, Daniella Fitria Praptono, Julia Sarisetiati and Reza Afisina. Photo: Jin Panji

not be exhausted; it is collected and stored in the lumbung instead. It has become something not intended for personal use, but to be used in times of scarcity—if there is a disaster caused by weather changes or by famine. By keeping the surplus in the lumbung and slowly consuming the resources available within, farmers also give the soil time to rest and recover. We see lumbung as a metaphor for sharing and a principle for collaboration. We are concerned with how resources—tangible and intangible ones—can be shared. The exchange and distribution of knowledge has always been core to our practice. We adapted this agrarian concept to an urban environment. We saw the living room of a domestic home as a lumbung—a space where various knowledge, skills and networks that circulate and shift are hosted. Lumbung is built on the initiative of people who have the same needs: those who try to organise themselves to share resources and have their own space, so that they can grow together along with the community around their living space. In the context of contemporary art and society, lumbung is an idea for not only mapping resources but also for identifying and understanding basic needs and self-limitation, to define the surplus from the resources (tangible and intangible) of each initiative/organisation to be shared with others. Lumbung has informed our idea for self-initiated and sustainable interdisciplinary spaces. It is where art meets social activism, management and also various local networks. It is central to our collective ruangrupa, and for understanding what is happening in our local environment and responding to it by initiating something together within our context. Lumbung is not a theme but a concept that is practised and operated in the journey to documenta fifteen and beyond.

NP Apart from sharing and sustainability, what other principles does lumbung highlight?

r Sharing and sustainability are principles to enhance wellbeing. We see the supporting systems for art as a means for focusing on wellbeing for the entire ecosystem. However, this also takes us to the principle of respecting different concepts of time. The modern emphasis on efficiency has ignored the richness of time in diverse cultures. Uncertainties and failure can be seen as luxuries that contemporary society compels us to do without. Money is not everything; time is what counts . . .

NP Do you also draw on older concepts of power, listening, gathering and leadership?

r We need to consider power to be not absolute. It is not embodied in structure; it is in rotation and is interchangeable. The ability to play a role in a different position with a good endurance to perform is what is needed. Sensibility towards the rotation is important. To move around leadership and followship is equally powerful. Good articulation and silence are similarly respected.

The term ‘majelis’ refers to a space where people are sitting side by side, sharing, discussing, speculating, solving problems, sharing food and humour without any time limits. In Jakartan slang, the word ‘nongkrong’ is used to describe this activity of spending time together in a friendly and comfortable atmosphere with old and new friends. It could even mean doing nothing collectively. There is a sense of mutually taking care of each other in aimless conversations.

The phrase ‘musyawarah-mufakat’ refers to an assembly in which a group’s members humbly gather to make decisions for the sake of the common interest. This is not through casting votes and going with the majority, but instead by talking things over to create an agreement. This can be held without a set timeframe and is very open in nature. The phrase ‘gotong royong’ can mean a form of mutual co-operation among a number of people to carry out a task deemed useful for the common good. This phrase is not only directed towards mutual co-operation, but gives emphasis on the active participation of an individual in a community, where they get involved and find positive values in the surroundings, issues and needs of those around them.

In sum, we are drawing on ideas that bring people together in more conversation and less authoritative processes. Conversations meander, decisions spring. We reduce individual control and ownership. We share power and authority, as well as respecting silence and absence. Ideas emerge organically without clear ownerships. It is a collage:

thousands of pieces of ideas come together. There's an openness to share, give and take, lose and find. Bad ideas are polished up with some imagination through conversations, forever making them better.

NP When did ruangrupa start, and what were the conditions that spawned its existence?

r ruangrupa started from a friendship among students at art schools in Jakarta and Jogjakarta in the 1990s. It formally came into existence in 2000, which coincided with the end of the Soeharto regime (1966–98) and the loosening of the restrictions against freedom of expression and public assembly.

NP What were the goals of the collective?

r The primary goal was to give space for discussion and experimentation with art. Before this period, it could be considered a subversive act to form an organisation or self-organised events without any permission from the authorities, and there was very rarely space dedicated for diverse art practices, especially for the young artists. The meaning of the word ruangrupa is literally 'visual space'. In the beginning, we usually met in our fellow members' living rooms or houses.

NP What other spaces did you seek to occupy or rather hang out in?

r Sometimes, we organised our programs in other art venues. After a while, we raised funds to rent our own space to gather and work in. There we began to organise workshops, exhibitions, discussions and publishing activities. Some of us had already collaborated on various projects during our art school time in the mid-1990s—mostly zines and music criticising the authority and establishment positions. The student movement reached a climax in 1998 and this led to the reformation. We were conscious that public space can never be taken for granted, as it can be taken away, sold off and controlled. ruangrupa thinks of public space as space where people can identify themselves as social beings. This is vital for any society, and the establishment of public space was one of the main reasons for forming ruangrupa.

NP Where does artistic practice end and public engagement begin?

r Slowly and informally, ruangrupa has become a kind of school for many people. However, we wanted to go beyond the idea of an art education that was focused on the development of individual talent and the spotting of budding geniuses. Believing that art and artists can no longer exist for their own sake, we practicise collectivity and working collaboratively as methods to take a stand in society. We established [the public learning space] Gudskul [in 2018] to encourage the initiating spirit in artistic and cultural practices. Using this approach, artists then simultaneously and organically act as producers, mediators, distributors and networkers. We designed the Gudskul as a space for study, achieved through collective practice simulations, advocating the importance of processes by means of critical and experimental-based learning and sharing. Gudskul promotes collaboration and self organisation, providing a collective learning space as well as a contemporary art ecosystem that is built on friendship, equality and solidarity.

NP Were there similar groups and collectives in Indonesia that shared these goals?

r There were numerous initiatives across the many cities in Indonesia. At least, two common tendencies could be observed among these organisations and groups. First, a collective's artistic practices, whether collaborative or by individual members, constituted their artistic statement as a group. Second, they played the role of a support system within the art ecosystem, through activities or programs that raised public awareness. Almost all of these collectives started in the residential houses of the participants and organisers. The activities were wide ranging, including exhibitions, workshops, festivals, discussions, publications, film and video screenings, website development, archiving and research. Central to all these collectives was the desire to meet and discuss in comfortable spaces and to then let things happen.

NP These spaces mixed the private and the public, the domestic and the civic, politics, art and life. Was this because of the absence of institutional spaces, or because it was attractive to meet in people's living rooms?

r Residential homes were the starting point for these collectives and the centre of activities. Meetings most often took place in the living room, since it is the largest room in most Indonesian homes. Over time, they were adapted and domestic spaces became more public. Living rooms were converted to function as galleries, bedrooms as archives, studios and libraries. Typically, the converted residential building was located in a middle-class area—a secular area, a melting pot of people of various backgrounds (from white-collar types to factory workers). They were usually easy to find and rents were affordable. The group was responsible for the lease and raised funds to support the activities.

NP How did the groups survive financially? What sort of mix of private patronage, state funding and commercial opportunities enabled the groups to keep going?

r Most artists tended to come from the same social and economic class as their neighbours, and generally divided their time working in the creative and media industries as freelancers or were students. The collectives were also often located in working-class or mixed-use neighbourhoods and co-existed with small and medium businesses. This fitted in with the kind of independent enterprises.

Most of us are also very active, with individual projects in many diverse fields—visual arts, design, music, architecture, writings, research, or a mixture of everything—which enriches ruangrupa in practice. ruangrupa represents the intersection and interdependency between individual and collective senses. This is when we realised how lumbung works for us. Since the beginning, ruangrupa survived as a lumbung of collective resources, time, energy, ideas and also money, so for us ruangrupa has never been one main thing. Individually, we always do other things, and that is what makes our lumbung richer and sustainable.

By acting as a stand-alone citizens' initiative, the group rendered its vitality by becoming the supporting infrastructure for both art and the community. It envisioned itself as living among the people. The involvement of the surrounding residents could act as an artistic exploration strategy, with unmediated influences from the residents themselves.

The lack of funding and infrastructure support from the government does mean that all such initiatives in Indonesia are vulnerable. Spaces and programs can be easily lost, and people are overworked and underpaid. 'Sustainability' and 'independence' are two words that most often only cast a shadow. Independence is almost impossible to achieve when the choice depends only on foreign donor agencies and private sponsors, who often only focus on the production process not the sustainability process. All always return to zero and in a condition of uncertainty and vulnerability for the next steps.

Our biggest challenge is how to create a platform that is able to sustain this artistic practice and to translate it within the increasingly rapid changes in society. Through our expanded notion of artistic practices, we are attempting to build a new model that takes into account the economy, social, culture, politics, working ethics and collaborative habits. Only then can the separation between art and life be truly overcome.

NP Has the absence of formal arts infrastructure served as a burden, in the sense that it needed to be built, or an opportunity to reinvent it?

r The fact that it was non-existent meant that the thinking towards the better or even ideal living ecosystem has always been conducted by the bottom that is, of course, always hoping that the state would at some point embrace them, so that it really becomes the bottom-up system that any democracy is striving to achieve.

Our function is therefore as a kind of problem solver, and creating living spaces was sort of 'contextual responses'. It is interesting that these types of spaces are not relying on the state's infrastructures at all. Most of them are not even connected to their local arts committees. Unfortunately, there are not so many opportunities for independent arts organisations to partner with state institutions. What these circumstances really reflect is the failure of the state's central planning in facilitating the vast growth of ideas in different localities.

NP What happened to ruangrupa when it started to expand by linking up with other local initiatives?

r In 2018, when ruangrupa had a chance to rent a bigger space in Jakarta, we decided to evolve. So the idea is not merely about ruangrupa as a collective; instead, we have transformed into a collective of collectives together with Serrum and Grafis Huru Hara. We run a new space together, working with ideas of an ecosystem by putting various resources into a lumbung as a way to support and strengthen each other.

At the same time, we started to develop RURU Corps—an experimental unit business, functioning as a way to strive for sustainability beyond the dependence on external public, private and foreign funding. We were looking for ways to generate more income, so as to be more financially independent in the future—in short, to survive with what we already have, but also to run a space at a scale that allowed us to practice a form of institutional activism. Our RURU Corps experience had trained us to tend to this 'self-initiated institution' while using it to continuously appropriate and opportunistically turn our space of practice into a meaningful place of knowledge production. This led to working together with programmers and curators to experiment on how to sustain their programs, and to the creation of various forms of local creative markets and commercial creative services, such as website design, video making, event programming and festival organising.

NP How does ruangrupa operate in the public domain of a foreign city? What are the challenges as well as opportunities afforded by directing documenta fifteen?

r When we were invited to offer a proposal for documenta fifteen, we decided to respond with a counter invitation—for documenta to become part of our ecosystem, through collaboration inspired by and modelled after lumbung. As lumbung is a form of organisation for a common governance of resources, the question becomes: how can we govern these resources together? One answer is to keep extending the invitation to others. The lumbung—an ecosystem benefiting, contributing and caring for it—will be collectively built over the span of three years and beyond by different collectives and institutions from around the world. In our radar are groups from remote and rural areas in Spain, Italy, central and Eastern Europe. We imagine members from places such as Southern Africa and Mali that have deep experiences in Ubuntu or Maaya traditions of sharing, as well as from places like Colombia, Hungary and Palestine that are challenged by populism, neo-liberalisation and conflict, but that also have rich histories of resistance and creative practice.

The challenge for the artistic team of documenta and the different groups is to develop a common pot. Each group will bring distinctive resources and new surpluses will emerge. However, it will also require building trust and lasting relationships, which will rely on visiting each other and exchanging knowledge. In order to find mechanisms for distributing resources, the groups and institutions will meet regularly, forming 'majils' (assemblies). In turn, this will lead to inviting others to join as well. This will become 'Lumbung International', an incubator for a wider transformation that questions the current global art economy.

The new arts economy that we are aiming to build brings back art to its more useful function—the imagination and living with both the new and habitual ways of life—and ways of organising that are more just, humane and holistic. We are therefore looking for friends that focus their artistic experimentation, activism and/or imagination in the fields of (urban, rural, public) space, economics, education and ecology. Organisations that get involved in the building of this new arts economy cherish relations, generosity, and the search for the rebalancing of individual to collective needs. To start living and crafting this economy during the first phase, collectives and organisations are invited that already have this at the core of their mission, and can therefore enrich the lumbung economy from their own experiences and activities in their context and with their own resources.

NP Has the COVID pandemic disrupted your plans and what are the ways in which you can plan for people to hang out and share in the future?

r We have used the lumbung model to take care of each other during this crisis. At the beginning of the pandemic, our space could not be used in its normal way. It was becoming our surplus. We had to use it differently to contribute to the situation. So we transformed the auditorium into a small production place for hazmat suits and masks. We did fundraising to support the local medics and hospitals in the remote islands of Indonesia. Our friends worked from home or on rotation to minimise exposure.

Obviously, we had to cancel many events or rethink of how to host things on digital platforms. As we realised that things were not coming back to normal soon, we started to feel drained and frustrated, and decided that we needed to split ourselves into small groups in order to be more flexible, and thus started to see the whole organisation as a connection of small units. So we now co-exist in a physical and virtual way; even our majelis and markets are done virtually. The hanging out is still on rotation; a few friends are working at our space (Gudskul); and spontaneous Zoom links are open to anyone who would like to join, with no fixed schedule, topic, goal or time limit. It is still an open space where people can come and go; it does not replace the usual hanging out, but it keeps the conversations going, keeps us sane, and keeps us caring. I think this pandemic has taught us to not underestimate the power of hanging out.

Deficit and Care
Zara Stanhope*

* Dr Zara Stanhope is the Director of the Govett-Brewster Art Gallery/Len Lye Centre, New Plymouth, New Zealand. She previously held lead roles at the Queensland Art Gallery | Gallery of Modern Art (QAGOMA), Brisbane; Auckland Art Gallery Toi o Tāmaki; Adam Art Gallery Te Pātaka Toi, Victoria University of Wellington; Heide Museum of Modern Art, Melbourne; and Monash University Musuem of Art, Melbourne. She was the lead curator for New Zealand at Venice at the 58th Venice Biennale (2019) and for the 9th and 10th Asia Pacific Triennials at QAGOMA. A writer and editor, she has a doctorate from the Australian National University and is an adjunct professor in the School of Art and Design at AUT University, Auckland, and at RMIT University, Melbourne.

Many artists working today are pushing and prodding at the public body politic to draw attention to concerns that are significant now and for future generations. Such artists are crossing between gallery and public spaces to connect with communities—whether cultural, social, or interest-based—with the aim of generating visibility for subsidiary or alternative sections of society, groups who can be considered similar to Michael Warner's discursively formed 'counterpublics'.[1] Creating art that contributes to raising awareness and reflection in the interests of change, these artists attend to building cohesiveness in counterpublics or communities. This short text discusses an artist collective and a singular artist working in Aotearoa, New Zealand, who are engaging with and contesting normative conditions for workers and LGBTQI+ communities respectively, through public art that attends to the betterment of temporary communities at a local and national scale.

Based in Tāmaki Makaurau, Aotearoa, the collective Public Share and artist Shannon Novak connect with conventional and self-defined groups to build a sense of mutuality particular to site in physical and online space. They share the aim to highlight certain pressures imposed by mainstream social and economic systems that result in discriminatory forms of power that constrain the sense of self. Their collaborations stretch normative institutions from the inside.

Since 2014, Public Share—Monique Redmond, Harriet Stockman, Kelsey Stankovich, Deborah Rundle, Mark Schroder and Joe Prisk—have been

1 Michael Warner, Publics and Counterpublics, Zone Books, New York, 2005, p. 90.

meeting weekly to make ceramics, inspired by the sociality of creativity. From this base, they have developed occasional projects that are quiet performances of public connectivity and that generate reflection on the politics of working conditions. They are eager to foster the spirit of sharing they enjoy beyond the group, and an ethos of and invitation to exchange imbues their 'hosting' projects. They have organised event-based installations in construction site tea-rooms, art spaces and museums, and public places, drawing attention to the historical regulation of organised labour and marginalisation of women. Tea break events, for which the collective make and give away handmade ceramic plates, tumblers, mugs, and stirrers, publicly highlight workers' rights in Aotearoa and their precarity. The national history of labour regulations includes temporarily losing the two ten-minute prescribed tea breaks in 2015, rights hard-won by organised labour, until being reinstated in 2019.

Several events indicate the group's subtle highlighting of workers as a micro public. In 2014, the construction company Fulton Hogan gifted to Public Share a seam of clay that was exposed during the making of the SH16 Highway at Te Atatu. The artists used the material to create plates on which they served food for 110 morning tea imbibers in A Break in Proceedings later that year.[2] On a separate

2 A Break in Proceedings was part of the Engaging Publics/Public Engagement symposium, 13 September 2014, Auckland Art Gallery Toi o Tāmaki, of which I was a co-organiser. Irregular Allotments took place at the temporary Fulton Hogan construction site tea-room on 29 October 2014. See https://

occasion, Public Share held a morning tea for the sixty Fulton Hogan workers at the Highway worksite, denoting acts of unexpected generosity on both sides. Two other actions by Public Share involved providing morning tea at road construction cabins, including gifting the handmade mugs, aimed to generate tea-room sociality (SMOKO, 2015, and Out of Office, 2016). The group's engagements were situated between a freely given act of reciprocation for the construction company's gift and an implication of Aotearoa's economic reliance on construction to support its economy, including financing the state's social obligations. Public Share's undertakings highlighted a public of workers in whose wellbeing the population are implicated.

When working inside art galleries (e.g. Carried Forward, 2015), most of Public Share's actions have included providing food and making ceramics for non-art local publics. Subsequent Conditions, 2016, in Christchurch was a response to local residents who were found still suffering following the 2011 earthquake, after escape clauses in insurance contracts had left them without compensation. The collective served morning tea at sites where they had met residents and where the clay used to make the cups that were gifted to participants had been extracted. In 2019, the workers at The Dowse Art Museum—including contractors and volunteers—could agree to take a tea break using a ceramic cup made, and baking organised, by Public Share,

publicshare.co.nz/allotted-breaks/. Fulton Hogan have subsequently contacted Public Share after finding new clay seams for a future work; see https://publicshare.co.nz/a-right-stirrer/.

asserting the right to individual rest as a 'collective agreement with the artists'.[3] The mutual agreement aimed to complicate normative conditions of labour and issues of the integration of work and leisure.[4]

By gifting the purpose-made ceramics (and often all the elements of morning tea), Public Share's gestures are easily associated with concepts of the gift economy, a set of ideas described by anthropologists including Bronislaw Malinowski, Marcel Mauss, Arjun Appadurai and other thinkers investigating non-commodified exchange. If the gift becomes a frame through which to think differently about Public Share's actions, then it might add a set of questions to their generosity and to their concern of sharing their making with groups in public space, without expecting any kind of reciprocation. Their forms of exchange are based in temporarily locating participants with a common interest, a micro counterpublic, and in generating collectivity outside the debt/credit relations of the economy. Public Share's interest in provisional or short-term public sociality as a means to question the situation of labour and the future of work could be understood to offer a gift economy, with space for the emergence of social being.[5] Following this concern,

3 Collective Agreement, 2019, required Dowse staff to take a ten-minute break every four hours as part of The Future of Work curated by Melanie Oliver.

4 Recent projects creating spaces for discussion were Last Run, 2017, at Te Toi Uku related to the Crown Lynn Potteries; Notice of Intent, 2016, at The Blue Oyster Gallery on the topic of Dunedin rail; and Workers Club, 2017, at RM Gallery, Tāmaki Makaurau.

5 Elizabeth A. Povinelli, 'Routes/ Worlds', e-flux journal, no. 27,

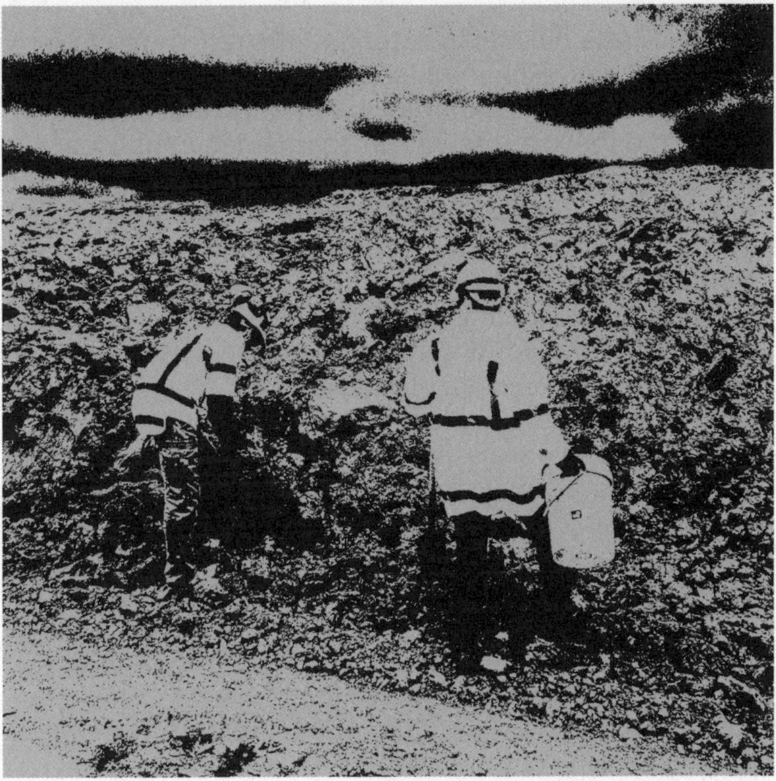

Public Share collecting clay from an infrastructure site in Waterview, Auckland, for the work SMOKO, 2015. Mugs produced from the clay facilitated morning tea events at the Performing Mobilities Assembly, Melbourne, 10 October 2015; and at the Well-Connected Alliance's Wiri site tearooms, Tāmaki Makaurau/Auckland, 13 June 2016. Photo: Public Share

Public Share have also extended the rejuvenating of work/life space beyond labour to the political life of women. Tumblers stamped with the various dates when the female vote was introduced in countries around the world were made for women participants, celebrating the 125th anniversary of suffrage (19 September 1893) at Aotearoa's Parliament in 2018, and at a public tea break event on the date women first voted (28 November 1893), addressing the continual deficit of power women endure with an excess of hospitality.[6]

Public Share explore questions about how to open space in normative frameworks to create a matrix of care for workers and women. Similarly, Shannon Novak's generosity toward engendering rights and acceptance for LGBTQI+ communities as part of his practice could be understood as a gift

September 2011, https://www.e-flux.com/journal/27/67991/routes-worlds/.

6 For OVER TIME, pt. 1, 2018, at Parliament, sixteen current and former Members of Parliament considered by Public Share to have contributed to women's rights in Aotearoa provided clay and soil from a site or person of personal significance. Clay was collected from the residences of two significant suffragettes, Meri Te Tai Mangakāhia and Kate Sheppard, for OVER TIME, pt. 2, 2018, held at Te Ngākau Civic Square, Wellington. The ceramic tumblers and stirrers were taken home after each event, along with a broadsheet with contributions from eleven writers published by Public Share to celebrate the legacy of women's rights as an excess of generosity. These events were part of the Ministry of Culture and Heritage's national program of events 'Suffrage 125—Whakatū Wāhine'.

obliging self-conscious attention to regard for others on the part of public and corporate domains. Novak's painting and environmental works, such as Nexus Central, 2018, at Pataka Art Space, Wellington, generate colourful ambient and cast light effects through prismatic, abstract vinyl work on windows.[7] Also located in commercial and public spaces, such as a ferry or corporate architecture, Novak's installations are encoded with site-specific meanings.[8] Significantly, the installation Litmus: Nelson, 2019, at The Suter Art Gallery, Nelson, was the first for Novak to publicly incorporate into the work his personal understanding of the local LGBTQI+ community's sentiment of both wellbeing and discomfort in their neighbourhood at the time.[9] Notably, the installation also introduced the Gallery as being a safe space for the LGBTQI+ community, indicated by the circular rainbow window graphic that is the mark of Novak's ongoing, not-for-profit project, the 'Safe Space Alliance'.

The Alliance helps to identify, navigate and create spaces in which bullying, violence, or hate speech towards the LGBTQI+ community are not tolerated. While Public Share draw attention to the minimum rest conditions for workers, the Alliance asks physical and digital spaces to, at minimum, uphold the Alliance's definition of a safe space and

7 See Shannon Novak, 'Nexus Central Installation', http://www.shannonnovak.com/works#/nexus/.

8 Extended Play on the Auckland/Waiheke Fuller Ferry was part of 2019 Sculpture on the Gulf.

9 Novak's understanding of local issues such as lack of visibility of LGBTQI+ communities was a factor in certain past public works, but not revealed.

to offer support, encouraging responsibility for rather than guaranteeing safety. Any organisation—regardless of scale, location or type—is welcome to apply to be listed on the Safe Space Alliance online directory, and there are no joining fees. The Alliance also recommends specialists in respective local LGBTQI+ organisations who can help identify needs and navigate change to ensure that facilities, staff and communications are inclusive and respectful; direct income to the community; and help in verifying the readiness of the organisation to be listed on the Safe Space Alliance website.[10] Listings are removed if reported unsafe until issues are resolved. Institutions ranging from major international art museums to sports and volunteer organisations have now made the commitment to part of the Alliance.

Developing and maintaining the Safe Space Alliance project as a potentially global initiative is demanding for Novak, with communities and individuals facing varied levels of acceptance and other complexities. Although unfortunately needed and in demand, its initiation and maintenance require a major act of munificence on Novak's part. But can such a practice escape the gift economy for the artist or participants? Anthropological lore would require that the giver receives more in return. Novak has said that he supports the Safe Space Alliance as a gift with a level of self-interest, which might change the world he inhabits as much as others. Novak agrees his reward is 'ultimately, saving lives'.[11] A number of his recent installations add highly coloured designs to architectural

10 See https://safespacealliance.com/.

11 Shannon Novak, email to author, 13 January 2021.

surfaces, a visual language that conveys the artist's visual mapping of the wellbeing and challenges facing a local LGBTQI+ community. Often, the abstract, colourful register of the health of a local LGBTQI+ community marking their level of discomfort is painted on a surface parallel to his image. If these works, such as Therapeutic Agent, 2020, at Puke Ariki, New Plymouth, Taranaki, is any guide, then there is much more to be demanded from public and private spaces and people in their future attention to how to behave with inclusiveness and equality. The consequent reactions and repercussions of the Safe Space initiative, like Public Share's morning teas, are potentially manifold for their counterpublics. A lens of gift relations cast over the logics of care of Public Share and Shannon Novak indicates how these artists' engagements with diverse social worlds in public space equate to a self-reflexive form of public art.

Twich Women's Sewing Collective: Activism through Enterprise, Social Change through Culture

Grace McQuilten*

* Dr Grace McQuilten is an art historian, curator, artist and senior lecturer in art history and theory at RMIT University, Melbourne, where she leads the Contemporary Art and Social Transformation Research Group in the School of Art. A researcher on the model of social enterprise in the arts in Australia, she has used the vehicle of art and design to advocate for social inclusion, with a particular focus on new migrant and refugee communities. McQuilten's most recent book is _Art as Enterprise: Social and Economic Engagement in Contemporary Art_ (IB Tauris, 2016), co-authored with Dr Anthony White. She is the founding CEO and a current board director of The Social Studio, a fashion and art based social enterprise working with young people from humanitarian migrant backgrounds in Melbourne.

The Twich Women's Sewing Collective is a Victorian-based social enterprise that uses art and fashion to engage with, challenge and transform mainstream representations of Sudanese Australian communities. A key feature of how they do this is through the occupation of public spaces. In this essay, I argue that Twich's engagement with diverse publics through both trade and cultural activity has an important political dimension, prioritising self-representation over being represented, and thereby challenging dominant (hegemonic) structures of power.

Using public space as a platform to challenge dominant constructs around race and migration has both political and aesthetic dimensions. With the predominance of socially engaged art practices in contemporary art discourse since the turn of the millennium, the links between artistic practice as social action and public practices with social justice imperatives have become clearer.[1] However, what is still missing in much of this discourse is attention to practices that emerge on the margins of contemporary art practice. A collective such as Twich, for example, emerges from an understanding of art that

1 See, for example, Karen van den Berg, Cara M. Jordan and Phillipp Kleinmichel (eds), The Art of Direct Action: Social Sculpture and Beyond, Sternberg Press, Berlin, 2019; Greg Sholette, Chloë Bass and Social Practice Queens (eds), Art as Social Action: An Introduction to the Principles and Practices of Teaching Social Practice Art, Allworth Press, New York, 2018; and Carol Becker, Thinking in Place: Art, Action, and Cultural Production, Routledge, London, 2009.

is inherently connected to culture, to daily life, and to trade—as opposed to art that has developed out of art school training or professionalisation. Twich also sits somewhat uncomfortably in the realm of community arts in that it was not initiated by a community arts organisation, local council or government. Instead, it is an example of a self-organised cultural and artistic group that uses material and aesthetic practices for both practical and political ends: to create employment and training opportunities for migrant women and to influence and potentially transform public perceptions about migrant Sudanese communities in Australia.

In thinking through Twich's engagement with its publics, I draw on Chantal Mouffe's approach to political public art articulated in Agonistics: Thinking the World Politically: namely, activating counter-hegemonic practices and giving voice to difference. Mouffe writes of politically engaged public art as follows: 'Its critical dimension consists in making visible what the dominant consensus tends to obscure and obliterate, in giving a voice to all those who are silenced within the framework of the existing hegemony.'[2]

Over the last two decades, there has been a rapid growth in the population of Sudanese migrant communities in Australia. This stems from humanitarian policies from the late 1990s and early 2000s that supported the intake of refugees fleeing the brutal civil war in Sudan (1983–2005) that resulted in the formation of South Sudan as an

2 Chantal Mouffe, Agonistics: Thinking the World Politically, Verso, London, New York, 2013, p. 93.

independent state in 2011.[3] The settlement of Sudanese migrants in Australia has been the subject of controversial public debate, played out in the media through the disproportionate reportage of gang violence, family violence, a consistent emphasis on perceived issues of cultural difference, and a generally negative portrayal of Sudanese communities' capacities to 'settle' or 'integrate'.[4] The resulting image of Sudanese communities in the Australian news media is one of violent, warring and criminal groups, no matter their age or gender. In the context of the COVID-19 pandemic, these media depictions extended negative stereotypes through reports that linked migrant and refugee communities with the spread of the virus, along with coverage of public housing tower lockdowns in Melbourne.[5]

Interventions and responses aiming to transform these negative representations of Sudanese Australian communities have arisen in cultural practices that draw on visual and material forms in public space. Such artistic strategies—particularly those at the forefront of popular culture—may not at first glance seem to have political intentions or implications. However, these

3 Australian Bureau of Statistics, Migration Review, Belconnen, ACT, 2007.

4 David Nolan et al., 'Mediated Multiculturalism: Newspaper Representations of Sudanese Migrants in Australia', Journal of Intercultural Studies, vol. 32, no. 6, 2011, p. 656.

5 Alicia Vrajlal, 'Australia's COVID-19 Racism Again Shows "Migrants Are Always Blamed" in a Crisis', Huffington Post Australia, 31 July 2020, https://www.huffingtonpost.com.au/entry/coronavirus-australia-racism_au_5f237ce8c5b656e9b0998d73.

projects take on different connotations when considered in relation to the ways in which contemporary politics play out through media, advertising and consumer culture.

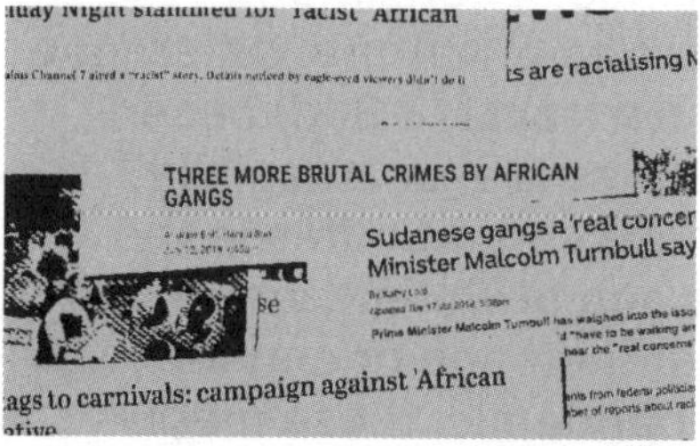

Figure 1: A selection of headlines from Australian newspapers on African gangs and racist rhetoric. Image: Greta Brereton

Twich Women's Sewing Collective began in 2011 in direct response to the challenging settlement environment encountered by South Sudanese communities. This fashion-based social enterprise was originally situated in Dandenong, a suburb in the south-east of Melbourne with high proportions of refugee and migrant communities. Since 2017, it has been operating out of its new store in Balaclava, a site the group was able to secure for lower rent, although the location is unfortunately less accessible for their community members. The Collective formed when a group of women from the Twich region and language group of South Sudan formalised a set of elaborate and sometimes painstaking art practices already occurring in their community, including weaving, beading, embroidery and textile design. What began with gatherings at home slowly evolved into more public-facing activities, including the creation of objects for both community-building and trade. The artists involved saw an opportunity to achieve multiple goals, including (1) generating much-needed income for older women in their community experiencing unemployment and underemployment, particularly those balancing motherhood and work; (2) providing a means with which to engage with younger men and women experiencing forms of social isolation and barriers to education and work by involving them in the fashion label, providing retail training and employment and collaborating with them to produce events; and (3) imparting aesthetic knowledge and demonstrating pride in their cultural background as a step towards redressing the negative stigma associated with media portrayals of youth violence and settlement problems.

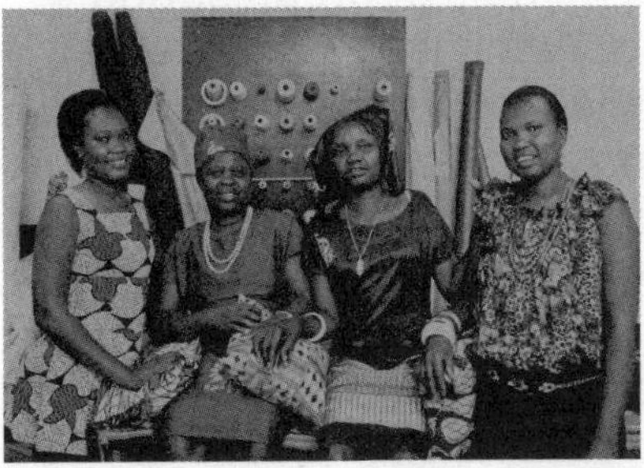

Figure 2: Founding members of the Twich Women's Sewing Collective, Nyachol John, Ayen Bol, Akech Majok and Abuk Bol (left to right). Image courtesy of Twich Women's Sewing Collective

The group of makers formed a non-profit social enterprise and opened the retail shop in central Dandenong, providing a public interface through which to engage with the broader community. From the outset, they adopted a 'hybrid' economic model that brings together income from a range of sources including philanthropic funds, small government grants, arts funding as well as revenue from trading. Combining a small business approach with artistic practice has therefore enabled the Collective to apply for different streams of funding that have overlapping benefits. The relation between their approach to creative activism and public space or public art can be understood in two ways. Firstly, their economic organisation as a social enterprise situates them firmly in a public space of exchange, both literally in terms of their retail shop and more symbolically in terms of their engagement with mainstream markets. Secondly, they engage more directly with public spaces through the presentation of public events that showcase their textile works alongside cultural dance, spoken word and performance.

In terms of their economic structure, as an incorporated association, the organisation operates on a membership model which has its roots in more cooperative or communal models of organisation from the 1970s and 1980s. Twich now consists of approximately fifty men and women from the South Sudanese community, who are overseen by an elected Committee of Management responsible for the organisation's strategic planning, decision-making and operational management. The five-person committee is made up of a mixture of younger and older women who are makers as well as managers. Major decisions are brought to the committee for discussion and debate, while the operations are handled in most part by the organisation's general manager, Abuk Bol. Trading revenue comes from the sale of specialist textiles imported from Africa, clothing, adornments and hand-beaded artefacts. Sales are made through the Twich retail shop (which also houses the studio and training space and provides an important interface with the broader public), at various art and craft markets in Melbourne, and through orders. Customers range from members of the South Sudanese community seeking specific products that are hard to access in Australia through to office workers and local artists. In addition, the Collective have generated income through the production, sale and hire of textile products for weddings, targeted specifically at the South Sudanese community across Australia. All of this trade contributes to approximately half of the organisation's running costs. The remainder is sourced through grants and donations, and is used to fund the training and work experience programs that the group delivers for new migrant community members.

These economic dimensions are important because in a strategic move, the Twich Women's Sewing Collective set out to go beyond a more conventional model of community organisation and to create direct employment and training opportunities through entrepreneurial activity. As Val Colic-Peisker and Karen Farquharson observe, 'structural equality and its crucial element—the employment success of skilled non-English speaking background migrants—is a domain where future multiculturalism will stand or fall'.[6] The entrepreneurial nature of the women involved and their active role in setting the organisation's direction serves to counteract the traditional model of welfare delivery, wherein a service provides 'assistance' to a client. As Slavoj Žižek argues in his critique of charity, this top-down model often implies a position of passivity or helplessness for the recipient of support, a position that can serve to reinforce, rather than ameliorate, disadvantage.[7]

6 Val Colic-Peisker and Karen Farquharson, 'Introduction: A New Era in Australian Multiculturalism? The Need for Critical Interrogation', Journal of Intercultural Studies, vol. 32, no. 6, 2011, p. 585.

7 Slavoj Žižek, 'First as Tragedy, Then

In addition to this reversal of the power structures of social welfare and migration settlement (where migrants are 'helped' by local citizens), the Collective also counteract and reverse negative representations of the South Sudanese community in popular media. Media portrayals of the Twich Women's Sewing Collective have tended to collapse back into tropes such as focusing on stories of hardship, suffering and trauma, including the narration of experiences of violence from the past. They also tend to portray Bol in terms of lack and disadvantage rather than highlighting her skills and experience.[8] As observed in a 2011 study of media coverage of the Sudanese community in Australia, the theme of violence is prominent, even in what might be considered as 'success stories'. While this may seem logical in the context of writing of the refugee experience, when considered collectively, these media representations influence the general public to associate the Sudanese community with violence and criminality. These perceptions have in turn been used by federal politicians and public commentators to reinforce

as Farce', RSA Animate Lecture, transcript, 24 November 2009, http://www.thersa.org/__data/assets/pdf_file/0008/1533626/RSA-Lecture-Slavoj-Zizek-transcript.pdf.

8 See Casey Neill, 'Life Held by a Thread', The Dandenong Journal, 27 October 2014, http://dandenong.starcommunity.com.au/journal/2014-10-27/life-held-by-a-thread/. See also Carolyn Webb, 'Fashion a Pathway to New Life for Refugee', The Age, 2 September 2014, http://www.theage.com.au/victoria/fashion-a-pathway-to-new-life-for-refugee-20140901-10axgc.html.

political decision-making about the intake of African migrants. In 2007, Immigration Minister Kevin Andrews announced a plan to reduce the number of African migrants, directly in response to perceived issues of Sudanese settlement:

> I have been concerned that some groups don't seem to be settling and adjusting into the Australian way of life as quickly as we would hope and therefore it makes sense to put the extra money in to provide extra resources, but also to slow down the rate of intake from countries such as Sudan.[9]

As a result of these public discourses, when Bol is interviewed by the media, she reorients the discussion towards the structural issues of employment for women in Melbourne and away from personal narratives of hardship and overcoming. She describes in one article that she wants 'to grow it [Twich] so they can employ more women',[10] and in another she emphasises the enterprise's creation of educational opportunities.[11] The Twich Women's Sewing Collective therefore engage with the political issue of Sudanese migration and settlement in Australia by counteracting negative media stereotyping and perceptions through the vehicle of

9 Farah Farouque, Andrea Petrie and Daniella Miletic, 'Minister Cuts African Refugee Intake', The Age, 2 October 2007, http://www.theage.com.au/articles/2007/10/01/1191091031242.html.

10 Abbie O'Brien, 'Cultural Threads', The City Journal, 27 October 2014, http://thecityjournal.net/gallery/cultural-threads/.

11 Webb, 'Fashion a Pathway to New Life for Refugee'.

material and cultural production rather than more conventional forms of protest or activism. The media sphere can be understood as a public sphere in and of itself—a public site that artists often use politically to subvert dominant power structures.[12] The potential of Twich's cultural activities to serve this transformative function is clear in the images associated with their events, which directly contradict the negative identifications found in mainstream media (Figures 3 and 4).

In their material form, the artworks and products generated by Twich further activate alternative constructions of Sudanese Australian culture. This fits within Mouffe's configuring of the political nature of art:

> Artistic practices play a role in the constitution and maintenance of a given symbolic order, or in its challenging, and this is why they necessarily have a political dimension. The political, for its part, concerns the symbolic ordering of social relations, and this is where its aesthetic dimension resides.[13]

As a result, Mouffe argues, there is no need to distinguish political and non-political art. The more important point of difference for Mouffe is the degree to which artistic practice enables opportunity for the generation of new subjectivities and new perspectives that differ from, and potentially transform, dominant ideological

12 See Nick Couldry, 'Speaking up in Public Space: The Strange Case of Rachel Whiteread's House', in Media, Voice, Space and Power: Essays of Refraction, Taylor & Francis Group, Milton, 2019, p. 96.

13 Mouffe, Agonistics, p. 91.

systems.[14] It is in this context that the Twich Women's Sewing Collective might be understood as a political collective in Mouffe's sense, while also operating in a dense social field shaped by organisational constraints and financial pressures that complicate a simple reading of their activities as purely a political gesture.

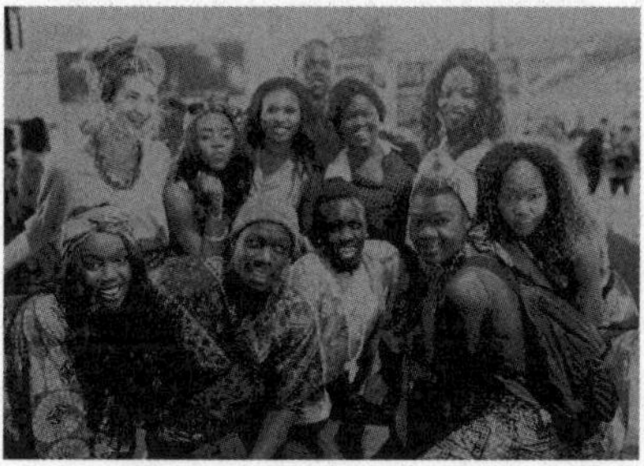

Figure 3: Models pictured together after the Twich Women's Sewing Collective runway for Cultural Threads, Dandenong Market, Victoria, 2014. Image courtesy of Twich Women's Sewing Collective

The activities of the Twich Women's Sewing Collective create a space from which Sudanese community members can articulate their own narratives about settlement and migration that run counter to dominant media discourse, while at the same time attempting (however difficult it may be) to effect real change in the form of employment outcomes, income generation and education. This includes active economic participation through trade, facilitating education and training opportunities, expressing cultural pride through the integration of traditional techniques and aesthetic elements, and disseminating positive images and stories of community cohesion through public events. From 2013 to 2014, the enterprise strategically activated key public spaces across vastly different demographic groups in Melbourne.

14 Ibid.

For example, in 2013, they were invited to present their work in a public event for the National Gallery of Victoria (NGV), a cultural cornerstone of Melbourne. At the time, the NGV had never before presented an exhibition of contemporary Sudanese art or material culture. For the event, the Collective presented a live showcase of their textile design and fashion pieces. A group of elder women also presented a traditional cultural performance involving percussion, dance and song, specific to the Twich language group and region in South Sudan.

The following year, the Collective held a major fashion parade and cultural showcase at the Dandenong Market, a fruit and vegetable market in the outer suburbs of Melbourne known for its affordable offerings and cultural diversity. In this showcase, young men and women presented a mix of traditional and contemporary weaving, beading and fashion pieces. This was followed by a hip hop performance, guest speakers addressing the positive contributions of the young Sudanese community, and elder women from the Twich community talking about cultural tradition. In these two examples of cultural and public spaces that attract audiences from different geographic and socio-economic backgrounds, Twich Women's Sewing Collective created spaces in which to express pride in their cultural differences while also engaging with different public audiences. For Mouffe, critical artistic practice is not determined by its degree of opposition or radicality. She 'challenges the idea that to be political means to offer a radical critique requiring a total break with the existing state of affairs'.[15] Instead, she argues

15 Ibid., p. 104.

that political struggle lies in the transformation and reconfiguration of dominant modes of representation. Artistic practice is a powerful means to effect this reconfiguration in Mouffe's account. She argues 'By constructing new practices and new subjectivities, [artists] can help subvert the existing configuration of power'.[16]

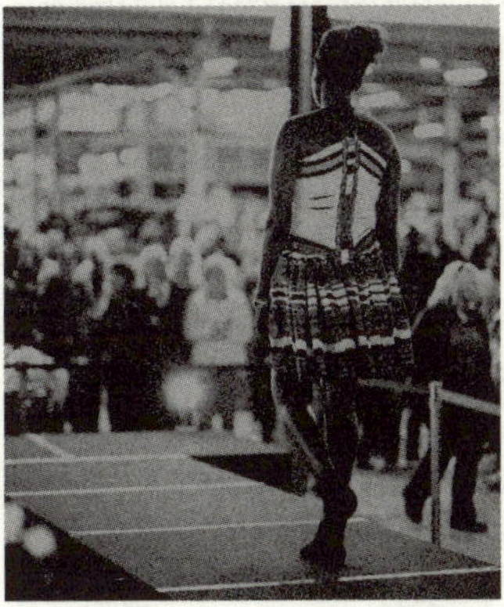

Figure 4: Intricate hand-beaded textile piece, Twich Women's Sewing Collective runway for Cultural Threads, Dandenong Market, Victoria, 2014. Image courtesy of Twich Women's Sewing Collective

In more recent times, the Collective have focused on public engagement through making, teaching and selling, moving away from staging these kinds of larger-scale 'events'. This is partly due to the needs of the group for income generation and partly because of the resource-intensive demands involved when staging public events. Both the NGV and Dandenong Market events were made possible with various kinds of structural and community support: in the former, the NGV provided funding fees for artists, models and musicians, and contributed human resources to programming the event; in the latter, the Collective received support from local council for funding artists and musicians,

16 Ibid., p. 105.

securing the venue and promoting the event. Without consistent funding and institutional support, any further events of this scale rely not only on volunteerism from Twich artists and community members but also on navigating complex power dynamics with institutions, bureaucratic structures (permits, funding applications) and the media (with which, as discussed previously, the Collective have an ambivalent relationshIp). Instead, Twich have continued to showcase their work in community-facing events such as South Sudanese cultural celebrations. Their public-facing activities have moved more towards the entrepreneurial aspects of their work, including the sale of goods at their own store (although it had to close temporarily due to COVID-19 restrictions in 2020–21); in other stores, including Space 2 B in St Kilda and The Social Studio in Collingwood, Melbourne; and at markets and cultural festivals. The advantage of these types of public activations is that the Collective are able to present their work on their own terms, and with a view to meeting the fundamental needs of the community for paid work, work experience and income.

A significant dimension of the Twich Women's Sewing Collective's approach, in this context, is that they resist being represented in favour of self-representation, along with their physical occupation of public spaces. Nyachol John, who is the business manager of Twich and a maker and creative producer, describes the role of these events beyond the aesthetic or promotional: 'We ran a fashion parade not only to let people see our cultural clothing, but to create a bond with the ... community and showcase the cultural diversity that is within Dandenong'.[17] Here, John articulates the role of creative practices in transforming dominant—hegemonic—constructions of the Sudanese Australian community. She speaks to Mouffe's idea of a radical form of democracy that harnesses the power of different and marginal voices in a transformational process, what she describes as agonistic, rather than consensus-based. Mouffe argues, 'The agonistic approach sees critical art as constituted by a manifold of artistic practices bringing to the fore the existence of alternatives to the current post-political order'.[18] What is crucial in Mouffe's formulation is that alternative, critical and radical transformation can emerge from within, rather than in opposition to, mainstream systems.

This position within commercial and cultural systems means that the Collective have to manage ongoing tensions that arise between pursuing economic outcomes, often precariously and in tough conditions, while simultaneously focusing on generating cultural value. Twich therefore occupy an ambiguous position in relation to both the commercial market and the arts sector. It is precisely in this complex position that they are effective in creating cultural change for the South Sudanese community in Australia; however, they do so with limited resources and in public spaces that are at best culturally complex and at worst openly hostile.

17 O'Brien, 'Cultural Threads'.
18 Mouffe, <u>Agonistics</u>, p. xvii.

Can You Be Your Whole Self Without Compromise?: Public Life, Public Accessibility, Public Art and Disability Justice

A Dialogue between Carmen Papalia* and Sam Petersen**

* Carmen Papalia is a Canadian artist who uses organising strategies and improvisation to address his access to public space, the art institution, and visual culture. His work, which takes forms ranging from collaborative performance to public intervention, is a response to the barriers and biases of the medical model of disability. As a convener, he establishes welcoming spaces where those from historically marginalised groups realise their desires for participation through processes rooted in activism, performance and institutional critique. Papalia is a 2019 and 2020 Sobey Art Award recipient. His work has been featured at the Solomon R. Guggenheim Museum, Tate Liverpool, Banff Centre for Arts and Creativity and Gallery Gachet, among other locations.

** Sam Petersen is an artist who works across sculpture, installation, performance and writing. Focusing on themes of identity, disability and sexuality, Petersen often explores the relationships between the body and built spaces, using materials such as plasticine, cling wrap and glitter to highlight the sensual and political aspects of matter and environments. Petersen's most recent exhibitions include My Pee Is Political (Darren Knight Gallery, Sydney, 2020) and Overlapping Magisteria: The 2020 Macfarlane Commissions (Australian Centre for Contemporary Art, Melbourne, 2020–21), where she presented an architectural intervention and lecture performance. For Petersen, spoken word is a powerful format for thinking through feelings, and a mode of addressing 'access, and the lack of it—to places, people's minds and opportunities'.

Editors' note: This is an edited transcript of a conversation that took place in November 2020 over video chat from the artists' respective homes in Vancouver and Melbourne.

Carmen Papalia: I got your talking points. There's a lot to get into; I feel like we have some of the same concerns when it comes to accessibility.

Sam Petersen: Thanks to you, I'm now doing visual descriptions of my work and it's a whole new dimension that I'm very excited about. I think I'm more of a writer than anything else and now I have more to write about. Would you like a visual description?

CP Yes, yes, awesome.

SP Yay. I have mousy brown hair, fair skin. I am wearing a green, black and white plaid shirt and a creamy T-shirt with a face-hugger on it and it's holding up a sign which says, 'Free mask'. I'm in a power wheelchair. Behind me there is blue sci-fi bunting on the wall.

CP I'm intrigued about the policy you are trying to advocate for so that folks who require care or need personal assistance can go to hospital during COVID with their assistants. It's necessary advocacy. I don't know if I shared much about my time in hospital, but I go two or three times a year with my blood condition. I have these really intense painful episodes that are completely debilitating and they can land me in the ICU. I went to the hospital just over a month ago. My wife had to drop me off because of COVID restrictions and I needed visual assistance. I also don't trust healthcare professionals, so it was this intimidating situation where I just had to lend myself to other people's care without even knowing them.

After I was released from the hospital, I was told that I was exposed to COVID in the Emergency Room, so I had to quarantine for two weeks when I came home from the hospital. Luckily, I didn't have COVID. I'd probably not be around if I got COVID.

SP Same, I don't trust healthcare professionals. They aren't given enough time to fully evaluate the situation.

I was terrified at the thought that I could get COVID-19 and would automatically get sent to hospital because my support workers didn't have the PPE to support me and I would have no contact with anyone who knew me. When you have a disability, you can be treated like nothing very fast.

The nurses are so busy and I require a long time for people to understand me. The nurses can get short with me and that can be impossible to deal with when I am sick. It gets to the point where I don't call on them even though I need to.

Even with the hoist and full body sling they use at the hospital to move me in and out of my wheelchair, I have experienced in previous stays that no one really knows how to use it [the hoist] except me, which isn't much help, and they just try to figure it out together. Last time my support worker had to tell them they hadn't put the sling on correctly before they tried to hoist me. I have had them use a sling back to front and another time, the wrong kind of sling.

The people at the top assure me the nurses know how to use a hoist, but I have seen that they don't.

This act of not believing me occurs too often. Nurses will tell me I look tired and put me to bed against my will at 5pm.

CP This relates to one of your points about being infantilised and also the patronising assistance that you get sometimes.

SP Definitely. Could you talk a bit more about coming up against this? Some people assume I can't make my own decisions and look to others or make decisions for me or often ignore me. This infantilisation is huge. Even with people I know, there is this condescension which leaves me out of decision making.

CP This is very much a problem that comes out of the medical model of disability—the idea that people need to be restored or fixed. It comes from the fact that for so long, people with disabilities have not had autonomy; they have not had the ability to self-determine as a community or as a culture. People with disabilities do require care from the medical establishment, but they don't have agency when they're in the care of the medical establishment.

It's intense. We have so many harmful ideas about disability in our culture. Some of them go back to the Bible, such as you're disabled because you have demons or you've sinned, and that [idea] has to be eradicated. I think those harmful ideas are embedded in the medical system. It's evident in these interactions, [in] the fact that when we seek care, it's a one-way relationship. You're supposed to be grateful for the care that you receive, even if it doesn't work for you. And you're not thought to have anything to offer in that interaction; you're just supposed to be a recipient. I think an ideal caring relationship is a reciprocal exchange. That's why I really appreciate care collectives and disabled folks supporting each other, mutual aid that grows out of the disability justice movement.

Disability justice involves building capacity for care within our communities, outside of institutions, outside of the government context, care that we lack on account of governmental failure and medical ableism.

SP That's what I see.

CP Especially in the mental health context, it's definitely about control. The medical-industrial complex is a carceral system in many ways.

There are a lot of people doing advocacy about the intersections of prison abolition and disability justice. There's a new disability justice organisation called the Abolition and Disability Justice Coalition. They emerged in response to the pandemic and the movement for Black lives. This group is addressing the medical establishment as a system of control and comes out of the anti-psychiatry movement, what people call the 'mad movement'.

For example, someone has to sign a paper in order for you to leave the hospital, right? You're being held—sometimes you're even being held in medical custody. There are situations where people are sedated and restrained against their will or don't have an advocate and then are completely coerced into procedures that they don't want, and that's a form of abuse. It's easy to see how these systems cause harm when you consider them in relation to the worlds we make for ourselves in community.

SP [When] I was in rehab, it was humiliating: I had to get clearance to go out on my own. A nurse said 'be careful' and they didn't understand why it was so upsetting.

Once, [when] I was about to have an operation, I moved on the operation table and all the nurses came and got on top of me to keep me still, like a boob blanket. They were scared I would fall off the table. One of them said, 'we better hurry up and put her to sleep'. I was indicating for my speech device because I needed to tell them that I was in an uncomfortable position and wanted to move a little. They were told about my communication device, but they didn't give it to me.

I felt so . . . I haven't got the words. Devastated maybe, and so angry. Like heat all through my chest.

I can see how it happened—they have a chronic lack of time, but that doesn't make it right. They haven't got time for me. They are always assuming the worst of me and others, and therefore seeing the worst of us.

CP You mentioned the term 'infantilised'. I really connected with that. This happens to me all the time: people will ask whomever I am with what I want instead of asking me. They won't talk to me because I'm being guided by a friend. It's like I can't make a decision for myself. I think the reason for that has something to do with the fact that disabled people are still underrepresented in public life. You still don't see too many disabled people out in public places, living full and interesting lives.

SP Yes, it's a vicious circle. People don't see us because so much is inaccessible and this in turn means they don't think of us, so things are not made accessible to us. Poverty can be a really big access problem, because we don't have access built into building laws. For example, many artists can't afford a wheelchair-accessible space, but what is the point if a significant part of the community can't attend? A local Melbourne gallery went from being a wheelchair-accessible gallery to a non-wheelchair-accessible gallery because they wanted to provide free rent to the artists. I peed on their doorstep in protest, but the fuckers liked it.

Poverty is a social construct just like disability is. I am so angry that we are sold this scarcity all the time.

CP There's a real inequality: why do we as disabled people have such low employment numbers? Do we have accessible work options, do we have workplaces that can accommodate the rhythms of our bodies or our capacities as they change and evolve? Very few workplaces are accommodating.

In Canada, I think the numbers are something like around 50 per cent of disabled folks have employment and less than half of the people who have employment have full-time employment. It's because we don't live in a culture where our government meaningfully supports us. It comes down to what we prioritise in our culture. We live under capitalism and that's what divides us.

If you think about ideas of productivity or what it means to contribute to one's society, people with disabilities are completely written off, they're often dismissed as people who are leaching on the system—taking resources instead of contributing. That's what it's reduced to. It would be different if we valued a basic level of social welfare, or we valued collectivism or collective health. Grassroots spaces that are dedicated to disability justice provide a context where care and support are prioritised and people can maintain their dignity.

It comes back to ableism. I learnt about the social model of disability when I was a young college student, and the idea that we are disabled by external conditions resonated with me. Your body is different than other people's bodies. You have pain—of course, those things are difficult—but the conditions that disable us are social, cultural and political.

[We need] a culture shift around ableism—ableist premises, ableist practices in health care and the cultural secctor—we need to embrace different ways of being in the world, not just different ways of learning and participating in the spaces meant for us. Can you be your whole self without compromise? For most people who are disabled, that's a 'no' in most situations, unless you're around people that you can trust.

SP I didn't learn about ableism until I was thirty-five. Like I could see it, but I didn't know it had a name. I went to uni but the books were so inaccessible to me.

There was student help, but they often didn't have good reading voices, or had a heavy accent, that made it hard for me to understand.

Yeah, people are so tired. Even me, I'm so tired of everything, so much ableism. I can only give out so much and the world doesn't listen.

CP Yeah, I feel that. That's why I'm an artist. It's the way that I can shift thinking and it gives me the ability to have agency. I get to propose the kind of world that I want to live in through my work, or make space for the critique that I want us to make more space for. I can advocate in the art context in ways that might influence the wider culture or even policy in some cases. Only as an artist can I replace my cane with a marching band and use that band to navigate the city. [For the public artwork Mobility Device, 2013, Carmen has collaborated with local marching bands in places such as Santa Ana, California and in New York for the High Line, to produce a site-responsive score that uses musical cues to direct Carmen's movements as he explores unfamiliar surrounds. The work creates an alternative and idiosyncratically sonic guiding system to his detection cane.] I want to live in that world, and I think that we really can through creative practice.

What is our position as disabled people in the wider culture; how do we interact with non-disabled people? It's usually in these very limited ways where people are trying to take care of us—it's not in a way that supports our autonomy. As an artist who makes work for public spaces, I can pose a vision for a future or a world that I want to live in where I don't subscribe to those ableist values of my body or my capacity or my productivity or whatever.

Art and creative practice offer so much possibility for us to radically re-envision what a museum could be or what it means to participate in one's community. What care could look like if it was more personal.

I don't know what I'd do if I didn't have art. I've been in dark places feeling completely limited in my ability to change things. I think this comes from my experience of being in hospital and being completely debilitated, and not able to advocate for myself when I'm having an episode, relying on people who are more bound to protocol than care. And that doesn't always go well—the care.

It makes me worried that I don't live in a culture that values my life. We still want to hide disability, but we need to use our presence and creative practice to center ourselves and disrupt public space. I think we do this anyway as disabled people. There's this great example from the United States, [where] these activists with ADAPT were protesting the cuts to the Affordable Care Act as a lot of disabled folks were losing basic services that they relied on, like in-home care. Some of the activists were wheelchair users, and cops were trying to arrest them, but they couldn't—they didn't know what to do with their chairs. It was this interruption of the process of being arrested.

I think we as disabled people make roadblocks in many ways. When I'm ordering a coffee, I have to ask for extra help or, 'What's on the menu?', etc., and people are frustrated standing behind me waiting in line. I'm taking forever. I think that's a place of possibility—that's why I made the work Long Cane, 2009. I created this absurdist fifteen foot [4.5 metre] white mobility cane that I would go on walks with, and it would take the entire sidewalk up and people would have to jump out of my way. It's like I'm inflicting disability on the wider culture.

I feel like people just have to deal with that discomfort. They have to deal with the messiness of the human body, the messiness of our experiences. That's part of humanity. We need to be able to be sick and messy and human—part of being human is having a body that is different.

SP Somebody once said to me, 'Why are you always stopping in the walkway?' The amount of obstacles I have to get through all the time! I love your cane. The sheer audacity of it.

I once created a rainbow burn out [Rainbow Burnout, 2012]—red, yellow and blue chalk mixed with water. I went round and round, right in the middle of the footpath.

CP I think about disability as a culture. I rarely see my experience or the way I understand myself reflected back to me in public or at a museum, and I want to see that more. It's important for

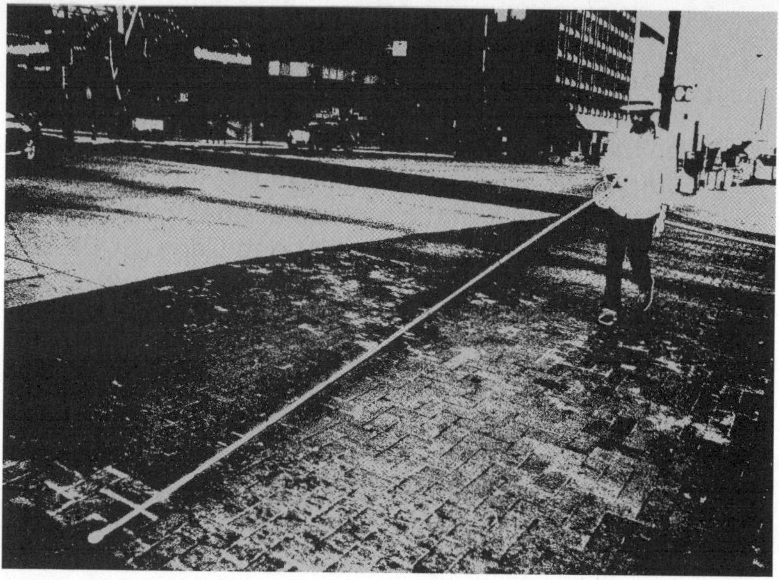

Carmen Papalia, Long Cane 2012, performance, duration variable. Photo: Kristin Rochelle Lantz, courtesy of the artist

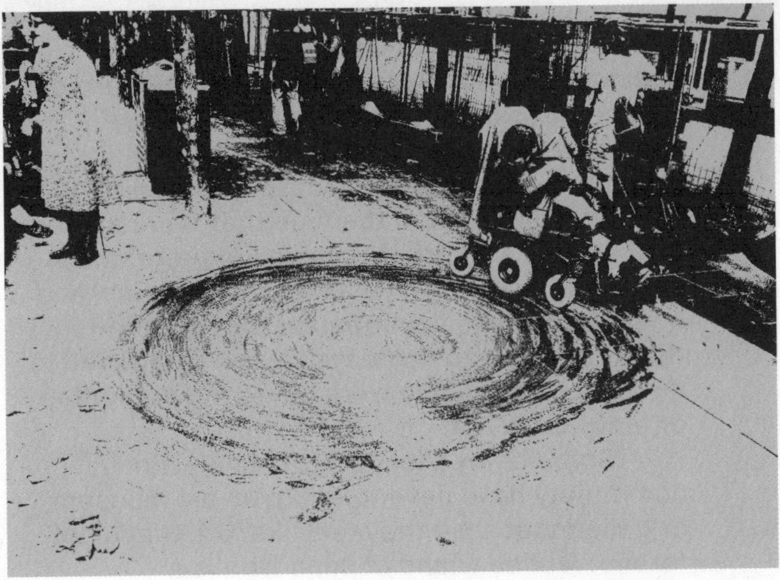

Sam Petersen, Rainbow Burnout 2011, performance with red, yellow, green and blue chalk and wheelchair, Swanston St, Narrm/ Melbourne. Image courtesy of the artist

us to occupy public platforms and start speaking for ourselves and defining the terms around our care and participation in these spaces, and not just as visitors. If you think about the ways museums have engaged people with disabilities from the time they were invited in, it was as a visitor. Accessibility programs in museums grew out of education programs, and it was a patronising model for participation that goes back to the ways we were engaged in medical settings. We were never the presenter or featured artist.

Some of my friends in the low-vision community have never been to an art museum or gallery because they feel like 'Oh, that's not for me'. A blind friend of mine who is a paralympic athlete was surprised when he asked what I was studying in grad school and I said art. These biases exist within the disability community. I think it's due to a tradition of exclusion: we could never imagine ourselves as artists because that experience was not available to us.

SP I'm not very comfortable saying I'm an artist because people see that as childish. Often, I say it anyway because I'm trying to break down the stereotype, but it's still there.

CP I hear this from some of my friends in the disability community who are artists as well. My friend in the UK who is a prominent disabled dancer and scholar told me about a doctor's visit where her doctor asked, 'What do you do for work?' and she explained, 'I'm a dancer' and he replied, 'Really? You're a dancer?' It's bias and it's a form of discrimination. It really limits your perception of self.

SP My work hasn't always been accessible in other ways, like visually, and I'm not sure how to make my art more accessible to non-artists. Maybe that's why I have been turning to spoken word. I can reach further into people's minds with words, make them squirm. And these works can live on YouTube, making them truly public.

CP It isn't your responsibility to make all your work accessible to everybody all the time. Some artists try to do that, but that's extra labour on you, the artist, where you're already concerned with your own access and trying to navigate the barriers that you encounter. It's the responsibility of the institution that's presenting the work to make it accessible to the publics they are catering to. Is it our responsibility, as disabled artists, to make our work accessible to the broader disability community? For me, I started making work in an effort to reach an uninformed, non-disabled audience. I wasn't trying to speak to disabled people when I was making that long cane, I was trying to speak to non-disabled people. I didn't initially think of disabled people as the audience for my work because I figured they already knew what I was trying to say.

When it comes to accessibility, the conditions and the people in the room are always changing—the biases that they bring with them, their politics, are always changing.

So the culture of whatever space we're talking about is always in flux. How can we ensure accessibility is available in all ways on an ongoing basis? I don't think it is possible. I think accessibility is temporary. It's something that has to be achieved collectively through an agreement with everybody in the room. I think of accessibility as a temporary, collectively held space.

In terms of the walking tours I lead [such as Blind Field Shuttle, 2010, a non-visual walking tour for groups of up to ninety people in which participants line up behind the artist, link arms, and agree to shut their eyes for an approximately one hour–long guided walk through cities or rural landscapes], people often ask, 'How do you address accessibility since people who use wheelchairs can't easily participate in that project?' In response, I usually offer an alternative one-on-one experience with eyes closed. I've also modified it in various ways for different audiences. Sometimes I lead walks where it's not everybody lining up behind me and linking arms with me leading at the front, but instead it's me facilitating an experience in a wide open space where participants can shut their eyes and roam independently. I try to figure out what I am offering, and who I am offering it to, and make it available in different ways based on the situation.

SP I know it's not my responsibility to make my work fully accessible, but I also think every iteration of the work is still the work, so I want a hand in that as much as I can.

My work is from the self, so I don't feel it is to any particular audience, but it's very angry and I don't tend to show anger to anyone who has disabilities. So, I guess it's for ables.

CP I have some questions for you, Sam, that I have posed to other disabled artists. Was there a place that you have worked or an experience that you have had as an artist that you would characterise as being accessible? Alternatively, was there a place or experience that was disabling?

SP My 2017 solo show at the old TCB Art Incorporated was located at an art space that was far from wheelchair accessible and didn't address many other accessibilities. It had a few flights of rickety stairs with no rails and no lift. The exhibition I made was called I'm Not There Because I Couldn't Be There.

CP I really like that. Not the lack of access, your title.

SP That was the reason I said 'yes' to having a show there—so I could make a statement about not being there. I had put plasticine on the back of blank canvases so that they couldn't see it. It was amazing how many people still asked at the opening, 'Where is Sam?' [In the gallery's Instagram posts about the exhibition, there were reminders that the gallery was not wheelchair accessible.]

They simply could not see the lack of access. I had them sprinkle yellow glitter all over the floor of the gallery (wee representations). I like to think that it was the last straw. They had been there for years, and mine was the last exhibition they showed there.

CP That's really funny and sad. It reminds me of an artist friend in New York, Shannon Finnegan. She was in a group show and the gallery was up a flight of stairs but there's another space at the bottom of these stairs. To address the inaccessibility of the venue, she established what she called the 'Anti-Stairs Club Lounge' which was this space that you could only access if you signed an agreement and vowed not to ever step foot in the gallery. If you agreed not to use the stairs, you would be invited into this comfortable space that was more accessible from a disability perspective.

SP Awesome.

CP Yeah, she also did this at The Vessel in New York City. This newly built performance venue is not fully accessible. The city funded it and it's supp-osed to be this exciting presentation space. Shannon hosted a protest there and had people sign declarations about not ever stepping foot into the venue as long as it was inaccessible.

SP Wow.

CP Another question: what actions are necessary in order to establish a context where the contributions of disabled artists/curators/creative practitioners can take root and thrive and become a vital part of the cultural ecology?

SP For people to slow down and respect everyone. I see that as the big thing stopping us.

CP Can someone who is disabled be separated from the effort to negotiate barriers in public life?

SP No, I can't separate art and activism. More people need to start by giving up space, space that isn't theirs to give.

CP I wonder if we can't separate art and activism because as disabled people who are trying to be self-determined and autonomous as artists and to make a statement about the world we want to live in, we are politicised. Because we're underrepresented, we don't hold a position of privilege in our communities. My friend in Portland who is a disabled dancer has observed, 'It shouldn't be radical to be independent as a disabled person', but that's where we're at because, given the circumstances, we are in survival mode most of the time.

Can you make art not about disability or your experience? I don't know if I can. For me, that wouldn't be interesting either because that would be a luxury. I don't think I can spend my time not making work about disability, not doing advocacy or something that improves my life or experience.

SP Totally.

CP When you think about accessibility or mutual support in the communities that you belong to/serve, what comes to mind? What does accessibility mean in your community and how is it practiced?

SP I am not really part of anything. Maybe I will be but I'm not counting on it. Community is where you feel safe and accepted and I have never felt that. Many people let me down and that isn't safe.

CP Do you have disability justice organisations or places that are radical, like grassroots disability-led spaces, in Australia? What's the scene? The sense that I get from other people is that it is limited. I didn't know about the disability arts movement until I met another disabled artist. I didn't know there was a world out there of radical disabled folks who loved parts of their experience and wanted to share that with others and felt proud to be disabled. I think it's internalised ableism that doesn't allow us to love our experience. I love the perspective that I have and the way that I can navigate the world because I am disabled.

There's even parts of my really severe pain condition that I love. It's made me a really good advocate for myself and a problem-solver, and it's brought me closer to other people. I make close relationships with people, I have to make relationships that are based on trust because I need their help, I need their support, and I need them to understand what I need when I'm in an emergency. I don't know if I'd have that sense of myself or that perception of myself if I didn't find other disabled people who were banding together and making art, posing these critiques and making space for these discussions.

You feel really alone sometimes, when you're not aware that others are out there, or you forget that others are out there. At my most isolated moments, I think about the fact that people like you are out there doing your work and you care about these things too. We're all contributing to parts of the same project. I need to stay connected to community to remember that there is progress. It's a hard thing though because we are very much underrepresented in the arts, in public life, especially now with COVID. People are less outside in public now, especially people with vulnerable immune systems. I would die if I got COVID. I have had to really limit my interactions.

There really is power in numbers and there's power in community, especially when it's a disability-led space.

SP Totally. Yeah, it is the connection with others and the lack of it for so long. It can still be overwhelming.

CP Do you know the Disability Visibility Project? It's a website and a podcast run by Alice Wong, an activist in California. It is such an affirming space for disability culture. When you're on the site, as a screen reader, all the images are described and they're described with care, and that non-visual experience is really considered. Alice is bringing her own experience and her perspective of disability to the site, and it's all content that is by and for disabled people and it's beautiful. It's a space where you can see the vibrancy of disability culture.

It makes such a difference when it's a space that's for and by disabled people. I think about stuff like disability on Twitter or disabled Twitter or whatever they call it, people make an effort to describe their images. They know who their audience is, it's other disabled people. I like that effort and practice because that's the kind of responsive, connected community that I want to be part of. For some of my disabled friends, these online spaces are some of the only places they can find connection with people like them.

SP Thank you, and there are some awesome people I know, it's just hard for us to connect.

CP I feel the same way. Before COVID times, it was hard to connect too, just getting coordinated to meet another group. I like to make the joke: 'How am I going to find another blind person anyway?'

SP Have things become more accessible for you during the pandemic?

CP Staying in touch with people has been easier. While it is just on Zoom, I've been talking to a lot of friends that way. In some ways it's completely restrictive too, and I feel super vulnerable now in terms of my health and the places that I can go safely.

COVID has been super destabilising on a major scale for so many reasons, and there's some potential there for things to change. I think when the world returns—I'll just say 'returns' because I don't like using the word 'normal'—I think people are thinking about how can we do things better, how can we accommodate people better? At a large scale right now, people are having to navigate their own vulnerability when they've never really had to think about it before and to deal with inconveniences that are out of their control.

That's the experience of being disabled: you're in a constant state of vulnerability, there's inconveniences, there's barriers that you just have to put up with, there's all these things out of your control. In some ways, it's great practice for people in general to have that experience of not having things instantly accessible for them. I've seen it shift the way people talk to each other too, just in meetings and stuff with people asking, 'How are you? How's everyone feeling today?' When did we even want to make space for the way people felt in a corporate setting before COVID? Now people are like, 'How are you feeling?' and people actually say that they're depressed, they say that they're feeling anxious, worried, they've had a death in the family.

There's a reason for people to offer care more than they did before, and I think that's a good thing. I read somewhere that times after pandemic have historically been times of social cohesion and that people are less likely to put up with inequality. It's hard to be hopeful right now and I obviously feel super depressed with what's going on over here. I heard in Melbourne there's no cases right now and people are back to their routines in some way. In Canada, it's pretty terrible. It's hard to keep that hopefulness, but what makes me feel not completely crushed is that the pandemic has been a time of communities coming together to support each other with all the mutual aid efforts, the free meal programs, the free counselling services that are becoming immediately available. I feel very lucky to be working as an artist right now, and to be honest I have [had] more work and more support to do the work I do since the pandemic. And I'm able to work from home, which is amazing. A lot of museums right now are asking, 'How do we do accessibility better?' They're actually asking the question, 'How do we do this?' and I feel like it's time that we tell them exactly how to do it, and it's not just about providing the basics or those conventional accessibility offerings or services. It's about radically re-envisioning what it means to participate—so you can participate on your terms.

How do you change or re-envision systems and practices so they're more supportive of the rhythm of the disabled body? What if a non-profit or a museum or a gallery or public art program or whatever was to, instead of trying to achieve growth on an ongoing basis, actually follow the rhythm of a disabled body and reassess what should be prioritised from season to season? For myself, my pain condition is triggered with changes in weather and barometric pressure. I work differently in the winter than I do in the summer. What if a gallery did the same thing? Maybe there's times where it wouldn't offer public programming because it needed to address its internal functions.

SP Totally. We used to live with the seasons. That slowing down doesn't happen anymore.

Note: Sam Petersen would like to inform readers that since this interview was recorded, a new disability justice group, the Australian Disability Justice Network (DJN), has formed. DJN is 'led by and for multiply-marginalised disabled people across so-called Australia', comprising members who have come together 'in the spirit of love and justice' to 'share space, organise, provide mutual aid, and care for each'.

For a New Lexicon and Other Attitudes
Tania Bruguera*

* Tania Bruguera is a Cuban artist and activist now based in the United States, where she is a senior lecturer in media and performance at Harvard University. Her performances, installations and Arte Útil (Useful Art) projects focus on the application of art to everyday political life, often intervening in institutional structures of collective memory, education and politics. A self-described initiator rather than author, Bruguera often collaborates with multiple institutions and individuals, and was named a 'Top 100 Global Thinker' by Foreign Policy magazine in 2015. Bruguera was the inaugural artist-in-residence at the New York City Mayor's Office of Immigrant Affairs. She established the Arte de Conducta (Behaviour Art) program at the Instituto Superior de Arte, Havana, in 2002; the Hannah Arendt International Institute for Artivism in 2015; and recently addressed the 13th Annual Geneva Summit for Human Rights and Democracy, in 2021.

Editors' note: This is an edited transcript of the keynote presentation Tania Bruguera gave at the Let's Go Outside: Making Art Public symposium.

I've been back and forth considering what to talk about today because I have had many different experiences in the public sphere, working in collective as well as public art. These ways of working are informed by different concepts but sometimes they mix together. One of the first things that I had to endure as an artist was the fact that I was defined by other people. I studied in a wonderful school, the School of the Art Institute in Chicago, which is one of the best art schools, but I entered the master program there already with experience. I knew where I was coming from and how my background informed my art.

This was many years ago; things have changed a little bit now. At that time, people didn't know much about Latin American art, and nothing about Cuban art. And one of the first important artistic experiences I had was to make the critics stop when they saw my work. They would struggle to define my practice and say, 'Oh yeah, you do performance. You are a feminist, you are this, you are that.' They were applying so many labels, but I felt they didn't know what I was doing or why I was doing it. So, I decided to start creating terms that defined my practice.

For me, [creating terms] is a political gesture but also a long-term performance that I enact with the critics. I came up with words and concepts that I felt were more complete in defining my practice, but also as a strategy to cause the critics to stop and say, 'What?' Most of my defining terms are in Spanish, such as Arte Útil, so the critics don't even know how to pronounce them properly—which I enjoyed. I want to talk about this as one of my practices.

I also want to say that in the public sphere, I use two techniques: one is to work with positive energy; one is to work with negative energy. When I work with positive energy—for example, the work I just did in Manchester [School of Integration, 2019, for the Manchester International Festival 2019 and Manchester Art Gallery]—everybody loves it, because everybody wants a future where actions are made that result in people being ethically and emotionally fulfilled, and where they are lifted out of their political frustrations.

In basic terms, this project involved inverting an integration school for immigrants; instead of the immigrants, asylum seekers and refugees being the ones being taught, they became the professors, teaching the local English people their knowledges and stories.

The School of Integration was a positive energy project. Why? Because everybody ends up happy. The community is happy because they are empowered. The people who came—even the English people—had to deal with a little bit of uneasiness, but then they said, 'Okay, we learnt something'. The institution is happy because this is a case study they can share with donors, the public, artists, etc. I think this is positive energy when the artist is fulfilling the hope of others.

I also work with negative energy—not so nice. Negative energy means when you are in the position as an artist to say what nobody wants to say; where you are going to have to confront public opinion; where you have to say things that people are literally going to try to stop you from saying—whether it's the curator you work with, the institution, or the public. I'm going to talk more about negative energy because I learn more from [these kinds of projects], although I have to do one positive project after a negative one, because the negatives are very hard.

The first thing I do with these kinds of negative energy projects is understand who my ally is. This is necessary when you're going to do critical work, whether it's institutional critique or political critique. These kinds of projects are a long journey where you sometimes don't have the answers and likely need to consult with, and listen to, others to understand what you should do and the best way to do it. In these circumstances, I think it is very important to understand the institution you are working with, and even the curator.

Right now, I'm working in New York because somebody invited me to do a project. I've been dying to do a project about Donald Trump since he was elected President. The institution is also keen to do something on Trump, but the curator is not the right person to help realise it. So, I decided that if the institution wants to work with me, I need to work with the education and social engagement curators. Why? Because I understand that the dialogue is going to be intense and severe, so you need people who understand how to facilitate that. The other thing that you need to understand when you do this kind of work, at least in my case, is that there is always a component of institutional education. I'm not saying that I know everything—I learn a lot through all of my projects—but you have to show generosity to the institution as well. They are sometimes in a very difficult situation. Sometimes, there are people who think like you but they can't do anything, so you also have to understand the people working in the institution. That's very important.

For me, art is not a process of producing something. I'm not interested in a result defining the process. I don't want to do something where we are ready before we start and know what is going to circulate, how it is going to circulate, what shape it has. I'm interested in understanding art as implementing a process. Why? Because in the social sphere, first of all you cannot impose the time of art. Today, ten minutes spent in front of an artwork is a long time. But you cannot implement a ten-minute socially engaged work. You can't change anything in ten minutes. It is important to understand that that's the process I have; it's an implementation process that defines the ethics of the project and where the energies are going to be.

I'm currently working on a book with Claire Bishop where we talk about a number of concepts.[1] But I want to talk about two specifically because I think they are quite current. The first one is Political Timing Specific, and the second is Arte Útil.

When I was younger, I felt that the term 'site-specific' was not enough, because while it included the cultural aspects of a given site, it didn't sufficiently address the political aspects. I'm a political artist. For people to appreciate my work, they need to understand the political sensitivities that are around at that time. For me, Political Timing Specific is a better term, as it describes work that is done in response to, and defined by, the politics of the time. So while the artist cannot force what you're seeing, the work absorbs the surrounding politics and its contradictions or impositions. I'm

1 Ileen Kohn and Donna Wingate (eds), Tania Bruguera in Conversation with/en Conversación con Claire Bishop, Fundación Cisneros, New York, 2020.

going to give two examples [of my work] and do a little test about which one you think is Political Timing Specific and which one is not.

One piece is Tatlin's Whisper #5 [2008]. It involved mounted police who had been invited to come to the Tate Modern's Turbine Hall to test their crowd control techniques with the museum's audience. The other piece is called Yo También Exijo [a 2014 restaging of the 2009 participatory artwork Tatlin's Whisper #6, originally presented at the tenth Havana Biennial where attendees were invited to step up to a podium and speak freely for one minute]—meaning 'I also demand'—which involved an invitation to people to go to Revolution Square in Havana and assemble and speak freely, after US President Barack Obama and Cuban President Raúl Castro had decided to re-open the relationship between the two countries. It's important to remember that in Cuba, to come out in public is different than it is in other places. The amount of people who attended that piece was amazing, given everybody was afraid.

The project started with a letter I wrote to Presidents Obama and Castro and Pope Francis, asking them what was going to happen now that relationships had re-opened. Because it was in Cuba, people were not happy or angry, they were just disturbed. They didn't know what was going to happen as a consequence of this new relationship; there was no explanation. In that moment when everything was changing, I felt that art had the possibility to enter and do what art does best, which is to give meaning to things. The aim was to test if free speech could happen. What happened was there was a consequence: eighty-three people were detained by the government. Which one do you think is Political Timing Specific: the first or the second one?

Audience member: Second.

Tania Bruguera: Second, okay, yes. Smart group. Well, part of what happens with Political Timing Specific is that the form of the work is unstable. Why? Because you don't define the next step and you don't define the meaning of the political gesture that others enact in response. And when I say 'others', I am not only talking about governments, I am also talking about people.

I think it's important when you do this kind of work to be open to what is happening and how people are reacting to it. But also to understand that making public art sometimes means making something public that is supposed to be private. That's also very negative energy. In this case, I was interrogated by the government more than thirty times.

In one of the interrogations, the interrogator, who was not very smart, recited to me the Wikipedia definition of Vladimir Tatlin, because I was using Vladimir Tatlin in the work's title. And she said, 'Oh, Vladimir Tatlin, but he's a revolutionary', and I said, 'Me too'. And then I thought, 'Oh great, I can have an educational moment now'. Some of the interrogators, not all of them, were up for this exchange. Others were very intense. As much as I could, I held these classes for my interrogator, where I taught them the difference between theatre and performance, between political art and socially engaged art and public art as well.

In the process, I said, 'Well, maybe what I should do is art. I should make this a permanent artwork'. I knew the Havana Biennial was coming, and I knew they [the government] were going to

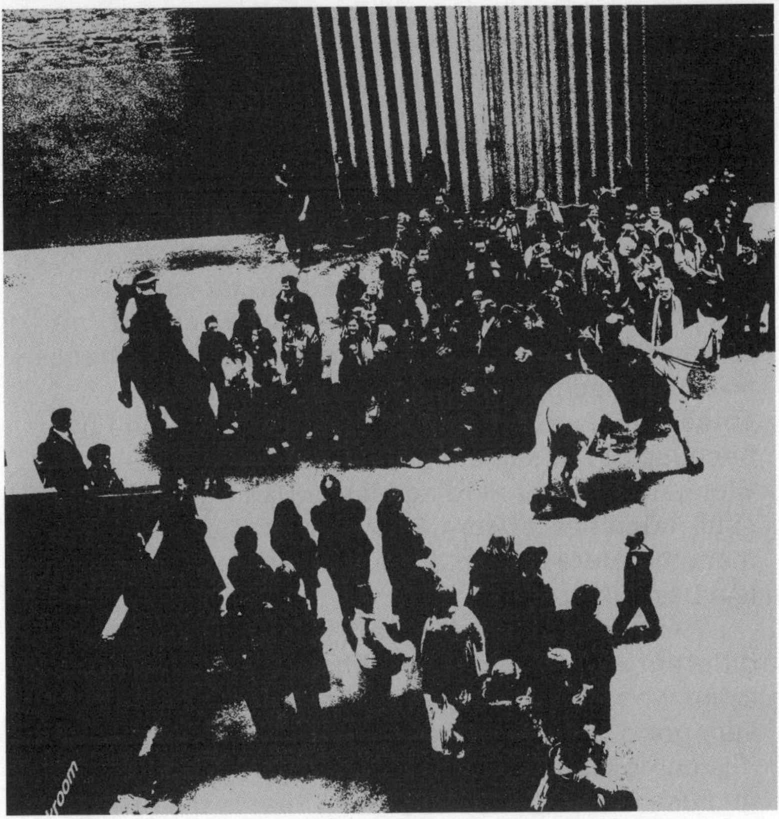

Tania Bruguera, Tatlin's Whisper #5 2008.
Performance, Tate Modern, London, 2008.
Image courtesy of Estudio Bruguera

create a fake case against me, so I decided to use their technique on myself. I self-surveilled myself by recording myself 24/7 while under house arrest as a performance to avoid the government implicating me in something that I hadn't done. And I was right. At some point, they accused me of making a scandal somewhere. I said, 'I'm sorry, I have the tapes. I surveilled myself, so you can see the tapes.'

I decided the performance was, as I call it, 'art for the not yet' or 'the yet to come'. The performance involved reading Hannah Arendt's Origins of Totalitarianism 24/7. Somebody told me, 'Don't do it because at the same time for the 2015 Venice Biennale they are reading Marx's Das Kapital' and I said, 'I don't care. Here, in Cuba, it has a different meaning. Here it is Political Timing Specific. There, it is a beautiful project.'

And for me, that is what makes my work different—it's my struggle with the art world. The artist who presented the reading of Das Kapital is a very good friend of mine and a great guy, but I think it is complicated how art takes the political meaning and use value out of everything. That is the struggle I have with the art world—where everything becomes beautiful and often un-useful.

In this case, I said, 'Okay, I cannot leave the house so I'm going to put a speaker directed outside and the voice can travel alone.' But of course, the government sent some guys who started operating jackhammers in front of my house so I could not be heard over them. So, I said, 'Okay, fine. You have to have lunch.' So, at lunchtime, I did the reading to them. What I like about this is that the piece made the government respond creatively. That's the Cuban government's artwork—sending the workers with jackhammers and making a hole in the street. It was very significant to me that as a political artist who is always trying to reach to the political with the means I have—which is not so much—that the political people then reached me, creatively. I was really very happy about that.

The second concept, Arte Útil, is one that I think comes out of being Cuban. I'm a very proud Cuban; I'm very proud of the original Revolution. Why? Because I think if you want to understand my work and all the art that comes from socialist places, you have to understand how we were educated. And we were educated asking ourselves for whom we do the work, and why we do the work—and it's never for you, never for your own pleasure. I know if you're a psychologist, you will not like that, but it is always this idea that you do things for others.

Arte Útil is more than me. I did a project at the Van Abbemuseum in Eindhoven out of which a group of people formed who also work on Arte Útil. It starts with a few guidelines. We don't call artists 'artists', we call them 'initiators'. Why? Because we want to acknowledge that artists don't own the whole content of the work. We don't see our work like art: we see it as case studies. Why? Because we think things can be improved and changed. We believe you can take somebody's idea and do it differently and appropriate it. We understand that spectators are 'users', that the museum is a civic space—which is easier said than done—and that the result of an artwork is not produced but implemented.

You might be like: 'Hey, Tania, you're inventing all these things. What are you talking about?' Let me prove that I have thought about it a lot. I made a diagram one day to explain to people what I was thinking. Basically, my work is situated in the tension between the information/the data and the affect/the emotions. This is the axis of my work and what I'm always struggling with is how much art and how much reality to include—hopefully it will meet in the middle. But the centre of the work is understanding that the work has a double ontology; it belongs to two worlds simultaneously. It comes from two places—either the political and the artistic, or the social and artistic—and it has to work in both.

I'm open to all art, but I personally don't like art that claims to be social or political but where people in politics or people who are in communities don't even know about it or don't understand it. I think such work must have a double language—a language where the public the artist is talking to can understand it, while simultaneously employing the language of the artist. This is because I think that public artists must contribute something to art, but they also have to contribute something to whatever sphere they're dealing with. This is not easy to do, but I try to every time.

I was very happy and feeling like I was a genius, because I had discovered Arte Útil—a new thing. Oh, beautiful ignorance. Then I started researching and I discovered that Arte Útil existed way before my original proposal. There are different cases where people have actually used the words Arte Útil, or 'useful art' in English. One case study is the artist Eduardo Costa who made a proposal in 1969 for a project in New York called 'Useful Art Works'.[2] Artist

2 Costa, in collaboration with Scott Burton, proposed that art would have a direct social impact and utility by improving city living conditions. See 'Useful Art Works', Arte Útil Archive,

Pino Poggi also wrote his first manifesto of 'Arte Utile' in 1965.[3] Then there was an architect Juan O'Gorman who in 1933 gave a lecture about artistic art and the 'arte útil'.[4] Of course, you also can go back to Ruskin and so on.[5] For me, discovering these precedents was a beautiful moment. What was beautiful about it was understanding that we had uncovered a parallel art history, with Arte Útil case studies going back to the 1800s. With colleagues at Van Abbemuseum, we worked towards coming up with a parallel timeline that demonstrated this practice had been done for many years.

The question we usually ask ourselves is 'What is art?' Alternatively, what we could ask ourselves is: 'What is art for?' And then you can see the same piece but understand something different. The only paintings we have in the archive of Arte Útil are the

Nr. 032, accessed 18 June 2021, https://www.arte-util.org/projects/useful-art-works/.

3 See Pino Poggi, 'Manifesto: Arte Utile 1', Arte Utile, accessed 18 June 2021, https://www.arte-utile.net/manifestos/manifesto-arte-utile-1/.

4 O'Gorman's lecture 'El arte "artistico" y el arte útil' (Aesthetic Art and Useful Art) was given at the National School of Plastic Arts (ENAP) in Mexico City on 9 June 1933 and self-published by the architect and painter in 1934. A reprint was published by the Instituto Nacional de Bellas Artes, Mexico City, in 2005.

5 John Ruskin's lecture 'The Relation of Art to Use' is included in his volume <u>Lectures on Art</u>, George Allen, London, 1904, pp. 115–49. See also 'Lectures and Other Essays', Arte Útil Archive, Nr. 118, accessed 18 June 2021, https://www.arte-util.org/projects/lectures-and-other-essays/.

Yirrkala bark petitions. [The Yirrkala bark petitions, 1963, named for the East Arnhem community in Australia's Northern Territory, asserted the Yolŋu right to traditional lands on the Gove Peninsula that had been excised without consultation for bauxite mining purposes. They were the first petitions recognised by the Australian Parliament to combine painting with typed text on paper, embedding Indigenous lore in the tradition of Commonwealth law.[6]] Works such as this mark for us the shift: you can look at something like this as a shape, as a form, as colours, as movement etc., but you can see it too in the context of how it was utilised.

The fact that this painting was used to negotiate politics is what makes it Arte Útil. Why? Because Arte Útil is when you use art beyond art itself, or you try to use art for other means. Why? Because I and the various curators who have worked on the concept with me at different institutions believe that art is a tool that can facilitate change in things that in other social and political spheres may be locked, or cannot be developed. That's the belief.

I'm going to give you a few examples of Arte Útil projects as the best way to understand it. This is a project from Núria Güell, which was made in the context of the banks in Spain evicting people from

6 See 'Yirrkala Bark Petitions signed', Deadly Story, accessed 18 June 2021, https://www.deadlystory.com/page/culture/history/Yirrkala_Bark_Petitions_signed and 'Yirrkala bark petitions 1963 (Cth)', Documenting a Democracy, Museum of Australian Democracy at Old Parliament House, accessed 18 June 2021, https://www.foundingdocs.gov.au/item-sdid-100.html.

their houses.[7] Núria together with a group of activists started researching the law and found out that, in Spanish law, to trespass is defined as breaking the lock.

So she, as an artist, decided she was going to do a project about this phenomenon and she hired a construction worker to take out all the locks from the houses from where people were evicted. Sometimes, she even took off the doors, because these were abandoned places. When activists were informed the piece was done, they informed the families and the families returned legally back to their houses. That 'wow' is the Arte Útil aesthetic. That moment where you think something cannot be changed, but it can if you believe art can help. That's what we call Arte Útil.

I'll give you another example. Rolling Jubilee is a project coming out of Occupy Wall Street, instigated by Strike Debt, a group of activists, artists and organisers who identified that one of the biggest problems in the US is student loans. They teamed up with a lawyer and an economist and people who know about how such loans and debt operate, and set up a structure in which they could legally copy how debt collection agencies buy up loans from banks.[8] It's one penny for a dollar, so with a million dollars, you can buy millions worth of debt.

7 See the descriptions of Intervención #1 (Intervention #1), 2012, on the artist's website and in the Arte Útil Archive, both accessed 18 June 2021, https://www.nuriaguell.com/portfolio/intervencion-1/, https://www.arte-util.org/projects/intervention-1/.

8 See 'The Rolling Jubilee', Arte Útil Archive, Nr. 161, accessed 18 June 2021, https://www.arte-util.org/projects/the-rolling-jubilee/.

In this case, Strike Debt set up a structure and invited people to give money through a crowdfunding platform, and with the money they bought and liberated by now more than $30 million worth of medical and educational loans.[9] And when they buy the loans, they find the people who hold the debt, and call them and say, 'You have been liberated'. And it's beautiful because it also makes you think: what is contemporary slavery? So, to undertake Arte Útil is to not be simply utilitarian. It's not just gross usefulness. It's not about you benefitting from it. It's about creating something that benefits other people, the people who are using the work.

These are independent groups and artists doing stuff, but my question is how can we do this better or long term or with more research but with institutions?

The challenge public institutions have is not only to change the way they talk about art or how they are using art, but also to counter their event-driven mentality. Institutions seem happy when they have many events and are satisfying this kind of culture we're living in, which is quick satisfaction and one thing after the other—you don't have to think about it, you don't have time to process your experience. What I would love is to see public institutions shift to the culture of implementation, understanding that maybe they do less but they do it for longer and make a long-term public commitment. And of course, when I say 'implementation', I mean social implementation—actions taking place in society.

9 See Rolling Jubilee website, https://rollingjubilee.org/.

We have resolved many issues in art, but I would love to see art that is implemented in reality—that doesn't have to be a shower curtain with an artist's drawing on it or a cup with an Andy Warhol design—but art that is actually centred in the ways people live their daily lives and that is generative.

And this raises the question of how to serve the people. For me, public art should not aim to be about a community that already exists, but instead to create a new community. What I can do is create new communities that would not have existed if the artwork had not happened. This results from the civic engagement that a community will have through the work.

I will finish by describing a project at the Tate Modern because it's an example of the kind of project where a new community is created. Working in the Turbine Hall is the one thing that every artist wants. But as soon as they invite you, you are like: 'Why? Why do I have to do this?' because it's very challenging. I had a lot of things I had to consider. The one thing I was clear on was that I was not going to do a super spectacular piece.

I decided that I wanted to ask the institution a question. The question was: how can an institution that is so powerful in the art world also be part of its surrounding community? People who have worked with me know that I spend more time imagining the audience than imagining the work I'm doing. I have this habit where I imagine every kind of potential person that will see the work and what their reaction will be.

In this case, however, it was impossible, because the audience for this is three million people. I cannot imagine three million people. Most of them are also passersby and tourists, so I decided I wanted to focus on the institution as a civic institution. I knew I wanted to do an invisible piece, one where people entering would ask: 'Where is the piece? Where is the art?' To me, it's the best question people can ask. I love that.

First, I looked back at all the projects that had been done in the Turbine Hall, and I said to the director Frances Morris: 'I want to do a social engagement project. I want to do a community-based project'. The result is [10,148,451, 2019] the first Tate Turbine commission that is community-based, meaning not working with the community but giving the community the power to decide what is going on in the space.[10]

It involved many different elements. [One was] a soundscape that was invisible; you couldn't really notice it and its technical components blended into the building.[11] We also had the element of a hidden image, where people had to work in order to the see the art. I finally did a painting, so now I can say I'm a painter.

I decided that one of the biggest models for community art is the mural. Instead of painting it on the wall, I wanted to do it on the floor—a mural that cannot be seen unless you are above it. We painted this huge mural. I worked with amazing curators including Catherine Wood, and director Frances

10 See 'Tania Bruguera: 10,148,451', Tate, accessed 18 June 2021, https://www.tate.org.uk/whats-on/tate-modern/exhibition/hyundai-commission-tania-bruguera.

11 The soundscape was designed to fill the hall with low frequency, unsettling energy that visitors would feel in their bodies.

Morris, and they were saying that only big dictators get such big portraits. I responded, 'Yeah, it's time for a normal person to get a big portrait too'.

We painted the whole floor with a special ink that is thermochromic [a heat-sensitive pigment that reacted to body heat when visitors worked together and lay on the floor to reveal the image]. I wanted people to walk onto the floor of the Turbine Hall without knowing that somebody's portrait was there; there was a story there that nobody was seeing, because I was talking about immigration and immigrant communities, and they are mostly invisible.

But the other thing that was interesting for me is that the work can only be seen through collective effort, because change can only be seen if we all work together. There is no one person who is going to change anything. I wanted to have a direct metaphor, let's say, where two hundred people needed to use their bodies together to heat up the floor, so viewers above could see the portrait.

Another part of the project was to make people cry for no reason. This piece has a lot to do with social media and specifically Facebook. It's my response to the way that Facebook users often behave 'correctly'. We have to 'like' something even when something is horrible, but what are we really doing? I wanted to create this situation where people had the physical reaction without having the emotional background for the reaction. So, I made people cry [in a small room containing an organic compound that induced tears in people's eyes]. They were also given a stamp on the back of their hand—and of course there are many historical precedents of stamps that I respect and am also interested in—that involved the number of people who had migrated last year, plus the number of migrants deaths so far that year.[12]

For me, it was very important that the piece had an unstable title. Every day, the title of the piece changed—on the website, physically through the stamp. Why? Because I wanted people who came to see the work to research the title of the day. To do this research, you had to go to the website of the International Organization for Migration (IOM)'s Missing Migrants Project. I wanted people to have this relationship with the piece.

The most important part of the work and why I feel it was good—what I liked, at least—was the creation of Tate Neighbours [a collective of twenty-one people who lived or worked in the same postcode as Tate Modern, and who represent the local community]. Over five months, we met every week for two hours, sometimes more, because I wanted to understand what was missing in the situation for them. Some of these people would never have met unless this project happened. They were people who had nothing to do with each other; one of them had never entered the Tate Modern, yet lived one block away.

As a group, we decided that this piece is about how to rethink the relation the institution has with social values. One thing that came up many times was the naming of the Tate Modern's buildings. For example, one building was named after a wealthy Russian philanthropist. We felt that, nowadays, a lot

12 The changing number that was also the work's title was created using data supplied by the International Organization for Migration (IOM)'s Missing Migrants Project. See https://missingmigrants.iom.int/.

of people buy their way in to public recognition and we wanted to go back to the times in which you had to do something amazing in your life for somebody to recognise you and to make the gesture of changing the name of a building for you.

As a result, we chose Natalie Bell, a social worker who had worked for thirty years in the neighbourhood around the Tate, literally saving the lives of hundreds of kids from the street. We decided to rename the Tate Modern's Boiler House 'Natalie Bell' and we made a plaque, copying the one that named the Russian donor. For us, it was very important to include the word 'contribution' and to rethink what that word means.

And of course, we changed the name everywhere—on all the printed material, elevators, etc. This made us very happy because we never thought it was going to happen. To get your name on a building or gallery requires donating £100 million, so in a way, the Tate Modern lost £100 million in order to do this piece. I think that's beautiful.

When the Tate Modern first heard about a re-naming, some were annoyed, because they were like: 'Oh my God, now who?' We took a long time to decide which person, but when we told them who it was, they were so excited. Frances, Tate Modern's director, has told me she has a problem now as the Tate staff don't want to remove the name. The name was supposed to remain for the few months of the commission, but it has been there for a year, and Frances told me recently that they're going to leave it for a little longer. I love leaving institutions with problems to solve.[13]

13 The building name remains as 'Natalie Bell' as of 12 January 2022.

What is most interesting with named buildings is that the people who give money are visible, which I think is also important, as well as people who contribute in other ways. At some point, the group wanted to take out the Russian donor's name and I said, 'No, it's more beautiful to see both his name and Natalie Bell on the buildings and to have this dialogue.'

To return to the portrait in the Turbine, [you may be wondering] who the guy painted so big on the floor is. The idea arose when we told Natalie Bell—who is an amazing person who totally deserved to have the building named after her—what we intended to do and she responded, 'Why are you doing this? I haven't done anything.' I'm like: 'You're crazy.' We talked to her and we said, 'Okay, give us an example of one of the hundreds of people you work with', and she gave an example of Yousef, a refugee from Syria who went to the United States, was deported, and arrived in the UK. He was living on the streets when Natalie met him, and due to her help he is now studying biomedicine. It is Yousef's image on the floor. For me, it was very important to highlight a positive story about an immigrant. It was important to have this kind of hope in the work. And, of course, people cried.

I hoped that there would be money from the commission to keep the group of Tate Neighbours together. It has not been possible, however, and we're struggling a bit to keep this group together. I also think that things should be done when they are needed. I think part of why we are in this empty culture of contemplation and beauty is because we do things that we don't need to do. Arte Útil is something for the 'not yet', so these are projects where you are trying to do work for what has not happened. What I and the communities involved in these projects want is to transform affect into political effectiveness. Thank you.

Our City in Summer

Mish Grigor*

* Mish Grigor's work is situated in an expanded performance practice that includes making theatre, curating events, holding public dialogues, creating socially engaged projects and occasionally publishing. She is co-director of experimental arts organisation APHIDS, one third of the collaboration POST with Zoe Coombs Marr and Natalie Rose, and she develops projects with other artists both as a collaborator and as a performer. Selected venues she has presented her work in include the Sydney Opera House; Malthouse Theatre, Melbourne; Sydney Theatre Company; Hong Kong Black Box Festival; Artshouse, Melbourne; Perth Institute of Contemporary Arts; Forest Fringe, Edinburgh; Battersea Arts Centre, London; La MaMa Experimental Theatre Club, New York; Taipei Performing Arts Centre; Adelaide Biennial of Australian Art; and Gabriela Mistral Cultural Center, Santiago.

Whenever I see a milk crate, I feel a tiny surge of adrenaline. It's a Pavlovian response, similar to when someone's phone plays the same tone as my alarm: a bothersome call to action. I have to remind myself—ignore the crate, keep walking, leave it.

This body memory stems from my life between 2008 and 2012, when I needed those interlocking plastic boxes—thousands of them. Because during each of those years, I spent the pre-summer months collecting (borrowing/stealing) crates to construct ad hoc banks of 'stadium' seating for DIY festivals across Sydney.

They were a free way to create audience zones for theatre shows, performances, visual art events and talks at semi-legal makeshift spaces across the inner-city suburbs of Sydney. I was in the liminal zone between art school and art life; and with a motley crew of friends—all young art makers and enthusiasts—I established programs of live events. Under the garishly valiant titles of The Imperial Panda Festival and Tiny Stadiums, we staged programs in carparks, empty shops, parks, and wherever we thought we could get away with it.

As an attendee on any particular day, you might climb into a hired van and hug someone in a bed for five minutes, reenact an old movie for a mini DV camera, or witness a Lady Gaga ghostwriter channelling freak spirits. There were sculptures strapped illegally to telegraph poles, works on paper suspended in trees, dance exchanges between bodybuilders.

There was a comedy show about comedy shows, a greenhouse that 'grew' human flowers, soap operas that were written as you watched them. There was smell-o-vision, a fake travel agency operated from old airline seats, suburbs mapped by cats. There were town hall meetings discussing imaginary issues, blobs of neon liquid squirted into dips in the road, miniature models of the streets surrounding the festivals.[1] And if you were sitting down, it would be on the uncomfortable but familiar plastic crenellations of a milk crate.

Inevitably, Australian politics of the day permeated the work—government apologies, leadership spills, debates about carbon price, and endless Middle Eastern wars all found their way into the shows—often imbued with the ironic criticality that dominated the counterculture of the time. We had finished university and stumbled into what seemed a disappointing world: the Sydney Olympics had happened and then just disappeared. 9/11. Iraq war protests. Prime Minister Julia Gillard was being endlessly heckled by opposition leader Tony Abbott—pre-misogyny speech.

Sydney's big art institutions—the Museum of Contemporary Art Australia, the Sydney Opera House, Art Gallery of New South Wales—seemed entirely out of reach for us. There were established Artist-Run Initiatives (ARIs) around, such as The Wedding Circle, Space 3, Knotspace—we attended their parties, but they largely ignored us. Independent theatre venues such as Belvoir's

1 Works in this description are by artists/collectives who represent a small sample of the extended community: SJ Norman, Kenzie Larson, Jen Jamieson, Bababa International, Nat Abbott, Jade Markham, Barbara Cleveland, Tiger Two Times, Team Mess, Lara Thoms, Imogen Semmler, Applespiel, Beth Arnold, Agatha Gothe-Snape, Keg de Souza with Simon Yates and Vanessa Berry, Lucas Ihlein, and Dan Koop.

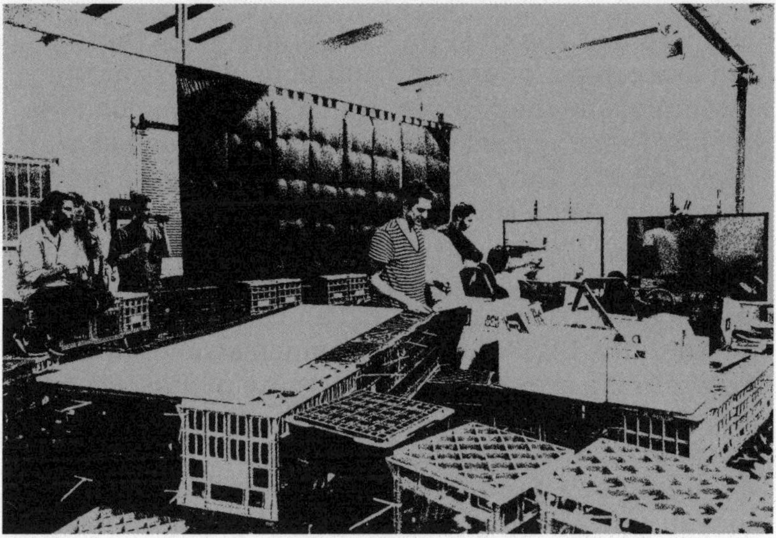

Lucas Abela, Vinyl Rally 2011. Interactive installation for The Imperial Panda Festival 2011 at 4 Lackey St, St Peters (Sydney). Photo: Lucy Parakhina

B-Sharp and The Old Fitz's Tamarama Rock Surfers felt like places for aspiring actors to impress movie directors, and they ignored us too. The communities around these venues were all a few years ahead in their careers. They were Gen X, while we were the as-yet-unnamed Millennials. They printed out flyers for events, while we invited people using the new online network, Facebook. To us, barely of legal drinking age, they seemed old and either much grottier (the DIY/ARI scene) or much cleaner (the actors). Like every generation of young turks, we felt a palpable need for a new way of making work in a place of our own.

Sydney's gentrification compounded this locked-out feeling. A change in licensing laws had caused pubs to be 'spruced up', turning them into shuttered pokies caves. Couches and sticky carpet were out, big sports screens and fluoro lighting were in. The vibe was hostile and the drinks were expensive.

Our solution was to make stuff in public space: nobody could lock us out, we needn't apply to participate and audiences would have no preconceived ideas about what belonged there. We saw it as a clean slate, artistically. We could engage with the histories of places, but we didn't need permission from any art world types. And—the best part—it was free. Like many artists in big cities before us, we eked out a practice in the context available to us. So, like the fungi growing in the bathrooms of the share houses we lived in, we proliferated.

A show called Guerrilla Gardeners on network television played a part too. It featured a group of gardeners who would illegally clean up public messes in disused corners or unloved gutters by putting up a pergola and planting a bed of peonies.

They monitored the spot to see if anyone noticed, or if people would start using the space in more visible and meaningful ways. If the cheesy hosts at Channel 10 can do it, we thought . . .

It was always hot when we held our festivals. The major festival, the Sydney Festival, had the slogan 'This Is Our City in Summer'. We would repeat the phrase like a mantra as we sweated through our events, carrying PAs up old stairwells, pushing audiences into tiny rooms without safety exits, and lying to cops about not selling alcohol. It was the punchline to everything that went right or wrong, a 'c'est la vie' of post-art school irony: 'Welcome, pull up a crate. This is our city in summer', we'd say with a shrug.

We wanted a city with an art world that we could be part of. We wanted somewhere we could afford to go. And we knew it couldn't last long—everything in public space erodes sooner or later. But for a while, we were happy to be organisers.

Eventually, we changed gear. We applied for local council grants and went into battle with them about their prohibitive restrictions. One artist collective wanted to run a forty-two-hour lecture reenacting architect/futurist Buckminster Fuller's 'Everything I Know' by camping out in a small park near a bus stop. The council said that this would require overnight security or it couldn't happen. The project got changed to something that could happen within the guidelines.

When I look back from my current, cranky mid-career position at the instant, pliant shifts we made, I'm vexed. Novices that we were, we often folded. The money from the council meant we could pay our rent—but we were realising that it came with more twists and turns than an F45 aerobics class.

It wasn't just the local council. We also benefitted from a surge of federal funding directed towards 'emerging' artists. Grants were often filtered through small organisations, such as Next Wave and PACT, which established programs that funnelled the money to both the artists and themselves. Programs called 'Spark' and 'Kickstart' lived up to their names, promoting skills development in practice-adjacent areas such as fundraising, marketing, and documentation.

ARIs tend to exist in the realm of the young, the uncouth but desperate, those of us content to put in seventy-hour weeks sans pay in order to make something great happen in a carpark. Eventually, curators from Artspace or Sydney Theatre Company started coming to our events, and then inviting us to show with them—hoping we would bring the energetic, scruffy hoards.

We found ourselves being subtly 'professionalised' and, willingly, we punks slouched towards where we are now—somewhat reluctant but perfectly performing neoliberal subjects. We maintain marketable, risk-assessed and budgeted art practices, complete with stakeholders and board approval. My projects are now viewed from a comfortable seat, in air conditioning, out of the rain. There are fewer roaches. No one is sitting on a crate.

With our new presentation environments—inside, insured, indemnified—the complexity of technical specifications went up, as did our output. The nexus between architecture and aesthetics has shifted my work's scale, sensibility, and durability. The artists I worked with now have international careers: collective Barbara Cleveland presented at the Biennale of Sydney. Claudia O'Doherty is a voice on the children's TV sensation Bluey. Zoe Coombs Marr has an Amazon comedy special. Nat Randall is touring New York's iconic BAM. Amy Spiers is editing this book. I feel like a proud mother: 'Look what we built! Jeez we had a ball, we lived on toast for a decade, but we are professionals now! Real artists in the real world!'

In Melbourne's seemingly endless 2020–21 lockdown, my neighbours started The Brunswick East Entertainment Festival—a series of semi-improvised dance performances held every afternoon on their front lawn, facing traffic and passing walkers out for their allotted one hour of exercise. It prompted me to reflect on the immediacy and availability of public space for artists to explode into, always there for us if we need to burst out of the doldrums of post-university slump or mid-lockdown ennui. I wonder if the temporary closure of institutions and suspicion of enclosed spaces will prompt new waves of work in the 'here' and 'available' arenas of public squares and dodgy parks.

I was also reminded of the infectious thrill of working without institutional frames—art for art's sake, for want of a more original phrase. When I'm asked to mentor young artists now, I'm always impressed by their intimate knowledge of funding structures, presentation contexts, and potential pathways overseas. But I worry that we're teaching them how to clamber up capitalism's ladders before letting them build a practice. Now that the current regime has all but completely obliterated funding for most emerging arts organisations and companies, I wonder if more of these artists will move towards quick and dirty ways of making and doing art together. Will our bums be on crates again? Or will they be deterred from the arts altogether?

Personally, I'm not rushing outside yet—but I do still have the taste for it. The legacy of those days remains the Janus-faced rush of stress and pleasure that a lone milk crate can still provide. I fancy I still have the indentations on my backside, gentle battle scars from one young artist's war of attrition in the art world of our city in summer.

A Letter to Folkestone
Madeleine Collie*

* Madeleine Collie is a writer, artist and curator who previously lived in Folkestone, UK, and now lives and works on the unceded lands of the Boonwurrung and Wurundjeri Woi Wurrung peoples of the Kulin Nation. She is a doctoral candidate in curatorial practice at Monash University. While in Folkestone, she led the collective memorial project The Ash Project (2016–19) and she was a curator for Custom Food Lab (2018–21). Her recent work includes Rumour of Waves with Amy Sharrocks, Nando Messias and Jade Montserrat and Disorganising Metabolisms with Meenakshi Thirukode (both 2020–21). She co-leads the Food Art Research Network.

When I first moved to Folkestone, people said, 'You wouldn't live there if it wasn't for the art.' I screwed up my nose at this, because there is obviously so much more to a place (to you, dear Folkestone) than sculptures and artworks. But I suppose on one level, it is true. I might not have known that Folkestone existed were it not for a trip to the Folkestone Triennial in 2014. And it was a magical trip. My friends and I walked all over, so I got to know the town really well. We stopped for ice cream. We had fish and chips in the wind. The town was less developed than it is now. We arrived by train and walked along back routes and grey footpaths towards Tontine Street. In an abandoned building, we climbed over broken bricks to see a temporary exhibition of Emma Hart's anxiety-riddled ceramics (Giving It All That, 2014). Trying to hide in corners, these clay outlines of wine glasses toppling, beads of sweat dripping—a comment on the performance of the self that one feels obliged to construct in art world openings and events—made me feel right at home. We looped back to take a ride on a precarious wind-powered lift (Ooze Architects and Marjetica Potrc, The Wind Lift, 2014) that offered trips to the top of the old viaduct, with views over the English Channel. We climbed into a bamboo building (Gabrielle Lester, The Electrified Line, 2014) that was perched on the dilapidated railway bridge. It was a structure built to give publics a sense of what the town might be like in a renovated future with access across the harbour. We walked along the harbour station past Paloma Varga Weiss's metal sculptures tinged with Verdigris from the salty air of four huddled travellers wrapped in a rug (Rug People, 2011). Through barricades and via a narrow walkway, we stopped to look through binoculars to see a line of Ian Hamilton Finlay prose. Affixed to the lighthouse at the end, the text reads Weather Is a Third to Place and Time (Ian Hamilton Finlay created posthumously with the artist's estate, 2014). It would take years before I really understood this fragment, to feel keenly how it describes a person's relationship to the elements when living on the edge of a changing stormy coastline, narrow sea and sharp chalk cliffs. At the end of the day, I felt that I had visited a place in which many stories might be possible.

When we moved to Folkestone three years later, we were lured by the prospect of a larger living space and the fact that it was closer to my new office in the middle of the Kent countryside. It was a Triennial year, and some of the vision that the artists had imagined for the town in 2014 had been realised. The walkway over the harbour was opening and the disused railway station was being restored. Access around the sea front had become smoother. Richard Woods's work Holiday Home, 2017, popped up in increasingly odd locations across the town. These too-small cartoon houses made of wooden ply caused a ripple of dissensus, as people wondered at the ethics of creating shelters in which no one could live at a time when Folkestone was facing an increasing homelessness crisis. The small harbour that the town centres on was once part of the infrastructure of the Venice Orient Express train route. However, when the Channel crossing was replaced, first by investment into the port at Dover in the 1970s and then by the Channel Tunnel in 1994, Folkestone town and its seafront went into a period of deterioration. The Triennial started in direct in response to this decline, founded by curator Andrea Schlieker on the invitation of Roger de Haan, a local

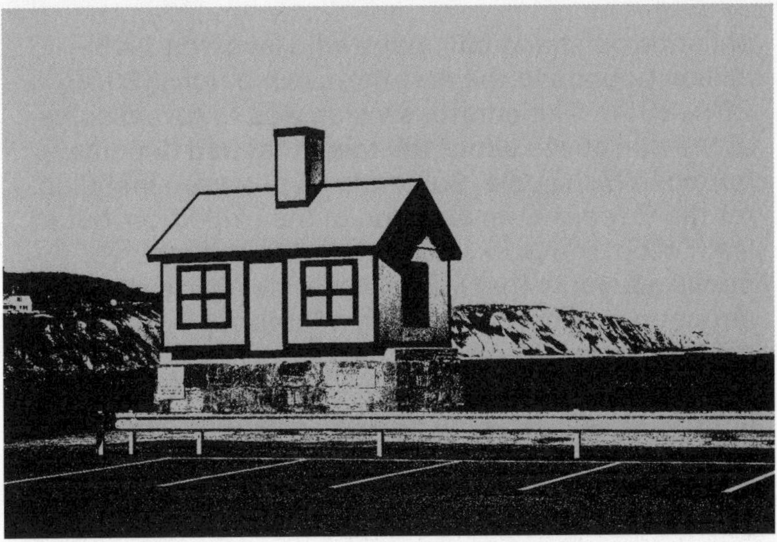

Richard Woods, Holiday Home 2017.
Commissioned by the Creative Foundation for Folkestone Triennial 2017. Photo: Thierry Bal

philanthropist and billionaire who invested £4.5 million pounds to the first three exhibitions (2008, 2011, 2014).[1] The curator's vision was to reveal some of the narratives about the town that had become buried in the rubble. Some works of art are installed for the three-month duration of the exhibition, but at least six of the works join a growing collection of public artworks that lays claim to being the UK's largest permanent collection of outdoor contemporary art.

Works by a range of high-profile British and international artists are located in various spots across the town. Examples on the seafront include a mermaid by Cornelia Parker (Folkestone Mermaid, 2011); a 'misremembered' lamppost by David Shrigley (Lamp Post, 2017); and a peace message in Morse code that flashes out to sea from the top of the grand hotel by Yoko Ono (Earth Peace, 2014). In the main street, a large neon by Nathan Coley towers over the street reading Heaven Is a Place Where Nothing Ever Happens, 2008, and A. K. Dolven's Out of Tune, 2011, a huge untuned bell suspended between two posts, frames part of the seafront. Lubaina Himid's Jelly Mould Pavilion, 2017, sits not far from the bell, a delicate, pastel-coloured form that the artist hopes provides a space to speak of the connection between memories of seafront fun fair—toffee apples and fairy floss—the slave trade, and sugar plantations. There is something of a surrealist stage set about the artworks in Folkestone, and as I write about them from Melbourne, with borders closed due

1 Nick Ewbank, Adventures in Regeneration, Nick Ewbank Associates, 2011, accessed May 2021, https://www.nickewbank.co.uk/projects/adventures-in-regeneration/.

to the COVID-19 pandemic, I imagine I won't be back there for some time. I conjure a future in which I return, thirty years hence. Coley's neon lights are out, or flickering softly; paint peels off murals; Dolven's bell and its huge posts are immersed in water; and only the top of Himid's jelly mould is visible. Because of de Haan's intent, the works of art in the collection have always held a tight accord with speculations on the town's future.

While there are many enchanting things about Folkestone, there is also a rub. On one hand, parts of east Folkestone have some of the highest rates of deprivation in the country; on the other hand, Folkestone is full of desirable real estate. Folkestone regularly makes it on to lists of the coolest places to live in Britain and, in 2020, Folkestone was listed in a Condé Nast travellers' guide as one of the best places in the world to work from home.[2] On the steps down to the sandy beach from the seafront esplanade there is a small baby's shoe made of metal and coated in paint (Tracey Emin, Baby Things, 2008). According to the artist, it is a pro-choice commentary on teen pregnancies in coastal towns. Because it initially looks real, I pointed it out to friends who came to visit, who would then try to pick it up. The first time it's charming—'Oh it's art!', they would exclaim—but as these encounters were repeated, they started to remind me that the subsidiary aim of such artworks might be to tempt new buyers, new families, new money to the town. In fact, in a Guardian article

2 Anna Hart, 'The Best Places in Europe for Remote Working', Condé Naste Traveller, accessed 20 February 2021, https://www.cntraveller.com/article/places-in-europe-remote-working.

published at the time, Emin acknowledged the link between poverty, her artworks and new money. She said to the journalist: 'I just hope they don't get vandalised or stolen. The young people of Folkestone should realise that the Triennial is going to bring in people and money which must be a good thing.'[3] The question about whether these artworks have a role in the gentrification of the town isn't really worth asking but it makes me reflect on the way in which the word speculative might have a double meaning here. These artworks are speculative both in the sense of imagining other futures and in the sense of foreclosing other possibilities. This artwork invokes a future in which the town is transformed, and teen pregnancies are a distant memory which lie trapped in this metal shoe. The public the artist imagines are not just the visitors who come each year or the people who live there throughout, but also a future public of art lovers and property speculators who might want to catch the wave of the town's changing fortunes.

Public art has a distinctly temporal dimension: not only does the sun rise and set across the artworks daily, but their spectral presences also wrap around the identity of the community. Some days, I would feel annoyed that there wasn't an artist-led library, kitchen, shelter, bakery, artist bank or community garden. Or would this too somehow play into the hands of speculative local improvement? I felt I wanted something more performative, activist or encounter driven, or gutsy. I

3 Mark Brown, 'Emin Leaves Trail of Baby Clothes through Folkestone as Britart Comes to Seaside', The Guardian, 14 June 2008, https://www.theguardian.com/artanddesign/2008/jun/14/art.

wanted to see projects that could be transformative for those who live and work in Folkestone—something that would get people talking to each other and that would activate community change at a time when people don't have much. However, these kinds of public art projects can also misfire, as Amy Spiers points out in relation to the media coverage of Michael Sailstorfer's Folkestone Digs, 2014. In this public provocation, bars of gold were buried in the sand for the public to find. This gesture produced images of families in austerity-stricken Britain digging deep in the sand to try to change their fortunes. Spiers observes, 'Surely it is incumbent on the politically engaged viewer to notice the unfortunate and uncomfortable implications of a public digging for gold.'[4]

On other days, I felt comforted, perhaps not by the curated selection of artworks but certainly by the communities of people that gathered in the town to live in the shadow of public art. I remember an autumn equinox event hosted by a local gleaner's network. Sol Calero's colourful seaside pavilion Casa Anacaona, 2017, was surrounded by fire pits along the beach. Calero made the pavilion with communities across the southeast of England as a 'social structure' in which many events might happen. It was a cold night and we warmed ourselves with spiced wine and hot soup as the pavilion was put to use as a community soup kitchen. In the darkness, groups of friends gathered. We told stories and ate food foraged from the

4 Amy Spiers, 'Blind Spots: The Unhappy Public in Public Art', in Civic Actions: Artists Practices Beyond the Museum, Museum of Contemporary Art Australia, Sydney, 2017, p. 146.

nearby hills. While the works of art may all be involved in a dance between competing visions of the future, what happens in, around and among them also exceeds the initial vision that the artist or their commissioners might have imagined. And the question I started with of whether Folkestone is a special place in spite of, or because of, public art doesn't seem so easy to resolve.

In 1863, Emily Dickinson wrote an eight-line poem called 'This Is My Letter to the World'. This brief, cryptic epistle asks for compassion from the reader for Dickinson's 'simple news that Nature told'. The poet acknowledges that she will never meet the people reading her words; these words are offered to a reader that the writer cannot see, to people she will never meet. While living in Folkestone, I wondered whether public art at its best is also 'a letter to the world', a letter to a public that the artist will never meet. In this way it is an anticipative gesture for a future world, a world transformed. A letter that will be read by communities that the artists will never encounter, a restless, changing multitude that makes up the many publics that contest, decry and live with the consequences of public art.

Folkestone is elemental in the best way—strong winds, freezing fogs, crisp sunny summers. I miss that uncanny sensation of walking along the sea edge, when you can barely see your hands in front of your face through the sea mists. The blue text on the lighthouse can just be seen through the brume—'Weather is a third to place and time'. This is my letter to Folkestone, a letter to a future public that will not respond, a love letter to the dramatic environmental and social forces that envelop the town.

Making Publics
Sean Dockray*

* Dr Sean Dockray is an artist and writer whose work explores the politics of technology, with a particular emphasis on artificial intelligences and the algorithmic web. A senior lecturer and head of Sculpture and Spatial Practice at the School of Art and Design at the Australian National University, Canberra, he is also a founding director of the Los Angeles non-profit Telic Arts Exchange, and initiator of knowledge-sharing platforms The Public School and AAAARG.ORG. Dockray is on the board of directors of the Melbourne non-profit arts organisation West Space, and his writing has been published in *Artlink*, *Frieze*, *Fillip*, *Cabinet* and *Volume*, and in the multi-author book *Contestations: Learning from Critical Experiments in Education* (Bedford Press, 2014).

If the 'public' is a thing at all, then it is not an unquestionably good one. At the beginning of Melbourne's second COVID-19 wave in July 2020, residents of nine public housing towers were forcibly removed from the public life of the city. Many were deprived of food, medication, and psychological support, all in the name of public health and the greater public good. This mobilisation of the public was not an exception, but an extension and amplification of Australia's ongoing history of dispossession, exclusion, and management of Asian, African, and Middle Eastern migrants and Aboriginal and Torres Strait Islander people.

As the virus spread, public spaces across the city began to quickly close off. Cultural institutions moved online or took some time to rest and regroup. Internal discussions veered between continuity and rupture. On the one hand were practical considerations of fulfilling promises made to funders, artists, and audiences. But on the other hand, the possibility to build something new, to dismantle competitive and exhausting structures, persisted. If the uncertain and improvisational moment opened by the pandemic is not the time for realising dreams of a different kind of world, then when will it ever be?

Zoom was the most prominent agent of a perverse continuity, reformatting any social encounter into a meeting, but maintenance of the status quo was assured by the entire apparatus of smartphones, WiFi, laptops, apps, social media, deliveries, and data centres. Art didn't move online so much as it was coerced by prevailing forces. If the place of public art has typically been outside of galleries and museums, then the widespread closure of those physical spaces and shift of programming during pandemic lockdowns to online platforms presents a problem: all art becomes public art. What is the usefulness of the term 'public' in a networked digital context, such as Zoom? Does the public even make sense here? Is it a concept worth holding on to?

One interesting case study that might help in considering these questions is the Biennial Live Event in the Everyday Digital (BLEED), co-organised by the Campbelltown Arts Centre and Arts House in Melbourne. This six-year project opened with a ten-week festival during Australian border closures and Melbourne's strict lockdown. It was conceived and planned, however, in the two years prior, allowing me to reflect on the differences between cultural programs that have proactively tested the digital waters and those that have fallen into them by circumstance. The premise of BLEED is to 'greet audiences where they already reside: online, hyper-connected and virtually networked', which inherits somewhat from avant-garde traditions of abandoning the stage or space of theatre to confront or activate its audience in a 'digital public sphere'.[1]

In some ways, this language feels dated. Even before Twitter flexed its muscles and banned the President of the United States, any semblance of a digital public sphere was smashed into thousands of algorithmically mediated discourses, filter bubbles, and fragmented, disconnected echo chambers. I wouldn't disagree that platforms have become sites for shared interpretation of events nor that they contribute to the production of public opinions, and I recognise the online condition that BLEED identifies. However, there is something post-public about the

1 'About BLEED', BLEED, accessed 11 January 2021, https://bleedonline.net/about-bleed/.

emergent political populism, surfacing fascism, and the media, surveillance, and communication environment within which it has flourished.

In contrast to BLEED's mostly apolitical scene setting, the actual artistic and discursive contributions to the program are deeply attentive to many of these questions. Paeonia Drive, 2019, by Angela Goh and Su Yu Hsin, and Jacqui Shelton's response, Not-Crying in the Park, 2020, produce encounters with systems of management and control of bodies and nature. Hannah Brontë shares the resistance in rest in mi$$-Eupnea, 2020. Alex Kelly and David Pledger organised an Assembly for the Future, which made space for citizens to propose and contest visions of the future, in Claire G. Coleman's provocation, for example, 'beyond whiteness'.

When Eduardo Costa, Raul Escari and Roberto Jacoby noted in 1966 that 'the public is not in direct contact with cultural activities but is informed of them through the media',[2] they positioned the media as a public space and repositioned all art, circulating as it does through media, as public art. Furthermore, artists have long been strategically situating their work within communication media, greeting audiences in the non-art spaces they already inhabit—think of mail art; Dan Graham's Homes for America, 1966–67; Chris Burden's TV Commercials, 1973–77; Olia Lialina's My Boyfriend Came Back From the War, 1996; and net.art more broadly. In a certain way, the idea of the online as a

2 Eduardo Costa, Raúl Escari and Roberto Jacoby, 'A Media Art (Manifesto)', in Alexander Alberro and Blake Stimson (eds), Conceptual Art: A Critical Anthology, MIT Press, Cambridge, MA, 1999, p. 2.

site for art rather than for just its documentation or publicity, and the fact that galleries, museums and festivals are figuring out how to present work for networked devices are pretty ho-hum. In other words, reaching audiences is less important than making publics.

A discussion of how the presentation of art might occur on a digital stage rented from Instagram or Zoom ought to acknowledge how the infrastructure of arts organisations has been absorbed into these same platforms, as well as those of Amazon, Google and Microsoft. Seen from this perspective, across whole organisations, the persistence of language like 'public' and 'private' in technical interfaces is used to facilitate access management, to define some activities as internal to the organisation with other activities as 'content'. That organisations have been pulled between continuity and rupture during the pandemic, between the maintenance of existing hierarchies and the production of new structures, is something often felt acutely at this moment of managing access. What if the institutions themselves were the work? Institutions can't be toggled public through the flick of a switch, but rather through developing processes, infrastructures, and communities that are empowered to act publicly.

Most frequently, the public is set in antinomy to private, but historically the public is the mediating term between private property and the common(s).[3]

3 I remember Jason E. Smith posing this relation in the process of writing the lecture 'There Is Nothing Less Passive than the Act of Fleeing' in 2010 with Matteo Pasquinelli, Caleb Waldorf and me.

If digital networks are confused for the public, then it's partly because these networks entangle both property and sharing. For public art to have any relevance amid digital platforms, then it will be more from making publics than from performing for friends and followers. Making publics isn't just about selecting a targeted audience or meeting old audiences in new spaces, but about creating or renewing communities, spaces and protocols collectively, conscious of the pull of algorithm. Making publics online today involves a choreography of withdrawal and engagement, it is a generous and generative act of making and sharing spaces, tools and concepts, such as Assembly for the Future or James Nguyen and Victoria Pham's RE:SOUNDING, since 2018, which creates a library of Đông Sơn drum sounds and proposes a community of shared use. Making publics is a constructive act of building interfaces to redistribute resources out of the control of institutions that have traditionally operated under the mantle of the public and from digital platforms that would 'disrupt' the public into the control of corporate monopolies.

Brian Fuata*

* Brian Fuata is an artist working with improvisation in the context of contemporary performance, public speaking and visual art, and in sites ranging from galleries and theatres to emails and text messages. Across performance, text, language, film and installation, his practice embraces a political ethos of horizontalism, where objects and ephemera—including personal and social histories—are given equal value. Fuata was the 2020 winner of the ANTI Festival International Prize for Live Art, and his most recent projects include the 10th Asia Pacific Triennial of Contemporary Art, Brisbane (2021-22) and a 2021 online residency with Western Front, Vancouver, involving the continuation of his longstanding email performance practice.

Beat cruising has often drawn out of me simultaneously multiple attentions, pulling me inside a granulated matrix of aesthetic experiences of bodies and obajects in libidinal space, variously rhymed and rhythmed accordingly. They have provided situations for, and of, loose art, the rare sensorial sublimities made through a shared cognisance between the Lover(s) and me. Saying nothing and everything in response to an invitation to think about whether there's a queer practice of public art, this performance text begins inside my home on a bright and temperate Saturday afternoon; it ends as its <u>header</u>.

Explicit Contents

I'm currently in what Buddhists term monkey mind, darting through life canopy that now includes readying myself to attend in person a 2021 performance by choreographer Rhiannon Newton titled Explicit Contents. 'Simian energy' is an impulse my mind raises typically before my live structured improvisations. Now embraced as a constructive technique, it aids in producing content—on a good day, there's at least one sensible point made apparent. So, with fingers crossed, let me pause here while I swing onto public transport en route to Newton's work.

I'm now in a moving carriage sitting backwards to the direction of the train, passing a station above which is a busy shopping centre containing what was once a popular beat made of its male toilet. The toilet block was small, the front door leading directly into a snug ablutionary alcove of approx. twenty square metres. Upon entering you were greeted by its tiny sink below a large mirror, to the right of which was the two-person urinal and to the right of that were two slim cubicles. The beat's popularity peaked when the cubicle doors were taken off by centre management as a homo deterrent. However, their censorious design instead renovated the room into a fantasy-irl sex-on-premises venue: a pornographic tableau free for two men by pretending to defecate—heads bowed, their waistbands sloped between knees and ankles both hands occupied with scrunched toilet paper (a prop). The first time I encountered this beat, and thereby learnt this double-act of waiting, both cubicles were transparently occupied. I walked in on the two actors at the time, initially taken aback with shame until I realised no shame in their eyes but the purity of purpose. In that precise second of locking eyes with the seated men—I realised I wasn't walking in on them, I was invited (albeit conditioned on physical appearances)—this performance was transmitted, absorbed and added to my extensive repertoire of beat acts. I didn't fuck then, saving it for the following week when time was on my side.

CLUP! (for my fellow worm, Frances K. Barrett) Last night's Explicit Contents began with the audience walking in on dancers Ivey Wawn and David Huggins under house lights. Dressed in work fatigues fit for release technique pressed against walls and floor, staged on and off stage, entering and exiting the theatre from its various doorways. Wawn and Huggins' gaze held for me along two planes: if their object of attention was human, either directly in the eye or above head height, non-human either directly centre or above it. Their dual looks rendered the theatre's thingness—its inside-outside dissolved. Today was Sunday / tonight was Sunday / today is Monday / tonight is Monday / today it's Tuesday evening . . . this text carries on. I took up a toilet seat, the other occupied, and waited. Each opening of the front door met with the shock of the general public-cum-audience-cum-performer walking in on my theatrical cheeky conceit was arousing. He entered and first gasped, then gasped again when He continued onto my cohort in the neighbouring cubicle. For namesake let's call He Jack. I could sense Jack was straight and also new to this beat. However, Jack, like me the week before but with more time on his hands having received the transmission, knew what to do. He stood with his back against the wall of the tight corridor, facing my open vestibule but slightly off enough for us to glean the contours of our edging bodies, Jack's head making minor shifts to catch my right thigh widening its spread for his view. We eventually emerged to brazen cruising with naked erections. After a while, with waistbands at our ankles we shuffled as if in a sack race, onto the silver Dad next door who bore an uncanny resemblance to a healthy William

Burroughs. William was highly strung markedly preferring to only watch, any move towards him was met with no words but a thunderous clap of his hands—CLUP! William was intense. As a formal sound effect, I found this CLUP! remarkably captivating. At first when William was visibly aroused we'd motion towards him then alas, CLUP! Our bodies stood in triangular formation, jerking, appearing as a unified trio until William's echoic CLUP! would make the relational construct appear: a duet watched by a single voyeur. William's CLUP! secreted our dynamic form similar to a moment on stage where Wawn and Huggins windmill their arms—dropping in and out of sync—each revolution read and re-read with different states of sound and light. Framed as a queer project, Explicit Contents with its ecological themes networking human and non-human actors in perpetual shiftings between situation and spectacle, makes affective moves to critique the binary domains of publics and art held inside and outdoors. Perhaps what I'm alluding to is why a queer public art when queerness senses queerness always-already happening? Queerness is out of time, out of sight even in clear lines of sight—centralising peripheral attention of the body to be here (or as Muñoz phrases, not yet here)[1] and elsewhere. If there was a 'Queer Public Art', would it necessitate a state sanctioned objecthood fixed to a singular identitarian remit? #queerpublicart #queer #art #CLUP!

1 José Esteban Muñoz, Cruising Utopia: The Then and There of Queer Futurity, New York University Press, New York and London, 2009.

Fine Arts

Years ago I went on a quasi date with this guy who had at the time recently graduated from art school. He majored in photography.

— What kind of art do you do Brian?

— Mainly performance.

— Omg. I. Love. Flash Mobs.

DL Empire Garden
around midnight in Brockwell Park, Brixton
by the roses a majesty of black men
huddled under hood
swatting heat through the lavender
fog lain on cobbled stone
the romance of this empire garden where inside
my bike and heavy chain cheers our night
his belt twice removed
head dreadlocked
head shaved
head uncut
head mean with love
head crystal clear
head, all lips
his name Jerome
the time is our hands

Film
OK. I will.
==
He sat about four chairs before me. I sat right at the back of the carriage, moved towards the aisle and started wanking myself over my shorts. He stood to turn, then came and sat directly in front of me. And the train announced its intentions and began to move. The trailing shadows of trees, clouds and buildings came all over his face. His blue eyes and red hair flickered and shone.
And shining. And shining. And shining. And shining. And shining. And shining.
==
I will. OK.
OK. I will.
==
He sat about four chairs before me. I sat right at the back of the carriage, moved towards the aisle and started wanking myself over my shorts. He stood to turn, then came and sat directly in front of me. And the train announced its intentions and began to move. The trailing shadows of trees, clouds and buildings came all over his face. His blue eyes and red hair flickered and shone.
And shining. And shining. And shining. And shining. And shining. And shining.
==
I will. OK.
OK. I will.
==
He sat about four chairs before me. I sat right at the back of the carriage, moved towards the aisle and started wanking myself over my shorts. He stood to turn, then came and sat directly in front of me. And

the train announced its intentions and began to move. The trailing shadows of trees, clouds and buildings came all over his face. His blue eyes and red hair flickered and shone.
And shining. And shining. And shining. And shining.
And shining. And shining.
==
I will. OK.
OK. I will.
==

Discrete Relations

Discrete Relations/Discreet Relations is an artwork by Agatha Gothe-Snape from 2019. A reversible worker's vest is one element of it. One side is metallic and highly reflective and the other is lined with thick cotton marked in floral pattern but embroidered in the same reflective material of the other side, in Helvetica all caps, is the work's title:

DISCRETE
RELATIONS

I happened to be wearing it one day at a beat inside Sydney Uni. The lover and I entered the cubicle and disrobed entirely except our shoes, our clothes heaped into signature mounds as if our bodies had instantly dissolved to scientifically reappear naked like Terminator's lightening arrival except there were two of us, and we both had poppers. Ag's artwork strewn on top of my clothes allowed my lover to witness her work:

DISCRETE
RELATIONS

'How apt', my lover said.

Biro

There was a period of toilet-based beat culture that involved communicating through wrapping a biro with tissue and passing it understall. This writing phenomena has since disappeared.

I recall being passed understall the initiating text, unwrapping the pen of its message. His hand was gracefully softened with age. The second vertical line in the letter 'H' topped with a desperate hole where the biro had broken through onto a soft lap. Beautifully drawn with a bad hand: Hello.

The cubicle door and walls, made with various materials from laminate, brick or ceramic tiles, was/is another surface for expression. There's the main surface in plain sight along with ingeniously discrete areas like along lines of mortar in-between brick or my favourite, at the base of the aluminum paper holder a slithered text uttering, Time. Date. Position. Viewing these works requires a physical re-positioning on or off the seat. Furthermore, with possible exceptions for remote suburban and regional areas encompassing truck stops and petrol stations perforating highways, media apps freed these text practices from practical comms (what I assert distinguished this visual culture from heteronormative economies of graffiti), these works are now free to exist in their ontological rhetoric, to be themselves, and perhaps free for innovation in form.

A, B, C and D at Camperdown Oval

Under one full moon at midnight, inside the football bleaches at Camperdown Oval, was a dance.

It was a company of four with members named A, B, C and D.

I was B.

Costumed by night sky, cruising felt like we were a rope team, where one move would push and pull the movement of the others. Eventual formations ranging from solo, duet, trio to ensemble. There were many plays. Here are two of them.

ONE ACT

A

B

C

D

A SISTER ACT

A

B

C D

Gmail

Fwd: A PERFORMANCE FOR THE ALL MEN IN MY EMAIL ADDRESS BOOK

6 messages

From: Brian Fu <█████>
Date: 19 July 2013 17:23:09 EDT

To: Adrian Burnett <█████>, "█████" <█████>, Adam Downer <█████>, Adam Jasper <█████>, Adam Micmacher <█████>, Adam Porter <█████>, Alasdiar McLuckie <█████>, Alec Thompson <█████>, "█████" <█████>, Alex Baker <█████>, Alex Davies <█████>, Alex Gearin <█████>, Alex Kershaw <█████>, Alex Kiers <█████>, Alex Pye <█████>, Alex White <█████>, Alex Wyatt <█████>, Alun Davies <█████>, Andrew Batt-Rawden <█████>, Andrew Corsi <█████>, Andrew Haining <█████>, Andrew Mitchelson <█████>, Andrew Morrish <█████>, "█████" <█████>, Andy Ko <█████>, Andy Lysle <█████>, Angus Withey <█████>, "Anthony Whelan | BREENSPACE" <█████>, Aurelien Dufau <█████>, Ba Ba Ba International <█████>, Barry Keloudis <█████>, Bastian Fox <█████>, Ben Connors <█████>, Benjamin McCready <█████>, "Benjamin.M Forster" <█████>, Bennett Miller <█████>, "█████" <█████>, Benny Nemerofsky Ramsay <█████>, Box Copy Admin <█████>, Brad Haylock <█████>, Bradley King <█████>, Bradley Vincent <█████>, Brendan Huntely <█████>, Brent Clough <█████>, brent taylor <█████>, Brian Carbee <█████>, "█████" <█████

████>, Cameron Power <████>, Carlos Gomes <████>, Channon Goodwin <████>, Charles Dennington <████>, Charlie S <████>, Chase Gordon <████>, Chris Brown <████>, chris petro <████>, Chris Ryan <████>, Christoph Sharp <████>, Christopher Hanrahan <████>, Christopher Hodge <████>, clinton richards <████>, Conrad Barrett <████>, Costa Georgiadis <████>, Craig Bender <████>, Craig Burgess <████>, David Cross <████>, Daniel Satele <████>, Damien Minton <████>, Dan Taulapapa McMullin <████>, Daniel Rodriguez <████>, David Capra <████>, David Clarkson <████>, David Mills <████>, David Simota <████>, David Williams <████>, Davide Savorani <████>, Dean Walsh <████>, Derek Kreckler <████>, Domenico Declario <████>, dickhunter <████>, Dominic Fitzsimmons <████>, Dominic Kirkwood <████>, Douglas Lance Gibson <████>, Duckie Performance Group <████>, Eddie Sharp <████>, Eden Falk <████>, Eduardo Wolfe-Alegria <████>, Edward Scheer <████>, Fernando do campo <████>, Fernando Quesada <████>, Freckles Finn <████>, George Edgerton-Warbuton <████>, George Pizer <████>, George Tiliniakis <████>, Glen Henderson <████>, Grant Stevens <████>, Greg Semu <████>, "████" <████>, Guillermo Gomez Pena <████>, "████" <████>, Harley Stumm <████>, Heath Franco <████>, Iakovos Amperidis <████>, Ian Milliss <████>, Ianto Ware <████>, Inigo Ugarte <████>, Ioane Lafoai <████>, Ivan Cheng <████>, "J.D. Reforma" <████>, Jack Jeweller <████>, Jackson Slattery <████>, jacopo romoli <████>, Jakob Oredsson <████>, "James @ Queen St Studio" <████>, James

Brennan <████>, James Brown <████>, James Cunningham <████>, James Fuata <████>, James Newitt <████>, James Winter <████>, Jamie North <████>, Jason Hood <████>, Jasper Susi <████>, Jeff Khahn <████>, Jeff Stein <████>, Jeffrey Hamilton <████>, jim singline <████>, Jim Wafer <████>, Jo Parro <████>, Joel Glazebrook <████>, "████" <████>, John A Douglas <████>, John Tonkin <████>, Jon Hunter <████>, Jonathan James <████>, Jonny Seymour <████>, "████" <████>, Josh Wright <████>, Joshua Sofaer <████>, Jude Emmett <████>, Julian Maynard Smith <████>, Julian Talarico <████>, Justin Miles <████>, Justin Shoulder <████>, Kaiserin Magazine <████>, Keith Armstrong <████>, Keith Gallasch <████>, Kenzee Patterson <████>, Kernow Craig <████>, Kevin Platt <████>, Koji Ryui <████>, Kym Lenoble <████>, Lachlan Verco <████>, Larry Vaux <████>, Lee Wilson <████>, Leigh Rigozzi <████>, Lemi Ponifasio <████>, Leo Tanoi <████>, Leon Ewing <████>, Léuli Eshraghi <████>, Levon Brodelouw <████>, Liam Benson <████>, Lachlan Anthony <████>, Lucas Abela <████>, Lucas Big Fag Press <████>, Lucas Liccini <████>, Luke George <████>, Malcolm Whittaker <████>, Manuel Vason <████>, Manuel Vason <████>, Marcus Whale <████>, Mark Feary <████>, Martin del Amo <████>, Marty Jay <████>, Martyn Coutts <████>, Mathieu Gallois <████>, Matt Vaughan <████>, Matte Rochford <████>, Matthew Day <████>, Matthew Hanson <████>, Matthew Prest <████>, Matthew Tumbers <████>, Michael Dagostino <████>, Michael Drebert <████>, Michael Moran <████

████>, Michael Poetschko <████>, Michael Snape <████>, Michael Wynne <████>, Mickie Quick <████>, Morten Søndergaard <████>, Murray Hewitt <████>, Nathan Babet <████>, Nathan Gray <████>, Nicholas Coyle <████>, nicholas de jong <████>, Nick Herd <████>, Nick Tsaldaris <████>, Nick Wales <████>, Nick Wishart <████>, "████Garner" <████>, Nigel Kellaway <████>, Oliver Watts <████>, PERICICH <████>, Padraic Murphy <████>, Pat Macan <████>, Patrice Pauc <████>, Paul Cordeiro <████>, Paul Dwyer <████>, Paul Gazzola <████>, Paul Wells <████>, Peco Shopovski <████>, Pete Volich <████>, Peter Bodkin <████>, Peter Braithwaite <████>, Peter Lankas <████>, peter lenaerts <████>, Peter Mcarron <████>, Peter Panagioti Polites <████>, Peter Shopovski <████>, Phil Spencer <████>, Phineas Hartson <████>, Richard McBride <████>, Reuben Keehan <████>, Richard Tipping <████>, Robert Hartig-Prym <████>, Robert Heathcote <████>, Robert Milne <████>, Robert Pacitti <████>, Robin Dingeman <████>, Ross Gibson <████>, Ross Gibson <████>, Ruark Lewis <████>, Ryan Burrett <████>, Ryuichi Fujimura <████>, Adrian Burnettdt <████>, "████" <████>, "Adam Downer" <████>, "Adam Jasper" <████>, "Adam Micmacher" <████>, "Adam Porter" <████>, "Alasdiar McLuckie" <████>, "Alec Thompson" <████>, "Alex Baker" <████>, "Alex Davies" <████>, "Alex Gearin" <████>, "Alex Kershaw" <████>, "Alex Kiers" <████>, "Alex Pye" <████>, "Alex Wyatt" <████>, "Alex White" <████>, "Alun Davies" <████>, "Andrew Batt-Rawden" <████

>, “Andrew Corsi” <>, “Andrew Haining” <>, “Andrew Mitchelson” <>, “Andrew Morrish” <>, “Andy Ko” <>, “Andy Lysle” <>, “Anthony Whelan | BREENSPACE” <>, “Aurelien Dufau” <>, “Ba Ba Ba International” <>, “Bastian Fox” <>, “Barry Keloudis” <>, “Ben Connors” <>, “Benjamin McCready” <>, “Benjamin.M Forster” <>, “Bennett Miller” <>, “Benny Nemerofsky Ramsay” <>, “Blair French” <>, “Brad Haylock” <>, “Bradley King” <>, “Bradley Vincent” <>, “Brendan Huntely” <>, “Brent Clough” <>, “brent taylor” <>, “Brian Carbee” <>, “” <>, “Cameron Power” <>, “Carlos Gomes” <>, “Channon Goodwin” <>, “Charles Dennington” <>, “Charlie S” <>, “Chase Gordon” <>, “Chris Brown” <>, “chris petro” <>, “Chris Ryan” <>, “Christian Thompson” <>, “Christoph Sharp” <>, “Christopher Hanrahan” <>, “Christopher Hodge” <>, “clinton richards” <>, “Conrad Barrett” <>, “Costa Georgiadis” <>, “Craig Bender” <>, “Craig Burgess” <>, “” <>, “” <>, “Damien Minton” <>, “Dan Taulapapa McMullin” <>, “Daniel Rodriguez” <>, “Daniel Satele” <>, “daniel stricker” <>, “David Capra” <>, “David Clarkson” <>, “David Mills” <>, “David Simota” <>, “David Williams” <>, “Davide Savorani” <>, “” <>, “Dean Walsh” <>, “Derek Kreckler” <>, “” <>, “Dominic Fitzsimmons” <>, “Dominic Kirkwood” <

██>, “Douglas Lance Gibson” <██>, “Eddie Sharp” <██>, “Eden Falk” <██>, “Eduardo Wolfe-Alegria” <██>, “Edward Scheer” <██>, “Fabian Barraza” <██>, “Fernando do campo” <██>, “Fernando Quesada” <██>, “Freckles Finn” <██>, “George Edgerton-Warbuton” <██>, “George Pizer” <██>, “George Tiliniakis” <██>, “Glen Henderson” <██>, “Grant Stevens” <██>, “Greg Semu” <██>, “██” <██>, “Guillermo Gomez Pena” <██>, “██” <██>, “Harley Stumm” <██>, “Hayden Fowler” <██>, “Heath Franco” <██>, “Iakovos Amperidis” <██>, “Ian Milliss” <██>, “Ianto Ware” <██>, “Inigo Ugarte” <██>, “Ioane Lafoai” <██>, “Ivan Cheng” <██>, “J.D. Reforma” <██>, “Jack Jeweller” <██>, “Jackson Slattery” <██>, “jacopo romoli” <██>, “Jakob Oredsson” <██>, “James @ Queen St Studio” <██>, “James Brennan” <██>, “James Cunningham” <██>, “James Brown” <██>, “James Fuata” <██>, “James Longbottom” <██>, “James Murnain” <██>, “James Newitt” <██>, “James Winter” <██>, “Jamie North” <██>, “Jason Hood” <██>, “Jasper Susi” <██>, “Jeff Khahn” <██>, “Jeff Stein” <██>, “Jeffrey Hamilton” <██>, “Jim Wafer” <██>, “jim singline” <██>, “Jo Parro” <██>, “Joel De Sá” <██>, “Joel Glazebrook” <██>, “██” <██>, “John A Douglas” <██>, “John Tonkin” <██>, “John Waring” <██>, “Jon Hunter” <██>, “Jonathan James” <██>, “Jonny Seymour” <██>, “██” <██>, “Josh Wright” <██>, “Joshua Sofaer” <██>, “Jude Emmett” <██>, “Julian Talarico” <██>, “Justin Miles” <██

████>, “Justin Shoulder” <████>, “Kaiserin Magazine” <████>, “Kane Hill” <████>, “Kedar Vishwanathan” <████>, “Keith Armstrong” <████>, “Keith Gallasch” <████>, “Kenzee Patterson” <████>, “ken shimizu” <████>, “Kernow Craig” <████>, “Kerry Brown” <████>, “Kevin Platt” <████>, “Koji Ryui” <████>, “Kym Lenoble” <████>, “Lachlan Verco” <████>, “Larry Vaux” <████>, “Lee Serle” <████>, “Lee Wilson” <████>, “Leigh Rigozzi” <████>, “Leo Tanoi” <████>, “Leon Ewing” <████>, “Léuli Eshraghi” <████>, “Levon Brodelouw” <████>, “Liam Benson” <████>, “████” <████>, “Lucas Abela” <████>, “Lucas Big Fag Press” <████>, “Lucas Liccini” <████>, “Luke George” <████>, “Luke Waterlow” <████>, “Malcolm Whittaker” <████>, “Manuel Vason” <████>, “Marcus Whale” <████>, “Mark Feary” <████>, “Mark Mason” <████>, “Martin del Amo” <████>, “Marty Jay” <████>, “Martyn Coutts” <████>, “Mathieu Gallois” <████>, “Matte Rochford” <████>, “Matt Vaughan” <████>, “Matthew Day” <████>, “Matthew Hanson” <████>, “Matthew Nicholson” <████>, “Matthew Prest” <████>, “Max” <████>, “Michael Dagostino” <████>, “Michael Drebert” <████>, “Michael Moran” <████>, “Michael Poetschko” <████>, “Michael Snape” <████>, “Michael Wynne” <████>, “Mickie Quick” <████>, “Mitch Cairns” <████>, “Morten Søndergaard” <████>, “Murray Hewitt” <████>, “Nathan Babet” <████>, “Nathan Gray” <████>, “Nicholas Coyle” <████>, “nicholas de jong” <████>, “Nick Herd” <████>, “Nick Tsaldaris” <████>, “Nick Wales” <████>, “Nick Wishart” <████>, “Nick Tsaldaris” <████>, “████Garner” <████

███>, "Nigel Kellaway" <███>, "Oliver Watts" <███>, "P E R I C I C H" <███>, "Padraic Murphy" <███>, "Patrice Pauc" <███>, "Pat Macan" <███>, "Paul Cordeiro" <███>, "Paul Dwyer" <███>, "Paul Gazzola" <███>, "Paul Wells" <███>, "Peco Shopovski" <███>, "Pete Volich" <███>, "Peter Bodkin" <███>, "Peter Braithwaite" <███>, "Peter Fimmano" <███>, "Peter Lankas" <███>, "peter lenaerts" <███>, "Peter Mcarron" <███>, "Peter Panagioti Polites" <███>, "Peter Shopovski" <███>, "Phil Spencer" <███>, "Reuben Keehan" <███>, "Richard McBride" <███>, "Richard Tipping" <███>, "Robert Hartig-Prym" <███>, "Robert Heathcote" <███>, "Robert Milne" <███>, "Robert Pacitti" <███>, "Robin Dingeman" <███>, "Ross Gibson" <███>, "Ross Gibson" <███>, "Ruark Lewis" <███>, "Ryan Burrett" <███>, "Ryuichi Fujimura" <███>, "Sam James" <███>, "Sam Pettigrew" <███>, "Samuel Hodge" <███>, "Samuel Phelps" <███>, "Scott Donovan" <███>, "Scott Elliot Millington" <███>, "Sean Rafferty" <███>, "Sebastian Goldspink" <███>, "Shane Haseman" <███>, "Shawn Ross" <███>, "Simon Casson" <███>, "Simon Mitchell" <███>, "Simon Mitchell" <███>, "Stephen Q. Wye" <███>, "Stephen Russell" <███>, "Steven Latimer" <███>, "Stuart Bailey" <███>, "Taliu Aloua" <███>, "Tang Fu Kuen" <███>, "Teik Kim Pok" <███>, "Theron Schmidt" <███>, "Thomas Jeppe" <███>, "Tim Barber" <███>, "Tim Derbyshire" <███>, "Tim Derricourt" <███>, "Tim Silver" <███>, "Todd McMillan" <███>, "Tom Burless" <███>, "Tom Cole" <███>, "Tom MacDougall" <███>, "Tom Smith" <███>, "███

████" <████>, "Tony Mighell" <████>, "Tony Osborne" <████>, "Tony White" <████>, "Tristan Meecham" <████>, "Travis Raymond" <████>, "Troy Saxby" <████>, "████" <████>, "Wade Marynowsky" <████>, "Yanni Kronenberg" <████>, "Angus Withey" <████>, "████" <████>, "Lemi Ponifasio" <████>

LADIES AND GENTLEMEN

TO ALL THE MEN IN MY ADDRESS BOOK, HERE NOW ON STAGE DRESSED ALL IN WHITE, PLACED GHOSTLY BESIDE YOUR HOUSE.

SOME OF YOU KNOW EACH OTHER AND/OR ME, OTHERS NOT AT ALL, EITHER ME OR ANY OF THE GUYS NEXT TO YOU.

FOR THOSE UNKNOWN AND UNKNOWING, I HAVE SOME IDEA OF HOW SOME OF YOU HAVE COME TO BE HERE, OTHERS I HAVE NO CLUE - I'M THINKING POSSIBLY ABSORPTION THROUGH MUTUAL CONNECTIONS OR ONE-OFF ENCOUNTERS BRUSHED THROUGH OFFICIAL CORRESPONDENCE RANGING FROM TAX AGENTS, TO GENERAL ENQUIRIES WITH BUSINESSES, ACADEMIC INSTITUTIONS, CULTURAL INSTITUTIONS OR GROUP SITUATIONS, SEXUAL ONE NIGHT STANDS, AND/OR PROFESSIONAL ACQUAINTANCES, ETCETERA.
ALL OF YOU PLEASE KNOW, I MEAN NO HARM.

THIS VERY TEXT BELONGS TO A SERIES OF EMAIL PERFORMANCES IMPROVISED BY MOOD AND PLACE AND IN THIS TIME PARTICULARLY, MEMORY AND A COLD STUDIO FLOOR IN WOOLLOOMOOLLOO.

THIS PERFORMANCE IS NOTHING MORE THAN A MENTION OF A SONG BY A QUEER PUNK BAND I LISTENED TO WHEN I WAS VERY YOUNG. IT ENDS WITH AN EPILOGUE.

i couldn't fit everyone in. so there are two performances.

show I. NAMES A - R
show II. NAMES S - Z

THIS IS DEDICATED TO ALL THE WOMEN IN MY ADDRESS BOOK WATCHING IN SINGLE CHAIRS IN BCC.

GATHERED UNDER A SIMILAR PREMISE, BUT RATHER THAN TO BE SEEN ON STAGE - TO WATCH IN YOUR OWN TIME AND SPACE, CLOSE UP

CURTAINS OPEN

PANSY TWIST

BY

HUGGY BEAR

1994

POST SCRIPT:

NO NOSTALGIA NO POETRY NO POET NOPE

CURTAINS CLOSE 3:19AM – 7:15AM JULY 20 2013
SYDNEY

LOVE BRIAN

Monash University Museum of Art
900 Dandenong Road, Caulfield Campus
Caulfield East VIC 3145
Australia
monash.edu/muma

Monash University Museum of Art (MUMA) is a public museum and site for contemporary art, art-led education and research on Monash's Caulfield campus. Alongside exhibitions, education programs, events and publications, MUMA curates and manages the University's art collection and public art program. Monash has a long engagement with public art, from commissions for new buildings realised in the 1960s to the development of a public art masterplan and suite of architecturally embedded and public realm projects over the last decade.

Monash Art Projects
900 Dandenong Road, Caulfield Campus
Caulfield East VIC 3145
Australia
monash.edu/mada/research/labs/monash-art-projects

Monash Art Projects (MAP) was established in 2012 in the Fine Art department of Monash Art, Design and Architecture, with a goal to connect our community of artists, architects, designers, thinkers and makers to public art opportunities. Working with a diverse range of practitioners in the development and production of numerous permanent and temporary public art projects, MAP also runs workshops, oversees the Graduate Certificate of Public Art, consults with multiple stakeholders and communities, advocates for opportunities, and publishes widely.

Let's Go Outside: Making Art Public Symposium
30–31 August 2019, The Pavilion, Monash University, Caulfield Campus

Presenters: Esther Anatolitis, Dr Marnie Badham, N'arweet Dr Carolyn Briggs AM, Nicholas Baume, Dr Sarah Breen Lovett, Tania Bruguera, Clothilde Bullen, Dr Rebecca Coates, Megan Cope, Professor David Cross, Dr Sean Dockray, Mikala Dwyer, Field Theory (Sarah Rodigari and Jason Maling), Emily Floyd, Mike Hewson, Barbara Flynn, Kaye Glamuzina, Agatha Gothe-Snape, Jefa Greenaway, Dr D Harding, Jonathan Jones, Clair Korobacz and Julian Rickert, Alana Kushnir, Talia Linz, Dr Brian Martin, Professor Callum Morton, Mardi Nowak, Dr Jess Olivieri, Open Spatial Workshop, Professor Nikos Papastergiadis, Jarrod Rawlins, Lynda Roberts, Anne Robertson, ruangrupa (Ade Darmawan), Beth Sometimes, Dr Amy Spiers, Joe Toohey, Ronnie van Hout, Katherine Wilkinson

Thank you to all MUMA staff who were involved in the symposium, especially Kate Barber, Trent Crawford, Hannah Mathews, Alicia Renew, Rachel Schenberg and Warisa Somsuphangsri.

Let's Go Outside: Art in Public is published by Monash University Museum of Art, Monash Art Projects and Monash University Publishing.

ISBN 978-1-922633-17-0
First edition of 700

Editors: Charlotte Day, Callum Morton and Amy Spiers
Managing editor: Melissa Ratliff
Designers: Stuart Geddes and Žiga Testen
Printer: Printgraphics Printgreen, Melbourne
Cover printing: Matte Gold, Melbourne
Copyediting and proofreading: Evie Franzidis

A catalogue record for this work is available from the National Library of Australia.

This project has been supported by the Henry Moore Foundation.